Chad

WORLD BIBLIOGRAPHICAL SERIES

General Editors:
Robert G. Neville (Executive Editor)
John J. Horton

Robert A. Myers   Hans H. Wellisch
Ian Wallace   Ralph Lee Woodward, Jr.

John J. Horton is Deputy Librarian of the University of Bradford and currently Chairman of its Academic Board of Studies in Social Sciences. He has maintained a longstanding interest in the discipline of area studies and its associated bibliographical problems, with special reference to European Studies. In particular he has published in the field of Icelandic and of Yugoslav studies, including the two relevant volumes in the World Bibliographical Series.

Robert A. Myers is Associate Professor of Anthropology in the Division of Social Sciences and Director of Study Abroad Programs at Alfred University, Alfred, New York. He has studied post-colonial island nations of the Caribbean and has spent two years in Nigeria on a Fulbright Lectureship. His interests include international public health, historical anthropology and developing societies. In addition to *Amerindians of the Lesser Antilles: a bibliography* (1981), *A Resource Guide to Dominica, 1493-1986* (1987) and numerous articles, he has compiled the World Bibliographical Series volumes on *Dominica* (1987), *Nigeria* (1989) and *Ghana* (1991).

Ian Wallace is Professor of German at the University of Bath. A graduate of Oxford in French and German, he also studied in Tübingen, Heidelberg and Lausanne before taking teaching posts at universities in the USA, Scotland and England. He specializes in contemporary German affairs, especially literature and culture, on which he has published numerous articles and books. In 1979 he founded the journal *GDR Monitor*, which he continues to edit under its new title *German Monitor*.

Hans H. Wellisch is Professor emeritus at the College of Library and Information Services, University of Maryland. He was President of the American Society of Indexers and was a member of the International Federation for Documentation. He is the author of numerous articles and several books on indexing and abstracting, and has published *The Conversion of Scripts and Indexing and Abstracting: an International Bibliography*, and *Indexing from A to Z*. He also contributes frequently to *Journal of the American Society for Information Science*, *The Indexer* and other professional journals.

Ralph Lee Woodward, Jr. is Professor of History at Tulane University, New Orleans. He is the author of *Central America, a Nation Divided*, 2nd ed. (1985), as well as several monographs and more than seventy scholarly articles on modern Latin America. He has also compiled volumes in the World Bibliographical Series on *Belize* (1980), *El Salvador* (1988), *Guatemala* (Rev. Ed.) (1992) and *Nicaragua* (Rev. Ed.) (1994). Dr. Woodward edited the Central American section of the *Research Guide to Central America and the Caribbean* (1985) and is currently associate editor of Scribner's *Encyclopedia of Latin American History*.

VOLUME 177

Chad

George Joffé
Valérie Day-Viaud

Compilers

CLIO PRESS
OXFORD, ENGLAND · SANTA BARBARA, CALIFORNIA
DENVER, COLORADO

British Library Cataloguing in Publication Data

Chad. – (World bibliographical
series; vol. 177)
I. Joffé, E. G. H.   II. Valérie Day-Viaud.   III. Series
016.96743

ISBN 1–85109–231–5

ABC-CLIO Ltd.,
Old Clarendon Ironworks,
35A Great Clarendon Street,
Oxford OX2 6AT, England.

———

ABC-CLIO Inc.,
130 Cremona Drive,
Santa Barbara,
CA 93116, USA

Designed by Bernard Crossland.
Typeset by Columns Design and Production Services Ltd, Reading, England.
Printed and bound in Great Britain by Bookcraft (Bath) Ltd., Midsomer Norton.

Please renew/return items by last date
shown. Please call the number below:

Renewals and enquiries: 0300 123 4049

Textphone for hearing or
speech impaired users: 0300 123 4041

www.hertsdirect.org/librarycatalogue
L32

THE WORLD BIBLIOGRAPHICAL SERIES

This series, which is principally designed for the English speaker, will eventually cover every country (and many of the world's principal regions), each in a separate volume comprising annotated entries on works dealing with its history, geography, economy and politics; and with its people, their culture, customs, religion and social organization. Attention will also be paid to current living conditions – housing, education, newspapers, clothing, etc.– that are all too often ignored in standard bibliographies; and to those particular aspects relevant to individual countries. Each volume seeks to achieve, by use of careful selectivity and critical assessment of the literature, an expression of the country and an appreciation of its nature and national aspirations, to guide the reader towards an understanding of its importance. The keynote of the series is to provide, in a uniform format, an interpretation of each country that will express its culture, its place in the world, and the qualities and background that make it unique. The views expressed in individual volumes, however, are not necessarily those of the publisher.

VOLUMES IN THE SERIES

1 *Yugoslavia*, Rev. Ed., John J. Horton
2 *Lebanon*, Rev. Ed., C. H. Bleaney
3 *Lesotho*, Shelagh M. Willet and David Ambrose
4 *Zimbabwe*, Rev. Ed., Deborah Potts
5 *Saudi Arabia*, Rev. Ed., Frank A. Clements
6 *Russia/USSR*, Second Ed., Lesley Pitman
7 *South Africa*, Rev. Ed., Geoffrey V. Davis
8 *Malawi*, Robert B. Boeder
9 *Guatemala*, Rev. Ed., Ralph Lee Woodward, Jr
10 *Pakistan*, David Taylor
11 *Uganda*, Robert L. Collison
12 *Malaysia*, Ian Brown and Rajeswary Ampalavanar
13 *France*, Rev. Ed., Frances Chambers
14 *Panama*, Eleanor DeSelms Langstaff
15 *Hungary*, Thomas Kabdebo
16 *USA*, Sheila R. Herstein and Naomi Robbins
17 *Greece*, Richard Clogg and Mary Jo Clogg
18 *New Zealand*, R. F. Grover

19 *Algeria*, Richard I. Lawless
20 *Sri Lanka*, Vijaya Samaraweera
21 *Belize*, Second Ed., Peggy Wright and Brian E. Coutts
23 *Luxembourg*, Carlo Hury and Jul Christophory
24 *Swaziland*, Rev. Ed., Balam Nyeko
25 *Kenya*, Robert L. Collison
26 *India*, Brijen K. Gupta and Datta S. Kharbas
27 *Turkey*, Merel Güçlü
28 *Cyprus*, P. M. Kitromilides and M. L. Evriviades
29 *Oman*, Rev. Ed., Frank A. Clements
31 *Finland*, J. E. O. Screen
32 *Poland*, Rev. Ed., George Sanford and Adriana Gozdecka-Sanford
33 *Tunisia*, Allan M. Findlay, Anne M. Findlay and Richard I. Lawless
34 *Scotland*, Eric G. Grant
35 *China*, Peter Cheng
36 *Qatar*, P. T. H. Unwin
37 *Iceland*, John J. Horton
38 *Nepal*, John Whelpton
39 *Haiti*, Rev. Ed., Frances Chambers
40 *Sudan*, Rev. Ed., M. W. Daly
41 *Vatican City State*, Michael J. Walsh

Contents

Contents

Abbreviations

Journals/Revues

B.I.F.A.N.   Bulletin de l'Institut Français d'Afrique Noire
C.O.M.   Les Cahiers d'Outre-Mer

Institutions and Professional Bodies

B.R.G.M.	Bureau de Recherches Géologiques et Minières, Orléans
C.B.L.T.	Commission du Bassin du Lac Tchad
C.E.A.N.	Centre d'Etudes d'Afrique Noire, Bordeaux
C.E.F.O.D.	Centre d'Etude et de Formation pour le Développement
C.E.R.D.I.	Centre d'Etudes et de Recherches sur le Développement International, Clermont-Ferrand University, France
C.H.E.A.M.	Centre des Hautes Etudes sur l'Afrique et l'Asie Modernes, Paris
C.I.D.A.R.C.	Centre d'Information et de Documentation en Agronomie des Régions Chaudes, Montpellier, France
C.N.R.S.	Centre National de la Recherche Scientifique
D.O.S.	Directorate of Overseas Surveys, Southampton
E.P.H.E.	Ecole Pratique des Hautes Etudes
F.A.O.	Food and Agriculture Organization
I.A.M.M.	Institut d'Agronomie Méditerranéen de Montpellier
I.E.M.V.T.	Institut d'Etudes Médico-vétérinaires Tropicales
I.I.S.S.	International Institute for Strategic Studies
I.N.H.	Institut des Sciences Humaines

Abbreviations

I.N.S.H.	Institut National pour les Sciences Humaines
I.N.T.S.H.	Institut National Tchadien pour les Sciences Humaines
K.I.T.	Koninklijk Instituut voor de Tropen, Amsterdam
L.A.C.I.T.O.	Laboratoire de Langues et Civilisations à Tradition Orale
L.A.P.E.P.M.O.	Laboratoire d'Anthropologie, Préhistoire et Ethnologie des Pays de la Méditerranée Occidentale
O.E.C.D.	Organization for Economic Cooperation and Development
P.N.U.D.	Programme des Nations Unies pour le Développement
S.E.L.A.F.	Société d'Etudes Linguistiques et Anthropologiques de France
S.G.A.	Service Géographique des Armées

Other

F.A.N.	Forces Armées du Nord
FROLINAT	Front de Libération National du Tchad
G.U.N.T.	Gouvernement d'Union Nationale de Transition
M.R.E.	Ministère des Relations Extérieures
U.J.T.	Union des Journalistes Tchadiens
U.N.I.R.	Union Nationale pour l'Indépendence et le Rassemblement

Research centres and libraries used

London

BL (British Library)
SOAS (School of Oriental and African Studies, University of London)

Paris

BDF (Bibliothèque de la Documentation Française)
BDIC (Bibliothèque de Documentation Internationale Contemporaine.
  Université de Paris-Nanterre)
BIBLIOTHEQUE CUJAS
BU (Bibliothèque Universitaire, Nanterre)
CEA/EHESS (Centre d'Etudes Africaines – Ecole des Hautes Etudes en
  Sciences Sociales)
CHEAM (Centre des Hautes Etudes sur l'Afrique et l'Asie Modernes)
CRA (Centre de Recherches Africaines)
IGN (Institut Géographique National)
Musée de l'Homme
ORSTOM (Office de la Recherche Scientifique des Territoires d'Outre-
  Mer)

Introduction

Chad is one of the largest states in Africa with an area of 1.284 million square kilometres. Located in Central Africa, it stretches from the arid Sahara in the north down towards semi-tropical fertile savannah and woodland in the south. The central part of the country is a semi-arid steppe zone dominated by Lake Chad. The Chari and Logone rivers drain into the lake which lies on the borders of Chad with Nigeria and Niger.

The population of Chad, estimated at around 5.5 million, is ethnically one of the most diverse in Africa. The sedentary Sara of the densely populated south make up 20 per cent of the population; the Sudanic populations of the central part of the country are mainly nomadic or transhumant; and the sparsely populated northern Saharan edge of Chad, between the Tibesti and Ennedi massifs, is peopled by the Tubu, Touareg and Wadai. Although French and Arabic are the official languages of the country it is estimated that some 100 local languages are actually in use.

This diversity of populations and languages is reflected in Chad's culture and religious practices. In the far north, although the region is ostensibly part of the Muslim world, older traditions still persist, and Arabic is not widely spoken in Tibesti or Ennedi. Along the Saharan edge, however, Arab populations which have migrated into the region from Libya and Sudan tend to be most numerous and the dominance of Arabic and Islam is reflected in the old central sultanates of Kanem, Baguirmi and Ouaddai. Further south, however, animism and Christianity predominate, so that around 50 per cent of the population are animists, 45 per cent Muslim and the rest Christian.

In economic terms, Chad is one of the poorest countries in the world, with an average income in 1985 estimated at only $120 per year. The economy is dominated by subsistence farming and pastoralism. In the Sara-dominated south of the country, cotton cultivation continues to be a major commodity. It is normally exported to Europe, and provides an economic base for 40 per cent of the population, generating 25 per cent of public-sector income. In the west and east, pastoralism has traditionally generated export revenues as a result of livestock commerce with Nigeria, Sudan and the Central African Republic. Only four per cent of GDP is generated by industrial activities and there is also a very small oil sector in Kanem and around Lake Chad. Indeed, what economic activity there is can be traced back directly to Chad's colonial past under French rule, as can the current political crisis that faces the country.

The pre-colonial reality

Before the French occupied what has now become modern Chad – during the colonial period it formed part of French Equatorial Africa – there was no political entity which approximated to the modern state. Instead, there were three zones of population settlement in which different types of political structure existed. Furthermore, these structures often extended beyond the boundaries of the modern state, thereby providing a demographic, ethnic and sociological continuity with its modern geographical environment.

In the north of Chad – the semi-arid and arid zone shading northwards into the Sahara desert and including the two great mountain massifs of Tibesti and Ennedi – there was a scattered nomadic and transhumant tribal population, probably equivalent to around five per cent of the total population of the modern state. It was divided between two major tribal groups. The first was the Tubu, who were found around the Tibesti massif but also in Borkou and reaching across the modern border westward towards the Bilma and Kawwar oasis chains. They were divided between the Tedaga and Dazaga. Some of the Tubu, particularly those in the Tibesti massif, also migrated northwards as part of their nomadic cycle and traded with Murzuq and Kufrah in southern Libya. The second group comprised the Bideyat and the Zaghawa, both different branches of the Beri, who were located around the Ennedi massif and extended into Darfur. Both groups were the remnants of one of the three great Saharan tribal groups – the Moors, the Touareg and the Tubu – and had formed part of one of the early imperial systems of the southern Saharan fringe, the Zaghawa empire of the eleventh century.

Intermixed with these groups were two others: the sedentary Kanouri and Kamadja, found in Bourkou and in Bilma or Kawwar, and various Arab tribal communities. One Arab group was derived from the Awlad Sulayman of the northern Fezzan who moved southwards into the northern part of the Kanem region after being displaced from Libya in 1842 by the Ottomans – that is, after the second Ottoman occupation of Libya in 1835. Another group which, like the first, came from Libya but, unlike it, was sedentary, was made up of traders located in the major oasis complexes of Borkou. It replicated many of the major tribes of Libya itself, such as the Qadhadhfa and the Zuwaya. The third group was composed of factions of eastern Arab tribes, such as the Djellaba, the Toundjour, the Djcheina and the Hassaouna, who had migrated westwards into the region over the previous millennium. The Djcheina and the Hassaouna fused in the fifteenth century into the Mahamid and became the major slavers of central Chad, thereby sustaining the trade routes across the Sahara which were controlled by the Tubu and Touareg.

The Arab tribes from Egypt and Sudan also created a series of small Muslim sultanates in central Chad – Kanem, Baguirmi (both remnants of the tenth-century Bournou empire) and Ouaddai. Their populations – probably around 15 per cent of the total population of the present Chad – were largely pastoralist, although there were also sedentary groups, such as the Hadjeray in what is today the Guera Prefecture. The sultanates acted as a barrier between the acephalous non-Arab populations of the Saharan fringe – largely animist in culture and linked into the far-flung subsistence economy of the Sahara with migratory and trading links into the Fezzan and Kufrah – and the sedentary agriculturalist populations of the extreme south of Chad. By the nineteenth century, the Sultanate of Ouaddai had also enforced its control over the Beri and had begun to Islamize them.

These populations – mainly acephalous decentralized animist communities based on lineage affiliation – were dominated by the Sara who also extended into modern Cameroon and Central Africa. The Sara formed a complex and hierarchical village-based society, dominated by a system of chiefs. The other major southern group were the Moundang, who were derived from the Fulbe populations of West Africa. Unlike the situation further north, there was no centralized authority and the southern part of Chad was constantly ravaged by slavers, particularly towards the end of the nineteenth century. Indeed, the first French advance into Chad was directed against the major Sudanese slaver, Rabih, who had conquered the sultanates of Kanem and Baguirmi and was preparing to turn against Ouaddai. His defeat at French hands occurred close to the site of the capital of modern Chad, N'Jamena.

Islam also came to the Tubu, largely as a result of the expansion of the Sanusi Order southwards from Jarabub and Kufrah at the end of the nineteenth century. The Sanusi Order, founded in the early nineteenth century and originally based along the eastern Libyan Mediterranean littoral at al-Bayda, was a powerful agent of

Introduction

Islamization amongst the Sa'adi tribes of Cyrenaica and also came to control trade routes and to administer tribal life from its *zawiya*-s which were dotted throughout Cyrenaica and extended into the Fezzan, Tripolitania and even Egypt. It maintained an uneasy *modus vivendi* with the Ottoman administration of the Mediterranean coast of Libya, whereby the Ottomans tacitly ceded administrative authority for the interior to the Sanusi Order. The Order also became a powerful agent for resisting colonial penetration, particularly through its migration southwards into Chad where, in addition to penetrating the Tubu and Beri regions, it also established a presence in Ouaddai. By the end of the nineteenth century, it had begun to prepare resistance to French penetration eastwards and northwards.

The colonial period

The French occupation of modern Chad slowly developed over the first two decades of the present century. In part it was a response to the need to protect French colonial acquisitions in West Africa and was carried out with very small logistical and military resources. The conquest actually took fifteen years to complete between 1900 and 1915 and, after a hiatus during the First World War, a further forty years were spent organizing the administration of the new colony. In part the conquest corresponded to the grander design of linking together the two components of the new French colonial empire created during the nineteenth century: French West Africa and French North Africa. The extent of the French advance into Chad was governed by the 1898 Anglo-French Spheres of Influence Agreement which, according to the subsequent 1899 Declaration, divided Central Africa between the two countries along a line, '. . . which shall start from the point of intersection of the Tropic of Cancer with the 16th degree of longitude east of Greenwich . . . shall run thence south-east until it meets the 24th degree of longitude east of Greenwich . . .'. It was only after the First World War that a very limited French presence was permanently established in the extreme north of what was to become known as the BET (Borkou–Ennedi–Tibesti) Region.

The French presence was felt in various ways in Chad. First, it defined a territorial extent and administrative boundaries to the new political entity. Many of the new territorial limits to the new colony resulted from internal French colonial administrative decisions, although some arose from international delimitation: the boundary with Cameroon was agreed between France and Germany, those of Nigeria and Sudan with Britain, and Italy agreed the boundary of Libya. Interestingly enough, although imprecisions still exist in most of these boundary definitions, they have not (for the most part) been the source of significant dispute between the modern independent states of this part of Africa. But this cannot be said to be true of Chad's boundary with Libya. Although this was originally defined in the 1898 and 1899 agreements between Britain and France, the section between the 16th and 24th degree of longitude east of Greenwich was essentially redefined by a 1919 Franco-Italian Exchange of Notes, after Italy had ousted the Ottoman empire from Libya in 1911 but before the subsequent Italo-Sanusi wars had been ended. The redefinition occurred because the original 1898 agreement was not accompanied by a map and France was able to unilaterally redefine the boundary in favour of its new colony by insisting that the two lines of longitude involved were linked by a line running east-south-east, rather than south-east. This had first been suggested in a secret Franco-Italian agreement drawn up in 1902 which actually referred to the non-existent 1898 map as its spurious justification. The section to the west, from the Tummo oasis to the 16th line of longitude east of Greenwich, was established by the 1919 protocol.

This arrangement was modified on two subsequent occasions: in 1934, Italy and Britain reached agreement on the so-called 'Sarra Triangle Dispute', which involved the portion of land to the north of the 1919 line and between the 22nd and 24th lines of longitude east of Greenwich. The following year, Italy and France negotiated and ratified an agreement – the Mussolini–Laval Agreement – which ceded a strip of territory one hundred kilometres deep south of the 1919 line to Italy. This strip of territory has since become known as the 'Aozou Strip'. The justification for this seems to have been a French desire to settle Italian claims to rights for its citizens in Tunisia – a French colony but in which the Italian community was the largest European element – as well as removing irridentist Italian claims to Nice, and as a means of diverting Fascist Italy away from close treaty links with Nazi Germany. In the latter respect, French policy failed, for two years later Italy signed the Pact of Steel with Germany and the instruments of ratification of the Mussolini–Laval Treaty were never exchanged.

Nonetheless, until 1955, the Franco-Italian border in Central Africa was conventionally assumed to be the new line established by the Mussolini–Laval Treaty. It was only after the independence of Libya in 1951 and the signing of a Franco-Italian Friendship Treaty in 1955 that the issue of the 1935 treaty re-emerged. This required Libya to recognize existing boundary agreements. At French insistence, in a subsequent exchange of notes in 1956, the various treaties considered to define the boundary were listed but no specific boundary definition was provided. The result of this has been that Libya has never accepted the 1919 line as its boundary with Chad, arguing instead that no boundary has ever been properly delimited and that the closest approach to such a delimitation is the 1935 Mussolini–Laval Treaty.

One reason for this view has been that Italy never defined the southern limits of its Libyan colony in its Treaty of Peace with the Ottoman empire at the end of its initial occupation of Libya in 1912. Libya considered that both the penetration of the Sanusi Order into northern Chad – where it established a significant administrative role between 1890 and 1913 – and a belated Ottoman presence there between 1908 and 1912 provide it with a claim based on *uti possidetis juris* to a large area of Northern Chad. Libya also argued that the French occupation of Northern Chad – of the BET region – was never 'effective' in the sense that a permanent and effective administrative presence was established. Its more limited claim to the Aozou Strip was, therefore, a concession. Chad, of course, basing its case on the 1955 Franco-Libyan Treaty and its rights as a successor state to France, did not agree.

The issue was eventually debated before the International Court of Justice at The Hague. In early February 1994, the Court decided to accept the 1955 Franco-Libyan treaty as legitimizing the international boundary as then accepted. Libya's claim to the Aozou Strip was thus rejected. The Libyan government, surprisingly, accepted the Court's decision and has since evacuated the Strip and signed a binding boundary agreement with Chad.

The colonial period and internal change

Even though the French presence in the BET region was always minimal and was mainly concerned with attempting to preserve a fragile peace while leaving local society relatively untouched, the same was not true of central and southern Chad. Indeed, even in northern Chad, sporadic attempts were made by the authorities to interfere with the traditional migratory links between the Tubu and southern Libya, and to prevent Beri movement in and out of Darfur in Sudan. The French military and administrative presence was, however, far too weak for this to be done by direct control and French administrators had to depend on local power structures, such as the Derde of Tibesti, for this purpose. The result was that control of the northern borders was ineffectual and traditional migratory patterns persisted. Furthermore, French military control of the BET region ended only in 1964, four years after Chad had become independent.

In the old Muslim sultanates, the existing order was preserved and France ruled through a system of indirect administration. French officials introduced new taxation systems, for the colony had to be as financially viable as possible, and ended the tradition of the *ghazaw* southwards. Apart from these modifications, however, the old Muslim heartland of Chad was left relatively untouched, as was the traditional pastoralist economy based on transhumance. Indeed, the relative calm brought by French administration opened up possibilities of livestock trade southwards as well as eastwards into the Sudan.

In the south, however, particularly in the Sara heartland, the colonial experience brought dramatic change. The old village chieftain system was uprooted, as chiefs were replaced by personalities loyal to the new administration. In 1921, cotton cultivation was introduced into southern Chad, a development which had profound social and economic implications. First, the administrative system based on the new, compliant chiefs was redirected towards the creation of an economy based on cotton monoculture. Secondly, all French developmental interest in Chad was now directed towards the south. Thirdly, a monopoly private company, COTONFRAN (later known as COTONCHAD) came to dominate the national economy. This was accompanied by an administrative decision to favour the south in terms of educational facilities, in order to create a native administration based on the Sara, while the Muslim regions of the country were left to stagnate through social and administrative neglect. Southern Chad had now become the 'Tchad Utile' for France.

This development had two further consequences. First, it upset the pre-colonial social and political balance, in which the sultanates of central Chad had been the dominant element. Secondly, it increasingly integrated Chad into the political development of West Africa through Cameroon. After the creation of the French Union in 1946, political parties began to develop in West Africa. Political agitation for independence was first voiced through the Rassemblement Démocratique Africain, founded by Félix Houphouet-Boigny in 1951, and Chad was represented at its founding conference. A year later, the Parti Progressiste Tchadien was founded in N'Jamena by Gabriel Lisette, an administrative official from Guadeloupe. This became the dominant political formation in Chad and was dominated by Chad's southern Sara populations, although it was originally also open to persons from northern Chad, such as Abba Siddick. Most northerners, however, were gathered into a new party, dominated by the Muslim élite of the old sultanates, the Mouvement Socialiste Africaine, until they left it in 1958 to create the Union Nationale Tchadienne which was dominated by young activists and from which was to emerge the eventual national independence movement, FROLINAT.

Independence

The striking feature of Chad on the eve of independence was the fact that the pre-colonial disposition of power inside the new state had been inverted. Whereas power had originally been based in the central Muslim sultanates, with the north of the country isolated by its links into the Sahara and southern Libya and the south dependent and subjected to central domination, now it was the Sara-dominated south of Chad that controlled the political process and sought to control power once independence was granted. Furthermore, the old links outside the territory of the new state, which had defined political structures in pre-colonial times, had been disrupted by the administrative functions located within the new boundaries. The northern populations found their ability to maintain close links with southern Libya circumscribed, as did the populations of the eastern BET region with Sudan or those of the central part of the country with areas across the borders to the east and the south. Chad had become, as a result of the colonial experience, an embryonic unitary state, although it was far from being a nation as well. Its population of some three to four millions was dispersed over about 100 different ethnic and linguistic groups. There was also at least three distinct religious identities, and old political loyalties reinforced the ethnic and religious divides.

Not surprisingly, independence produced a southern Sara-dominated government under François Tombalbaye and, within five years, the precarious unity of the state collapsed as a Sara-dominated administrative structure alienated the large non-Sara minorities in the centre and the north of the country. The simple fact was that the administrative structure of Chad failed to coincide with any other political or cultural reality so that, once the Sara-dominated government faltered, its whole basis of legitimacy collapsed. The first sign of the troubles to come appeared in Mangalme in October 1965, with a tax rebellion amongst Moubi transhumants. Soon, in the wake of the withdrawal of French administrators from the BET region, tensions between the government administration and local political structures there generated a new dimension for the rebellion. Within one year, activists of the northern-dominated Union Nationale

Tchadienne had moved into active rebellion against the Tombalbaye government and, under the leadership of a Nigerian who had moved to Chad, Ibrahim Abacha, had formed a guerrilla movement, FROLINAT. The outbreak of Chad's first civil war was, in essence, an attempt to redress the geopolitical balance inside the country. The Sara-dominated government – in which President Tombalbaye was replaced by Felix Malloum in 1974 – now confronted an increasingly powerful armed opposition which, although it claimed to represent all Chadians, was actually dominated by the once-marginalized Tubu. Furthermore, the leadership of FROLINAT itself split along ethnic lines, between the Teda of Tibesti and the Daza of Faya Largeau in Borkou, represented by the son of the old Tibesti Derde, Goukouni Oueddei, and a French-educated Daza lawyer from Faya who had returned to Chad as a member of the administration and then defected to FROLINAT in 1971, Hissen Habré. This internal split had been powerfully aided by the former colonial power, France, which, in 1969, in response to a desperate plea from the beleaguered Tombalbaye government, had sent in troops to isolate FROLINAT within the BET. This, in turn, led FROLINAT to turn to Libya for aid. By the start of the 1970s, therefore, Chad had not only collapsed in civil war, it had also become the arena for a surrogate conflict between outside powers.

In late 1972, Libya unilaterally annexed the Aozou Strip, claiming that François Tombalbaye, while president, had recognized the validity of Libya's claim to the 1935 boundary line. This action was the direct cause of the 1974 split inside FROLINAT between supporters of Goukouni Oueddei, who was prepared to tolerate the Libyan action for the sake of Libyan support, and Hissen Habré who was not. Eventually Habré allied with the Malloum government but, in 1979, the combination of tensions inside N'Jamena and a FROLINAT Forces Armées du Nord (FAN) offensive under Goukouni Oueddei ended the southern-dominated Malloum regime. As a result of sustained prodding by Nigeria, the Organization of African Unity (OAU) eventually imposed a peace plan, the Lagos Accords, which provided for a transitional government, the GUNT, which was supposed to hold elections eighteen months later.

By March 1980, however, tensions between the two reunited wings of FROLINAT had broken out into renewed fighting which ushered in the second civil war. Libyan intervention in June ensured victory for the Goukouni Oueddei faction, but, within a year, Hissen Habré had amassed Sudanese and Egyptian support, because of the threat Libya was seen to pose through its presence in Chad. By 1982,

Introduction

Libyan forces in central Chad had withdrawn and the Oueddei government fell, to be replaced by a Habré administration dominated by the Daza Tubu. Twelve months later, a Libyan-backed rebellion led by Goukouni Oueddei had occupied all of Chad down to the 16th parallel and the Habré government had had to call on France once again. The USA, given its ferocious hostility towards the Qadhafi regime in Libya, had by now entered into the picture, competing with France to arm the Habré regime, and also bolstering Egyptian and Sudanese support for it.

In the early months of 1987, Libya suffered a staggering defeat at the hands of the Forces Armées Tchadiennes (FAT), led and trained by Habré's Zaghawa supporters, Hassan Djamous and Ibrahim Déby. Libya was left with a toehold on Chadian territory at Aozou and was eventually persuaded by Algeria and Morocco to place its claim before the International Court of Justice at The Hague. Habré, as victor in the conflict – Goukouni Oueddei had been eclipsed and many of his supporters had in any case defected to the Habré government in N'Jamena – was fêted in Paris and Washington.

The Habré regime was, however, in trouble. Ethnic tensions within Hissen Habré's own UNIR movement – between his own Daza faction and his erstwhile Hadjeray and Zaghawa allies – led, first, to a rebellion in Guera, the heart of Hadjeray country, and a year later, to a mysterious coup attempt in N'Jamena which left Djamous dead and Déby in exile. At the same time, tensions erupted over proposed political changes which seemed to threaten southern Chadian interests. Déby sought and obtained Libyan support and, operating through the Sudanese border at Darfur, amongst his own ethnic Zaghawa group, soon ousted Habré in December 1990. The Déby government is still in power, despite at least two coup attempts and hostile US and French pressure. At the same time, it is attempting to resist too close a Libyan embrace. Chad itself is bankrupt and prostrate after twenty-seven years of continuous warfare and is now struggling towards a more equitable, less tribally based government.

The bibliography

Since Chad was a French colonial possession, it is hardly surprising that the majority of works dealing with the country are in French. Many of these reflect the interests of former members of the colonial services there, particularly as far as sociology and anthropology are concerned. There is also, for the same reason, a predominance of French scholarship in the linguistics field. This is also why a surprisingly large proportion of the basic texts are in the form of articles – they tended to have been written by busy colonial officers – and often date from the period before 1960 – when Chad gained its independence – or from the early 1960s, when there was still a residual colonial presence in Chad, particularly in the north of the country.

More recent texts tend to concentrate on political issues, often related to the civil wars and the apparently insoluble problem of the relationship between the north and south of the country. In many respects, the colonial experience in Chad tended to reverse domestic political roles, promoting the interests of the southern Sara communities, which were linked, both politically and ethnographically, with neighbouring states such as Cameroon. Indeed, the first political movement which came to power after independence was an extension of the national movement in Cameroon (as is described above). It took over the pre-colonial dominance of the central Muslim sultanates and, interestingly enough, it was precisely in these areas that the civil war broke out. Similarly, the close commercial and social links that existed between southern Libya and northern Chad were broken by the creation of a colonial boundary that hardened into an international boundary after Libyan independence in 1951. The literature reflects these political developments.

Overall, it must be said that the bibliography of Chad is poor, although some categories – particularly in ethno-linguistics – are over-represented. Many of the journals in which material does appear are difficult to obtain, and many of the books are confined to narrow academic circles or are out-of-print. This situation reflects the fitful colonial interest in the country and the relative lack of commercial and political interest offered by Chad since independence. Even the convulsions of the civil wars that Chad has faced in recent years have generated relatively little interest as compared, say, with Algeria, Angola or South Africa. For those who would like to look into the archival sources of Chad's history – held in the state archives of Britain, France and Italy – we can do no better than recommend a close study of the proceedings of the Libya–Chad case before the International Court of Justice. Coverage of Chadian affairs by the foreign press is miniscule, despite the country's obvious strategic importance. Perhaps this reflects the fact that, even under colonialism, Chad was a distant, obscure land; a situation which has not changed since independence. This bibliography is designed to contribute towards countering that impression.

Introduction

Acknowledgements

We would like to acknowledge the continual courtesy and interest extended towards us, particularly to Valérie Day-Viaud, by the many libraries and academic institutions in which we had to carry out our basic research. We would also like to thank the patience and thoroughness of the editorial staff of ABC-CLIO Ltd for their vital support in seeing this project through to a successful conclusion.

The Country and Its People

1 **Au delà de l'actualité, le Tchad réel.** (Beyond the news, the real state of Chad.)
  Anon. N'Djamena: UJT, CEFOD, [n.d.]. 125p.
This illustrated booklet was written by six Chadian journalists, probably in 1991, and provides information on agriculture, the economy – especially transport – health and education, development and life in N'Djamena. It also contains interviews with four women from different social and ethnic backgrounds. It shows that, beyond the tragedy of war, Chadians are struggling to escape poverty and create conditions for the peaceful development of their country.

2 **La République du Tchad.** (The Republic of Chad.)
  Anon. Paris: La Documentation Française, 1967. 63p. (Notes et Etudes Documentaires, no. 3411).
A brief but concise overview of Chad which offers a short introduction to the geographical, historical, ethnographic and demographic aspects of Chad. It covers political and administrative institutions, economic and financial matters, cultural and social topics more comprehensively. Although this is by no means an exhaustive study, it constitutes a useful introduction to Chad, seen here essentially as a young, post-colonial nation striving to develop.

3 **Tchad.** (Chad.)
  Anon. *Le Courrier, Afrique-Caraïbes-Pacifique*, no. 102 (March-April 1987), p. 27-43. map.
This illustrated article approaches Chad from a simple chronological point of view which is devoid of analysis and provides a general overview of the history of Chad during the past twenty years. It contains an interview with Hissen Habré and an economic balance-sheet and it considers EC–Chad relations and economic cooperation.

1

4   **Country report: Cameroon, CAR, Chad.**
    Anon. *Economist Intelligence Unit.* quarterly.
This quarterly report deals with economic, political and social developments in Chad.
It is accompanied by a Country Profile each year which provides basic political and
economic information.

5   **Sud Sahara, Sahel nord. De l'Atlantique à l'Ennedi.** (Southern Sahara
    and northern Sahel. From the Atlantic Ocean to the Ennedi Massif.)
    Anon.   Abidjan: Centre Culturel Français, 1989. 241p. maps.
These are the proceedings of a meeting organized by the Centre Culturel Français
d'Afrique de l'Ouest in Dakar and Ouagadougou in 1987 and 1988 which brought
together specialists of the Sahel-Sahara region of central Africa. It contains illustrated
articles on the geography, history and prehistory, economy, languages, arts and
politics of this fragile region.

6   **Cameroon and Chad in historical perspectives.**
    Edited by Mario Azevedo.   Lampeter, Wales: The Edwin Mellen Press,
    1988. 212p. bibliog. (African Studies, Volume 10).
An interesting comparative study which focuses on Cameroon and Chad. Because of
their many contrasts and similarities, the author claims that they provide a realistic
view of the African continent as a whole. Each country is seen through its cultural
setting, economy, history, politics, health and education, and finally through the status
of women there.

7   **Les ombres de Kôh.** (The shadows of Koh.)
    Antoine Bangui-Rombaye.   Paris: Hatier, 1983. 158p. (Monde Noir
    Poche).
Koh is the exact replica of Bangui's village, where the spirits of the dead dwell, and
for Bangui it represents the past, the memory of the old, the history of the people. He
uses it here as a reminder of the importance of remembering the past, at a time when
Chad was being torn apart by civil war. This book, subtitled 'Chronicle', is a
recollection of Bangui's childhood, as well as a description of the daily lives of
village people.

8   **Le Tchad.** (Chad.)
    Christian Bouquet, Jean Cabot.   Paris: Presses Universitaires de France,
    1973. 127p. maps. bibliog. (Que sais-je?).
This is a very concise book which covers the most important aspects of Chad. It is
divided into two parts: the environment and the people, and the economy and its
problems. It provides a condensed introduction to Chad and its economy.

9   **Chad, a country study.**
    Edited by Thomas Collelo.   Washington: Federal Research Division,
    Library of Congress, 1990. 254p. maps. bibliog. (Area Handbook Series).
Completed in 1988, this is probably the most comprehensive and up-to-date work on
Chad. It examines its history, geography, society (including languages and ethnic

groups, religion, social structure, health and education), and its economy. It finally devotes a large section to national security which covers the internal and external conflicts of the last twenty-five years. An appendix clarifies the divisions of the principal armed factions between 1975 and 1987, and a series of tables of statistics completes the study.

10　**At the desert's edge. Oral histories from the Sahel.**
Edited by Nigel Cross, Rhiannon Barker. London: Panos Publications, [n.d.], p. 155-175. maps.

This interesting work contains one chapter on Chad, with interviews of five Chadian women and three men in which they describe their life, reminiscing about the past and comparing life then and now. It shows Sahelian perceptions of their changing environment and way of life and provides valuable first-hand material about Sahelian lives and the struggle to survive. The book is illustrated.

11　**The emerging states of French Equatorial Africa.**
Virginia Thompson, Richard Adloff. London: Oxford University Press, 1960. 595p. maps. bibliog.

A very thorough illustrated study dealing with the four territories which formed French Equatorial Africa: Middle-Congo (Congo), Gabon, Ubangui-Chari (Central African Republic) and Chad. It is primarily devoted to the federation, the last chapter being the only one to deal with individual territories. Economic and social topics are discussed alongside the political and economic development of the territories.

12　**Chad.**
Kaye Whiteman. London: Minority Rights Group, 1988. 16p. map. bibliog. (Report no. 80).

This report from the Minority Rights Group differs from other reports in the series in that it does not investigate the plight of a minority, although it does consider the Chadian crisis partly on the basis of ethnic factors. It contains a condensed version of Chad's history, geography, ethnicity and national unity up to Independence. The bulk of the report, however, is devoted to the civil war: the French intervention in 1969; the decline and fall of Tombalbaye; the period of disintegration in 1979, Habré's seizure of power; Operation Manta; and the dispute with Libya. The report is a narrative rather than an analysis of the Chadian crisis. It provides a clear summary of the situation of Chad since Independence.

Travellers' Accounts

13 **Sahara–Tchad (1898-1900). Carnets de route de Prosper Haller, médecin de la mission Foureau–Lamy.** (Sahara–Chad (1898-1900). Travel diaries of Prosper Haller, doctor on the Foureau–Lamy mission.) Edited by Jean-Claude Abadie, Françoise Abadie. Paris: L'Harmattan, 1989. 219p. (Racines du présent).

These travel diaries describe the expedition across the Sahara from the north to Zinder, around Lake Chad and down to Brazzaville.

14 **Carnets du Congo. Voyage avec Gide.** (Congo travel diaries. A journey with Gide.) Marc Allegret. Paris: CNRS, 1987. 297p.

A descriptive work by French cinema director Allegret who travelled with André Gide in Congo and Chad in the 1930s.

15 **Notes sur un voyage au Tibesti (Avril 1950). Tableau des clans.** (Notes on a journey through Tibesti (April 1950). Table of clans.) Jean d'Arbaumont. Paris: CHEAM, 1953. 70p.

This article is the result of a three-week journey through Tibesti, designed to investigate the Teda's social institutions, particularly in the notion of clan, to assess the degree of Islamization in Tibesti and the amount of Sanusi influence and finally to determine the region's food resources, the nature of exchange processes and the way in which both could be improved.

16 **Travels and discoveries in north and central Africa.** Heinrich Barth. London: Frank Cass, 1965. Vol. 1: 657p. Vol. 2: 709p. maps.

The illustrated journal of the famous German explorer's journey through Africa between 1849 and 1855. The first major Western traveller in this part of Africa, his journey took him from Tunis to Timbuctu, through the Libyan province of Fezzan, the Kanem, the Bornu and Baguirmi regions of Chad, and what are today Niger and Mali. Barth describes, in addition to the journey itself, the peoples he encountered, their traditions and their history.

17 **Bahr el ghazal, terre du Tchad.** (Bahr el-Ghazal, Chad.)
Julien de Cerf.   Monte Carlo: Regain, 1957. 190p.

An unusually frank and lucid study, by a man who travelled through the region of Kanem, north of the town of Moussoro, and who recounts his encounters with the local community. It depicts a changing society where slavery is becoming shameful and where a eunuch can still remember his own mutilation. It also describes the mundane and everyday events that punctuate the life of the people of Kanem. The book ends with the portraits of three administrators of the region: Audillière, Holsken, Ténal.

18 **John Olley, pioneer missionary to the Chad.**
J. W. Clapham, revised and amplified by Neville J. Taylor.   London: Pickering & Inglis, 1966. 139p.

A narrative in the manner of nineteenth-century travel accounts, tinged with a strongly religious outlook, this account of Dr. John Olley's life and work in Chad is a hymn of praise to the missionary and to Christianity.

19 **Mission au Tibesti. Carnets de route 1933-34.** (Mission in the Tibesti. Travel diaries.)
Charles Le Coeur, edited by Marguerite Le Coeur.   Paris: CNRS, 1969. 206p. map.

These personal impressions of ethnologist Charles Le Coeur contain detailed observations and descriptions of the environment, geology, topology and people, as well as their clothing and social customs. The travel diaries were written in the present tense. The illustrated book contains a map of North Africa from Morocco to the Darfur region and of the Tibesti with rivers, Teda terms throughout the text and tables of genealogies.

20 **Mémoires sur le Soudan. Géographie naturelle et politique, histoire et ethnographie, moeurs et institutions de l'Empire des Fellatas, du Bornou, du Baguermi, du Waday, du Dar-Four, rédigé d'après des renseignements entièrement nouveaux et accompagné d'une esquisse du Soudan Oriental.** (Memoirs on the Sudan. Physical and political geography, history and ethnography, morals and institutions of the Fellata empire, of Bornu, of Baguirmi, of Wadai, of Darfur, written from entirely new data and accompanied by an outline of eastern Sudan.)
Comte Escayrac de Lauture.   Paris: Arthur Bertrand, 1855-56. 184p. map.

An early work which is full of derogatory remarks and reflects the patronizing attitude of the late nineteenth century which believed that Africa was a vast territory with a people in need of a European master. Its usefulness is limited to providing an excellent example of the colonialist and self-righteous mentality of the time. It covers southwestern Chad as far north as Lake Chad.

21 **Le retour du Tchad, suite du voyage au Congo: Carnets de route.**
(Return from Chad, sequel to the journey to the Congo: travel diaries.)
André Gide. Paris: Librairie Gallimard, 1928. 247p. maps.

This travel diary by one of France's most famous twentieth-century writers, deals with only the southeastern part of Chad, most of the book being concerned with Cameroon. It offers an open-minded approach to its description of people and encounters with prominent individuals. It provides particularly good and vivid descriptions of the landscape.

22 **Théodore Monod.**
Isabelle Jarry. Paris: Plon, 1990.

A biography written from interviews (carried out by Jarry) with Monod, a biologist, a specialist in marine animal life, a desert traveller, a philosopher and a pacifist.

23 **Not by might, nor by power: story of the Paul Metzlers, 47-year missionaries to the heart of Africa.**
Joyce Metzler Baker. Schaumburg, Illinois: Regular Baptist Press, 1990. 225p.

Baker recounts the life of the missionary Paul Metzler and his wife Etienette, who were in Chad from the 1920s to the 1960s. The first draft of this biography was originally written by Hélène Metzler, their daughter, but she died before it was completed and the present author, her niece, took over the manuscript.

24 **Sahara and Sudan. Vol. 1: Tripoli and Fezzan, Tibesti or Tu. Vol. 2: Kawar, Bornu, Kanem, Borku, Ennedi. Vol. 3: The Chad Basin and Baguirmi.**
Gustav Nachtigal, translated from the German by Allan and Humphrey Fisher. London: C. Hurst & Company, 1974. Vol. 1: 460p. Vol. 2: 540p. Vol. 3: 519p. 1 map inserted at the end of Vol. 1 and 4 maps at the end of Vol. 3.

Nachtigal is probably the most famous explorer of Chad after Barth. He travelled through Chad between 1862 and 1867 and completed the work of Barth by visiting areas not seen by his predecessor. The Tibesti study, for example, is unique since no European had ever entered it and given a full account of it before and no European was to enter it again for over thirty years after Nachtigal. He describes the lands he visited and the people he encountered, giving very detailed and illustrated accounts of local traditions and practices.

25 **Chad.**
Alex Newton. In his: *Central Africa, a travel survival kit.*
Hawthorn, Australia; Berkeley, USA: Lonely Planet Publications, 1989,
p. 122-137. maps.
This travel guide provides general historical and geographical data as well as
practical information on travelling in Chad. N'Djamena, Lake Chad, Abéché and the
Tibesti are specifically described and details are given of their main attractions as
well as travelling tips.

26 **Sur les routes du Cameroun et de l'AEF.** (On the roads of Cameroon
and French Equatorial Africa.)
M. Rondet-Saint. Paris: Société d'Editions Géographiques, Maritimes
et Coloniales, 1933.
A colonial view of the region which is very patronizing when describing 'the locals'
and their traditions. It concentrates, however, on the colonial societies of AEF
[l'Afrique Equatoriale Française], with an emphasis on economic development
created by colonization.

27 **Méhariste et chef de poste au Tchad.** (Meharist and unit commander
in Chad.)
Guy le Rumeur. Paris: L'Harmattan, 1991. 188p.
An illustrated account of the life of a French meharist (the French Camel Corps
Section of the colonial forces) in northern Chad in the 1930s, which describes the
lives and customs of the Tubu. It is very informative on the life of French colonial
troops in isolated military units.

28 **Journal d'un safari au Tchad.** (Diary of a safari in Chad.)
Teddy Scheid. Brussels: La renaissance du livre, 1960. 183p.
This small book is a glorification of big-game hunting, which nonetheless prides itself
on its respect for animals. It recounts the safari of a Belgian couple and was written
by the wife, herself a hunter in Europe, but here only a photographer.

Geography

General

29 **Lanchad télédétection et géographie appliquée en zone sahélienne du Tchad.** (Lanchad remote sensing and applied geography in Chad's Sahelian zone.)
Claude Bardinet, Jean-Marie Monget. Paris: Ecole Normale Supérieure de Jeunes Filles, 1980. 543p. map. bibliog. (Collection Ecole Normale Supérieure de Jeunes Filles, no. 12).

This survey deals with the techniques involved in remote sensing. It discusses the Lanchad programme, the methodology for Landsat, Lanchad data analysis in spectral or taxonomic preliminary analysis, automatic cartography, spectral and geographical preliminary analysis, multi-spectral spatio-temporal analysis and geographical interpretation, and the remote sensing of Central African landscapes by Meteosat. The work includes a separate graphic and cartographic annexe which contains eleven satellite photographs and computer generations.

30 **L'Afrique Equatoriale Française.** (French Equatorial Africa.)
G. Bruel. Paris: Larose Editeur, 1935.

A general study of the geography, people, colonization and administration of the region, encompassing the modern territories of Chad, Gabon, the Central African Republic and Zaïre.

31 **French Equatorial Africa and the Cameroons.**
Edited by Lieut.-Colonel K. Mason. London: Naval Intelligence Division, December 1942. 524p. maps.

A very comprehensive study published during the Second World War for the exclusive use of officials. It deals with all aspects of the French Cameroons (Cameroon), Spanish Guinea (Equatorial Guinea), Gabon, Middle-Congo (Congo), Ubangi-Shari (Central African Republic) and the Belgian Congo (Zaïre), including

8

fauna and flora, history, diseases, ethnic groups, religions, communications, agriculture, ports, trade, mining, industry, geography, geology, finance and administration.

32   **Afrique Equatoriale Française.** (French Equatorial Africa.)
     A. Megglé.   Paris: Société Française d'Editions, 1931.

A study of the history of colonization, glorifying Brazza, Gentil and colonial activity in general, including the colonial administration of Chad. It also contains a brief geographical description and some basic information on the ethnic groups of the region. Good on natural resources and colonial infrastructure.

33   **L'Afrique Equatoriale.** ([French] Equatorial Africa.)
     Pierre Vennetier.   Paris: Presses Universitaires de France, 1972. 127p.
     maps. bibliog. (Que sais-je?).

Equatorial Africa covers Gabon, Congo, Cameroon, Central African Republic and Chad and was the name used by the French authorities which ruled over these territories until the 1960s. This study examines briefly the region's geography and ancient history and is devoted primarily to the economy.

34   **Afrique Equatoriale Française.** (French Equatorial Africa.)
     H. Ziéglé.   Paris: Editions Berger-Levrault, 1952. 199p.

This general work on French Equatorial Africa is divided into five parts: nature (geology, geography, climate, fauna, flora, coasts); people (demography, ethnic groups, social organization, beliefs, arts); history (pre-colonial and colonial); economy and infrastructure; politics (administrative organization). It gives a sober and very factual description of colonization.

Regional

35   **Le canton Diongor Abou-Telfan.** (The district of Diongor
     Abou-Telfan.)
     Alphonse Abras.   Fort-Lamy: République du Tchad, Présidence de la
     République, Ecole Nationale d'Administration, 1967. maps. 79p.

This document and the following items (36 to 74) all have a similar structure. Each deals with the population, language, geography, economy, social organization and some elements of ethnology and sociology of the 'canton' or district concerned. They are all available at the CHEAM (Centre des Hautes Etudes sur l'Afrique et l'Asie Modernes), Paris.

36   **Bededjia, Logone Oriental.** (Bededjia, eastern Logone.)
     Thomas Altoubam.   Fort-Lamy: République du Tchad, Présidence de
     la République, Ecole Nationale d'Administration, 1972-73. 55p.

37 **Le village de Maibo, sous-préfecture de Moissala.** (The village of Maibo, sub-prefecture of Moissala.)
Jacques Amos. Fort-Lamy: République du Tchad, Présidence de la République, Ecole Nationale d'Administration, 1968-69. 61p.

38 **Le canton de Mangalme, préfecture du Guéra.** (The district of Mangalme, prefecture of Guera.)
Mahamat Bachar. Fort-Lamy: République du Tchad, Présidence de la République, Ecole Nationale d'Administration, 1969-70. 75p.

39 **Le canton de Kokaga.** (The district of Kokaga.)
Maurice Bangui Dana. Fort-Lamy: République du Tchad, Présidence de la République, Ecole Nationale d'Administration, 1963-64. map. 27p.

40 **Le village de Maikirom, canton de Derguigui, P.A. de Bediondo, sous-préfecture de Koumra, Moyen-Chari.** (The village of Maikirom, district of Derguigui, P.A. of Bediondo, sub-prefecture of Koumra, Middle-Chari.)
Cyrille Banlongar. Fort-Lamy: République du Tchad, Présidence de la République, Ecole Nationale d'Administration, 1971-72. map. 130p.

41 **Le pays Boa. Le canton de Korbol.** (The Boa area. The district of Korbol.)
Radamane Barma. Fort-Lamy: République du Tchad, Présidence de la République, Ecole Nationale d'Administration, 1963-64. map. 37p.

42 **Le canton Dangaleat.** (The district of Dangaleat.)
Jacques Bilbil. Fort-Lamy: République du Tchad, Présidence de la République, Ecole Nationale d'Administration, 1967-68. 64p.

43 **Le canton Marba.** (The Marba district.)
André Boy. Fort-Lamy: République du Tchad, Présidence de la République, Ecole Nationale d'Administration, 1963-64. map. 43p.

44 **Le canton de Matekaga, sous-préfecture de Koumra, préfecture du Moyen-Chari.** (The district of Matekaga, sub-prefecture of Koumra, prefecture of Middle-Chari.)
Boguel Dimanche. Fort-Lamy: République du Tchad, Présidence de la République, Ecole Nationale d'Administration, 1968-69. 43p.

45   **Le village de Bedaya, sous-préfecture de Koumra, Moyen-Chari.**
      (The village of Bedaya, sub-prefecture of Koumra, Middle-Chari.)
      Ruben Djaibe.   Fort-Lamy: République du Tchad, Présidence de la
      République, Ecole Nationale d'Administration, 1970-71. maps. 65p.

46   **Le village 'hors-canton' de Beladjia.** (The 'out-district' village of
      Beladjia.)
      M. Djekilambert.   Fort-Lamy: République du Tchad, Présidence de la
      République, Ecole Nationale d'Administration, 1965-66. 61p.

47   **Le canton de Mondo (Kanem).** (The district of Mondo (Kanem).)
      Mahamat Djibert.   Fort-Lamy: République du Tchad, Présidence de la
      République, Ecole Nationale d'Administration, 1963-64. map. 31p.

48   **Le canton de Léré, sous-préfecture de Léré, préfecture de Mayo-
      Kebbi.** (The district of Lere, sub-prefecture of Lere, prefecture of
      Mayo-Kebbi.)
      Roger Djonfene.   Fort-Lamy: République du Tchad, Présidence de la
      République, Ecole Nationale d'Administration, 1967-68. 51p.

49   **Les villages de Kaga (Canton Goulaye) sous-préfecture de Lai
      (Tandjile).** (The villages of Kaga (Goulaye district) sub-prefecture of
      Lai (Tanjile).)
      Jacques Dono-Horngar.   Fort-Lamy: République du Tchad, Présidence
      de la République, Ecole Nationale d'Administration, 1970-71. 49p.

50   **Le village de Rapol, sous-préfecture de Beinamar, Logone
      occidental.** (The village of Rapol, sub-prefecture of Beinamar, western
      Logone.)
      Albert Doumaye.   Fort-Lamy: République du Tchad, Présidence de la
      République, Ecole Nationale d'Administration, 1972-73. 78p.

51   **Le quartier Mardjan-Daffack (Fort-Lamy).** (The Mardjan-Daffack
      area (Fort-Lamy).)
      Mahamat Faradjallah.   Fort-Lamy: République du Tchad, Présidence
      de la République, Ecole Nationale d'Administration, 1963-64.
      map. 24p.

52   **Le canton de Guegou, sous-préfecture de Léré, Mayo-Kebi.**
      (The district of Guegou, sub-prefecture of Lere, Mayo-Kebi.)
      Rebecca Gassinta.   Fort-Lamy: République du Tchad, Présidence de la
      République, Ecole Nationale d'Administration, 1971-72. 64p.

53 **Le canton de Maro.** (The district of Maro.)
Robert Kameldy.   Fort-Lamy: République du Tchad, Présidence de la
République, Ecole Nationale d'Administration, 1964-65. 55p.

54 **Le canton de Bao.** (The district of Bao.)
François Koumbairia.   Fort-Lamy: République du Tchad, Présidence
de la République, Ecole Nationale d'Administration, 1963-64. map.
55p.

55 **Le canton de Bessao.** (The district of Bessao.)
Philippe Mbailao.   Fort-Lamy: République du Tchad, Présidence de la
République, Ecole Nationale d'Administration, 1963-64. map. 30p.

56 **Le canton de Kyabe. Préfecture du Moyen-Chari.** (The district of
Kyabe. Prefecture of Middle-Chari.)
Robert Mbogo.   Fort-Lamy: République du Tchad, Présidence de la
République, Ecole Nationale d'Administration, 1969-70. 103p.

57 **Le canton de Mbalkabra. Sous-préfecture de Benoye, préfecture du
Logone occidental.** (The district of Mbalkabra. Sub-prefecture of
Benoye, prefecture of western Logone.)
Jacques Miagotar.   Fort-Lamy: République du Tchad, Présidence de la
République, Ecole Nationale d'Administration, 1964-65. 50p.

58 **Le canton de Mballa.** (The district of Mballa.)
Michel Miambe.   Fort-Lamy: République du Tchad, Présidence de la
République, Ecole Nationale d'Administration, 1964-65. 54p.

59 **Le village de Pare, canton de Bara, sous-préfecture de Moissala.**
(The village of Pare, district of Bara, sub-prefecture of Moissala.)
Raymond Mordjim.   Fort-Lamy: République du Tchad, Présidence de
la République, Ecole Nationale d'Administration, 1971-72. 132p.

60 **Bedaye, sous-préfecture de Koumra, Moyen-Chari.** (Bedaye, sub-
prefecture of Koumra, Middle-Chari.)
Daniel Mouadjidi.   Fort-Lamy: République du Tchad, Présidence de la
République, Ecole Nationale d'Administration, 1972-73. 118p.

61 **Les Daye de Bara II, canton Bara, sous-préfecture de Moissala, Moyen-Chari.** (The Daye of Bara II, district of Bara, sub-prefecture of Moissala, Middle-Chari.)
Alphonse Moudalbaye Belmond. Fort-Lamy: République du Tchad, Présidence de la République, Ecole Nationale d'Administration, 1971-72. 69p.

62 **L'Organisation cantonale au Tchad (partie septentrionale).** (District organization in northern Chad.)
Alphonse Moudalbaye Belmond. Fort-Lamy: République du Tchad, Présidence de la République, Ecole Nationale d'Administration, 1973-74. 32p.
This study is almost exclusively composed of tables which contain information on each district, its administrative centre ('chef-lieu'), population, the name of its chief, the date at which he took office, the number of villages and ethnic group.

63 **Ngoumou-Nanga (Sous-préfecture de Moissala).** (Ngou-mou-Nanga (Sub-prefecture of Moissala).)
Etienne Mouyo. Fort-Lamy: République du Tchad, Présidence de la République, Ecole Nationale d'Administration, 1963-64. map. 26p.

64 **Ngara.** (Ngara.)
Jacques Nabetimbaye. Fort-Lamy: République du Tchad, Présidence de la République, Ecole Nationale d'Administration, 1963-64. map. 47p.

65 **Le village de Bebo-Pen, canton de Bebo-Pen, sous-préfecture de Koumra, Moyen-Chari.** (The village of Bebo-Pen, district of Bebo-Pen, sub-prefecture of Koumra, Middle-Chari.)
Gaston Nadjiyo. Fort-Lamy: République du Tchad, Présidence de la République, Ecole Nationale d'Administration, 1971-72. map. 112p.

66 **Le canton de Béré.** (The district of Bere.)
Jacob Toumar Nayo. Fort-Lamy: République du Tchad, Présidence de la République, Ecole Nationale d'Administration, 1964-65. 73p.

67 **Le poste administratif de Doualat-Bedoto.** (The administrative post of Doualat-Bedoto.)
Christophe Ndeingar. Fort-Lamy: République du Tchad, Présidence de la République, Ecole Nationale d'Administration, 1963-64. map. 33p.

68   **Le canton de Bousso.** (The district of Bousso.)
     Abderahim Yacoub N'Diaye.   Fort-Lamy: République du Tchad,
     Présidence de la République, Ecole Nationale d'Administration,
     1963-64. map. 18p.

69   **Le village de Nankesse, sous-préfecture de Doba, prefecture du
     Logone oriental.** (The village of Nankesse, sub-prefecture of Doba,
     prefecture of eastern Logone.)
     Pierre Ngartori.   Fort-Lamy: République du Tchad, Présidence de la
     République, Ecole Nationale d'Administration, 1967-68. 49p.

70   **Kokaga ou Fort-Archambault de nos jours.** (Kokaga or Fort-
     Archambault (Sarh) today.)
     Jacques Ousmane.   Fort-Lamy: République du Tchad, Présidence de la
     République, Ecole Nationale d'Administration, 1965-66. 39p.

71   **Le canton de Michemire, sous-préfecture de Mousoro, préfecture
     du Kanem.** (The district of Michemire, sub-prefecture of Mousoro,
     prefecture of Kanem.)
     Oumar Outman.   Fort-Lamy: République du Tchad, Présidence de la
     République, Ecole Nationale d'Administration, 1967-68. 75p.

72   **Le village de Sateignan I, sous-préfecture de Moissala, Moyen-
     Chari.** (The village of Sateignan I, sub-prefecture of Moissala, Middle-
     Chari.)
     Rodou Renard.   Fort-Lamy: République du Tchad, Présidence de la
     République, Ecole Nationale d'Administration, 1969-70. 67p.

73   **Le canton de Peni.** (The district of Peni.)
     Simon Saringarti.   Fort-Lamy: République du Tchad, Présidence de la
     République, Ecole Nationale d'Administration, 1963-64. map. 38p.

74   **Donomanga.**
     Fidèle Yohaldengar.   Fort-Lamy: République du Tchad, Présidence de
     la République, Ecole Nationale d'Administration, 1963-64. map. 27p.

75   **Iles et rives du Sud-Kanem (Tchad): Etude de géographie
     régionale.** (Islands and lake banks of south-Kanem (Chad): a
     geographical study.)
     Christian Bouquet.   Bordeaux: CNRS, 1974. 200p. map. bibliog.
     (Travaux et Documents de Géographie Tropicale, 13).
     This illustrated study of applied geography in relation to the eastern part of Lake
     Chad in the Kanem region is enriched by the variety of perspectives used. The author

examines the geography of the region through the impact of agriculture and commerce which in turn involve the exploitation and use of the soil. The aim of the study is to define the possibilities for positive development of the region.

76 **Insulaires et riverains du Lac Tchad: Etude géographique. Tome I.**
(Lake Chad islanders and lakeside residents: a geographical study.
Vol. 1.)
Christian Bouquet. Paris: L'Harmattan, 1990. 415p. maps. bibliog.
Although the focus of this academic study is geographical, the author has also historical, ethnic and demographic perspectives. The second part, in addition to a study of the physical geography of the areas under observation, examines their agricultural and commercial activities. This volume deals with only the Lower Chari and the islands of Lake Chad and is illustrated with a number of photographs, diagrams and drawings.

77 **Le Bassin du Moyen Logone.** (The Middle-Logone Basin.)
Jean Cabot. Paris: ORSTOM, 1965. 237p. maps. bibliog.
This illustrated study of part of the Logone river (which flows from the southwestern border with the Central African Republic into Lake Chad) deals with the area between Gore in the south up to just north of Bongor and Yagoua, a region between fifty and two hundred kilometres wide on either side of the river. As a study of applied geography it represents a very thorough attempt to provide valuable information for development programmes carried out in the 1960s. Thus, the physical geography is complemented by a study of ethnic settlements, habitats, lifestyle and living standards as well as social structures. The colonial impact on agriculture is examined and the author concludes with a summary of the most recent (early 1960s) achievements and looks at the perspectives for the future.

78 **Borkou et Ounianga: Etude de géographie régionale.** (Borku and Unianga: a study in regional geography.)
R. Capot-Rey.   Algiers: Université d'Alger, Institut de Recherches Saharienne, 1961. 182p. map. bibliog.
Capot-Rey deals with geographical topics such as climate, relief, water, vegetation, as well as with the history, peoples and demography of the northern regions of Borku and Unianga.

79 **Lake Chad: ecology and productivity of a shallow tropical ecosystem.**
Edited by J. P. Carmouze, J. R. Durand, C. Léveque.   The Hague; Boston, Massachusetts; Lancaster, England: Dr W. Jung Publishers (a member of the Kluwer Academic Publishers Group), 1983. 575p. (Monographiae Biologicae, vol. 53).
The outcome of a research programme initiated by the ORSTOM Centre at N'Djamena and carried out between 1964 and 1978, this book contains, among other information, the result of new observations on Lake Chad. The research team studied the state of the lake known as 'Normal Lake Chad' before years of drought created the state known as 'Lesser Lake Chad' (a cyclic phenomenon which had already

occurred at the beginning of the century). The work is divided into five parts which deal with the lacustrine environment and its evolution; the main types of communities and their evolution during drought; the balance of the lacustrine ecosystem before and during a period of drought; and trophic relations.

80 **Les quartiers de Sarh, ex-Fort-Archambault (République du Tchad). Essai de définition des quartiers d'une ville tropicale.**
(The districts of Sarh, formerly Fort-Archambault (Republic of Chad).
A description of the districts of a tropical town.)
Jacques Chauvet. Bordeaux, France: Université de Bordeaux, 1974.
351p. maps. bibliog.

Chauvet's doctoral thesis deals with the second-largest town in Chad, situated in the southern Sara region, whose main characteristic is the ethnic diversity of its inhabitants. In relation to its demographic growth between 1955 and 1970 – the consequences of which are examined – the author establishes the various urban zones in terms of the district's morphology and ethnography. He analyses the main aspects of daily life in each zone, using the symbiosis between modernism and tradition as the main theme of the study.

81 **Le Ouaddai.** (The Wadai region.)
Capitaine B. de Courville. Paris: CHEAM, 1964. 8p. (no. 3971).

This short study of the Wadai region examines the geography of the region (relief, climate and fauna), discusses agricultural methods and deals with other topics such as markets, merisse (an alcoholic beverage), youth and the seasonal migration of Arabs in the region.

82 **Contribution à l'inventaire des ressources du Tibesti.** (Contribution to an inventory of the resources of Tibesti.)
J. M. Massip. Paris: 1969. (PhD thesis in Geography, Sorbonne, Paris).

Massip's doctoral thesis covers human, water, vegetal and underground resources, fauna and tourism, and their exploitation in this northern region of Chad.

83 **Rapport sur une mission exécutée dans le nord-est du Tchad en décembre 1966 et janvier 1967.** (Report on a mission carried out in northeastern Chad in December 1966 and January 1967.)
Théodore Monod. Fort-Lamy: INTSH, 1968. 115p. maps. bibliog.
(Etudes et Documents Tchadiens, Serie A, 3).

This report by Théodore Monod, a distinguished biologist, contains remarks and observations on geography, archaeology and biology made during a two-month journey in the little-explored east of the Borkou-Ennedi-Tibesti region (B.E.T.). It contains photographs and reproductions of prehistoric rock paintings, maps showing the itinerary of the mission, a short chronology, a list of prehistoric items, and of fauna and flora samples collected during the journey. The second appendix contains comments on a future project of international and interdisciplinary research in the southeast of the Libyan Desert. The report is completed by an extensive bibliography.

Atlases

84 **Geo Katalog. Band 2 Geowissenschaften.** (Geo list. Volume 2
geographical sciences.)
Anon. Stuttgart, Germany: Ausser-Europa, ILH GeoCenter, 1976. 6p.
(Section 568).

This publication contains lists of maps in French and German which relate to
geographical subjects, such as geographical handbooks, geology, hydrology,
mineralogy, geophysics, climatology, hydrography, and other subjects such as
archaeology and ethnography.

85 **Géocarte information. Niger, Tchad, Sierra Léone, Libéria.**
(Geo-map information. Niger, Chad, Sierra Leone, Liberia.)
Anon. Orléans, France: Bureau de Recherches Géologiques et
Minières, Service Géologique National, Département Documentation et
Information Géologiques, Cartothèque, 1985, p. 41-85. (Dossiers
documentaires sur la cartographie géologique mondiale).

A very useful document which contains a list of geological, mineral, hydrogeological
and hydrological, geophysical, structural, pedological, agro-pastoral, vegetation and
climatological maps.

86 **Inventory of world topographic mapping. Volume 2: South
America, Central America and Africa.**
Compiled by Rolf Bohme. London; New York: published on behalf of
the International Cartographic Association, by Elsevier Applied
Science Publishers, 1991, p. 294-8.

The chapter on Chad contained in this book presents brief information on the
mapping of Chad, together with a short bibliography and two index sheets illustrating
the status of the coverage of Chad for 1989.

87 **Atlas pratique du Tchad.** (A practical atlas of Chad.)
Jean Cabot, Christian Bouquet. Paris: Institut Géographique National;
N'Djamena: INTSH, 1972. 77p. maps.

This very useful atlas contains maps representing the entire surface of Chad and
illustrating such aspects as geology, pedology, hydrology, temperatures, archaeology,
languages, population distribution, crop distribution, cattle breeding, cotton crops,
pastoral movements, school equipment, medical equipment and tourist resources. It
also contains the maps of Fort-Lamy (N'Djamena), Fort-Archambault (Sarh),
Moundou and Abéché.

88 **Atlas historique et géographique de Sahr (Tchad) de 1899 à 1970.**
(Historical and geographical atlas of Sahr (Chad) from 1899 to 1970.)
Jacques Chauvet et une équipe de lycéens de Sahr (J. Chauvet and a
student group from Sahr). Sahr, Chad: Centre d'Etudes Linguistiques,
1984. 94p. maps.
This roneotyped work traces the history of the southern town of Sahr from its creation
as Fort-Archambault by Gentil in 1899 and studies its social geography. It contains
eleven black-and-white sketch maps and eleven annexes which describe many aspects
of the town, from its ethnic and social divisions to its basic infrastructure.

89 **Elevage et potentialités Sahéliennes. Synthèses cartographiques.**
Tchad. (Sahelian cattle breeding and potentials. Cartographic
synthesis. Chad.)
IEMVT, BRGM. Wageningen, Netherlands: Centre Technique de
Coopération Agricole et Rurale, 1986. 41 maps.
This atlas contains eleven maps on a 1:500,000 scale, two on 1:1,500,000, fourteen on
1:3,000,000, one on 1:5,000,000, one on 1:6,000,000 and twelve on even smaller
scales. The maps illustrate diverse themes such as pastoralism and vegetation,
pastoral potentials, minerals in natural grazing grounds, subterranean waters,
migration axes and Sahelian grouping centres, main animal husbandry species and
veterinary infrastructure, as well as maps on the distribution of various cattle parasitic
afflictions.

Maps

90 **Tchad. Carte Administrative.** (Chad. Administrative map.)
Anon. Paris: MRE, 1984. 1 map. Scale: 1:6,000,000.
The latest available map of the administrative divisions of Chad, created under the
Habré regime. This map and those which follow (items 91 to 112) have been chosen
to give an overview of the kinds of maps of Chad that are available. They do not
cover the numerous historical maps and itineraries, nor do they include town maps.

91 **Organisation Administrative.** (Administrative organization.)
Anon. Paris: IGN, 1960. 1 map. Scale: 1:7,500,000.
The original administrative divisions of Chad as set out at Independence.

92 **Tchad, Carte routière au 1:1 500 000.** (Chad. Road map,
1:1,500,000.)
Anon. Paris: IGN, 1974. map with legend.
This map shows roads and tracks, relief and vegetation, as well as the location of
hotels, religious buildings, hospitals, post offices, aerodromes, wells and rivers.

93 **Tchad. Carte Routière.** (Chad. Road map.)
    Anon. Paris: IGN, 1968. 2 maps. Scale: 1:1,500,000.
This map is the precursor road map to the 1974 road map (q.v.) and was prepared by
French cartographers.

94 **Tchad. Carte Routière.** (Chad. Road map.)
    Anon. Brazzaville: IGN for Shell, 1962. 1 map. Scale: 1:1,666,666.
A map prepared by the official French Cartographic Institute for the Shell oil
company as part of the attempt to attract interest towards oil prospecting in Chad.

95 **Etude de la moyenne vallée du Chari, rive gauche. Carte ethno-
    démographique.** (A study of the Middle-Chari Basin, west bank.
    Ethno-demographic map.)
    Anon. République du Tchad, Ministère de l'Agriculture et de la
    Production Animale, 1968. Scale: 1:200,000.
This map shows the location of fourteen ethnic groups including the Sara, the Masa
and the Kanuri. It also contains basic information such as roads, towns and villages,
small town clinics and airfields. The map is part of the study *Les populations de la
moyenne vallée du Chari. Vie économique et sociale*, by Claude Arditi (q.v.).

96 **Bassin du Tchad. Carte forestière sommaire. Agriculture.** (Chad
    Basin. Summary forest map. Agriculture.)
    Anon. Paris: IEMVT, 1980. 1 map. Scale: 1:1,000,000.
This is one of the few maps to provide a comprehensive, if cursory, view of
vegetation cover in Chad.

97 **Esquisse de la couverture végétale du Tchad en relation avec les
    sols au sud du 16ème parallèle.** (A sketch of the vegetal cover in
    relation to soil constitution, Chad, south of the 16th parallel.)
    J. Pias. Paris: ORSTOM, 1968. 1 map. Scale: 1:1,500,000.
The map provides information on the relation between vegetation and soil type for the
southern half of Chad.

98 **Synthèse des études agro-pastorales. (Bassin du Lac Tchad).**
    (A synthesis of agro-pastoral studies. (Lake Chad Basin).)
    Anon. Paris: IEMVT, 1979. 1 map. Scale: 1:1,000,000.
One of the most important areas in Chad, in terms of agricultural potential, is the
Lake Chad basin, even though the lake itself is shrinking. This map reflects this
potential.

99 **Pâturages du sud-ouest du Tchad.** (Grazing lands of southwestern Chad.)
IEMVT.   Paris: for the Ministère de l'Agriculture, de l'Elevage, Eaux et Forêts, Pêche et Chasses (Ministry of Agriculture, Livestock Breeding, the National Commission for Forestry, Fishing and Shooting), 1976. 2 maps (north and south). Scale: 1:500,000.

Pastoral agriculture is extremely important in Southern Chad as livestock exports have traditionally formed an important part of the economy there. This is part of a series of cartographic studies carried out in France for the Chadian government preparatory to plans for development.

100 **Ensembles pastoraux du Kanem et du lac – 1976.** (Pastoral areas: Kanem and Lake Chad – 1976.)
IEMVT.   Paris: for the Ministère de l'Agriculture, de l'Elevage, Eaux et Forêts, Pêche et Chasses (Ministry of Agriculture, Livestock Breeding, the National Commission for Forestry, Fishing and Shooting), 1976. 1 map. Scale: 1:500,000.

This map is similar to the preceding entry (q.v.), but covers the Lake Chad–Kanem area in the north-west of the country.

101 **Carte hydrogéologique de la République du Tchad.** (Hydrogeological map of the Republic of Chad.)
Schneider.   Orléans, France: BRGM, 1969. 1 map. Scale: 1:1,500,000.

The relative paucity of water in Northern Chad and the restricted level of access to water in the central part of the country, has led to considerable speculation over additional water sources. This map provides a general overview of the situation.

102 **Carte hydrogéologique.** (Hydrogeological map.)
BRGM.   Paris: Ministère des Travaux Publics, 1966-68. 6 maps. Scale: 1:500,000.

This six maps which make up this series provide a very detailed view of the hydrology and underlying geology of Chad.

103 **Carte géologique de la République du Tchad.** (Geological map of the Republic of Chad.)
Schneider.   Orléans, France: BRGM, 1964. 2 maps (north and south). Scale: 1:1,500,000.

A general geological study of Chad.

104 **Esquisse géologique des formations tertiaires et quaternaires du Tchad au sud du 16ème parallèle.** (Geological sketch of Tertiary and Quaternary formations south of the 16th parallel.)
J. Pias. Paris: ORSTOM, 1967. 2 maps. Scale: 1:1,000,000.
This geological map of Chad covers the southern half of the country.

105 **Borkou – Ennedi – Tibesti. Géologie.** (Borku – Ennedi – Tibesti. Geology.)
Anon. Paris: Service Géographique de l'A.E.F. pour la Direction des Mines, 1958. 2 maps (west and east). Scale: 1:1,000,000.
The Borku–Ennedi–Tibesti (BET) region of Chad, in the north of the country, is the most lightly populated part of the country, but it is believed to contain significant mineral deposits. The two maps included here provide valuable insights into the regional geology in the light of these claims.

106 **Emi Koussi Tibesti-Sahara. Topographie.** (Emi Koussi Tibesti-Sahara. Topography.)
Anon. Bern: E. Collioud et Co. Druck mit Unterstutzung die Fritz Thyssen-Stichtung durch FA, 1969. 1 map. Scale: 1:25,000.
The topography of the central and northern regions of Tibesti form the subject of this map.

107 **Structure pétrographique du Tibesti.** (Petrographic structure of the Tibesti.)
Anon. Section Cartographique de l'A.E.F., [approx. 1937]. 1 map. Scale: 1:1,000,000. (From old French Equatorial Africa maps, 3rd series, page 24).
This study of rock structures in the Saharan massif of Tibesti reflects the anxiety of the French colonial administration to find some justification for its commitment to preserving a French presence there.

108 **Bassin alluvionnaire du Logone et du Chari. Région au nord et à l'est du lac Tchad.** (Logone and Chari alluvial Basin. Northern and eastern Lake Chad region.)
R. Deruelle. Paris: ORSTOM, Société Nouvelle de Cartographie, 1958. 1 map. Scale: 1:1,000,000.
A study of the topology and morphology of one of the most important demographic regions of Chad.

21

109 **Etude pédologique du bassin alluvionnaire du Logone-Chari.**
(Pedological study of the Logone-Chari alluvial basin.)
Anon.   Paris: ORSTOM, 1954. 3 maps. Scale: 1:200,000. (One
234-page vol., 3 pedological maps.)
A soil study of this important region which is a significant agricultural centre for
south-western Chad.

110 **Carte pédologique du Tchad.** (Pedological map of Chad.)
J. Pias.   Fort-Lamy: ORSTOM, 1970. 2 maps. Scale: 1:1,000,000.
A soil map of Chad providing important information for developmental purposes.

111 **Bassin du Lac Tchad.** (Lake Chad Basin.)
Anon.   N'Djamena: CBLT; PNUD; UNESCO, 1968. Series of 12
maps. Scale: 1:500,000.
This map series was prepared by a UNESCO-piloted project in 1968 to provide
complete information on the Lake Chad region. Apart from describing the limits on
mapping techniques (Map 1), the series covers topography, hydrogeology,
geophysics, rainfall patterns, hydrology, vegetation and geology.

112 **Bassin du Lac Tchad (Synthèse Hydrologique).** (Lake Chad Basin
(Hydrological synthesis).)
Anon.   N'Djamena: CBLT; PNUD; UNESCO, 1966-68. 3 maps.
Scale: 1:1,000,000.
These three maps form part of the preliminary work for the *Bassin du Lac Tchad*
study in 1968 (item no. 111). They cover the geology, hydrogeology and surface
hydrology of the region.

Geology

113 **Génèse et évolution de deux toposéquences de sols tropicaux du Tchad, interprétation biogéodynamique.** (Genesis and evolution of two Chadian tropical soil toposequences. Biogeodynamic interpretation.)
G. Bocquier.   Paris: ORSTOM, 1973. maps. bibliog. (Mémoire, no. 62).

This illustrated study is concerned with the two areas of Kosselili and Mindera and examines the morphological organization of their soils. It then gives some general interpretations on the formation and the evolution of the two sequences. It contains a very extensive bibliography.

114 **Contribution géophysique à la connaissance géologique du bassin du lac Tchad.** (Geophysical contribution to geological research in the Lake Chad Basin.)
P. Louis.   Paris: ORSTOM, 1970. 311p. maps. bibliog. (Mémoire, no. 42).

The research described in this volume was started in 1959. It begins by showing the characteristics of the geophysical study undertaken by the ORSTOM in the Chad Basin which described the main structural features of this region. This is completed by a series of geological comments on the geophysical documents examined in the first part. Three maps are included at the end of the volume.

115 **L'erg de Fachi-Bilma (Tchad–Niger). Contribution à la connaissance de la dynamique des ergs et des dunes des zones arides chaudes.** (The Fachi-Bilma erg (Chad–Niger). A contribution to the knowledge of erg and dune dynamics in hot and arid zones.) Monique Mainguet, Yann Callot. Paris: CNRS, 1978. 184p. maps. (Service de Documentation et de Cartographie Géographiques. Mémoires et Documents, Année 1978, Nouvelle Série, Vol. 18).

This study is divided into two parts: the first deals with ergs [shifting sand-dunes] in general and the second with the erg of Fachi-Bilma, situated in northern Chad. Its overall aim is to establish a method of analysis using photo-interpretation and cartography and to provide a geomorphological map (1:1,000,000) to be compared with satellite photographs in order to build a systematic cartography of the Sahara's ergs.

116 **Contribution à l'évaluation de l'évaporation de nappes d'eau libre en climat tropical sec. Exemples du Lac de Bam et de la Mare d'Oursi (Burkina Faso), du Lac Tchad et d'Açudes du Nordeste brésilien.** (Contribution to an assessment of evaporation from water pools in dry tropical climates. Case studies of Lake of Bam and Oursi Pool (Burkina Faso), of Lake Chad and Lake Açudes in the Nordeste region of Brazil.) Bernard Pouyaud. Paris: ORSTOM, 1986. 254p. bibliog.

This study is divided into five parts: hydropluviometric and climatological data, assessment of evaporation; theories of evaporation of a water pool in the atmosphere; assessment of evaporation of large water pools from measurements on evaporation trays; a finer approach of evaporation: Lake of Bam; and a general conclusion.

117 **Biographie d'un désert.** (Biography of a desert.) P. Rognon. Paris: Plon, 1989. (Collection Scientifique).

A geological history of the Sahara which concludes by discussing present problems and hopes for the future protected from desertification. It makes relatively easy reading without excessive use of scientific terminology.

118 **Etudes des diatomées et paléolimnologie du bassin tchadien au cénozoïque supérieur.** (Studies on the diatomites and palaeolimnology of the Chadian Basin during the Upper Cenozoic.) Simone Servant-Vildary. Paris: ORSTOM, 1978. 346p. (Vol. 1). (Vol. 1 & 2, Travaux et Documents, no. 84).

This research was originally presented as a doctoral thesis. Volume one examines the evolution of the associations of diatomites in the ancient and recent Quaternary and concludes by describing the main facts of that period, their palaeoecological interpretation and the flora of the ancient Plio-Pleistocene, the Ghazalian, the end of the Pleistocene and the Holocene epochs. The second volume is made up entirely of illustrations to accompany the first volume.

Flora and Fauna

119 **Mes éléphants du Tchad.** (My elephants of Chad.)
H. Oberjohann, translated by Henri Daussy.   Paris; Grenoble, France:
B. Arthaud, 1952. 195p. (Les clefs de l'aventure).
Written when elephant hunting was still fashionable, this illustrated book of
adventure tells how the author, a big-game hunter, captured elephants in order to send
them to European zoos, and discusses various aspects of the life of elephants.

120 **Lexique des plantes du pays sar. Plantes spontanées et cultivées.**
Tome 1: noms sar – noms scientifiques. Tome 2: noms scientifiques
– noms sar, avec indications d'utilisation. (Sara plant lexicon.
Naturally occurring and cultivated plants. Vol. 1: Sar names –
scientific names. Vol. 2: Scientific names – Sar names, with
indications of use.)
Pierre Palayer.   Sahr, Chad: Centre d'Etudes Linguistiques, Collège
Charles Lwanga, 1977. 82p., 78p. bibliog.
This is the first lexicon on plants found in the Sara area of southern Chad. The first
volume contains Sar names in alphabetical order and gives a brief description of each
plant, while the second one is organized according to the alphabetical order of the
scientific names and describes each plant's use in the Sara region. The first volume
contains over 800 names, while the second one consists of only 496. This is due to the
existence of several synonyms in Sar for a single scientific species.

121 **Faune sauvage du Tchad.** (Wild fauna of Chad.)
G. Pécaud.   *Bulletin de la Société des Recherches Congolaises*,
no. 10 (1929), p. 47-108.
In spite of the large variety of animals described here, this study is specifically
directed to game hunters. It lists mammals and birds and each of these groups is

divided into orders, families and sub-families in which a brief description of each animal is given.

122 **Les systèmes de défense végétaux pré-coloniaux (Tchad et Nord-Cameroun).** (Pre-colonial vegetal defence systems (Chad and north Cameroon).)
Christian Seignobos. Montpellier, France: Annales de l'Université du Tchad, September 1978. 93p. map. bibliog. (Série Lettres, Langues Vivantes et Sciences Humaines).
Seignobos examines vegetation as a means of defence. The work describes its origins, and studies several types of defensive systems as well as the magic power of hedges and plants.

123 **Paysages de parcs et civilisations agraires (Tchad et Nord-Cameroun).** (Park landscapes and agrarian civilizations (Chad and north Cameroon).)
Christian Seignobos. Montpellier, France: Annales de l'Université du Tchad, September 1978. 93p. map. bibliog. (Série Lettres, Langues Vivantes et Sciences Humaines).
This study begins with an explanation of the concept of park. The author then proceeds to analyse the value and significance of parks and finally he examines the consequences of their absence in Chad and the mechanisms of their destruction.

124 **Des fortifications végétales dans la zone soudano-sahélienne (Tchad et Nord-Cameroun).** (Plant fortifications in the Sudanese-Sahelian zone (Chad and north Cameroon).)
Christian Seignobos. *Cahiers ORSTOM, Série Sciences Humaines*, Vol. XVII, no. 3-4 (1980), p. 191-222. maps.
The author examines here how the transformation of plant fortifications into enclosures frequently concealed the original role played by these installations. He explains how certain natural, historical or geo-strategic conditions favoured the setting up of such systems which were indispensable, given permanent conditions of insecurity in the region.

Rapport sur une mission exécutée . . . 1966 et 1967.
See item no. 83.

Prehistory and Archaeology

125 **Les peintures rupestres archaïques de l'Ennedi.** (Archaic rock paintings of the Ennedi region.)
Gérard Bailloud. *Anthropologie*, vol. 64, no. 3-4 (1960), p. 211-34.

Bailloud relates the prehistories of the Tassili region of Algeria and of the Ennedi massif in northern Chad and shows that the artefacts and paintings found in the Ennedi are much older than previously thought. Four sites are described in detail, and a number of others are briefly described.

126 **Tibesti: Carrefour de la préhistoire saharienne.** (The Tibesti: crossroads of Saharan prehistory.)
Pierre Beck, Général Pierre Huard. Paris: Arthaud, 1959. 293p. maps. bibliog.

The first global description of the largest and most isolated Saharan massif. It is divided into two parts, the first by zoologist Pierre Beck, who describes the volcanic chain, the flora and fauna and the 10,000 Tedas who live in this northern region of Chad. In the second part, General Huard gives an overview of a 7,000-years-old past with the help of archaeological artefacts, objects and rock-paintings left by hunters and shepherds. The book also examines relations with the Tassili massif and the Nile and finally unveils the origins of the Teda race, with the help of anthropometry, blood groups and palaeoethnological data.

127 **Rock drawing from southern Libya and northern Chad.**
Pavel Cervicek. *Annali*, vol. 44 (1984), p. 11-28. map.

This short article is very rich in illustrations of the rock-drawings found in southern Libya and northern Chad. The text is limited to description, dating and location of the rock-drawings, and engravings without interpretation.

128 **Mission paléontologique dans le nord de la république du Tchad.**
(Palaeontological mission in northern Chad.)
Yves Coppens. [n.p., n.d.]. 6p.

The mission was organized at the request of the Centre National de la Recherche Scientifique (CNRS) and the Mission Hydrogéologique de l'Institut Equatorial de Recherches et d'Etudes Géologiques et Minières and was carried out between 20 January and 30 March (presumably around 1958-59). It sought to complete the knowledge (acquired from previous missions in 1955 and 1957) of the fauna of the beginning of the Quaternary period in Central Africa and to try to link this fauna with its modern counterpart.

129 **Fouilles dans la région du Tchad. Première partie, Deuxième partie (Midigué).** (Excavations in the Chad region. Part One, Part Two (Midigue).)
M. Griaule, Jean-Paul Lebeuf. *Journal de la Société des Africanistes,* Part One: Vol. XVIII (1948), p. 1-116. Part Two: Vol. XXX (1950), p. 1-152. maps.

This article is the result of research missions carried out in July 1936, between January and August 1937, January and February 1939, during the Sahara–Cameroon and the Lebaudy–Griaule missions. It deals with the Sao civilization which existed in southern Chad and provides a general view of this vanished population with the help of artefacts found in forty-four excavation sites.

130 **Ossements anciens de Mdaga.** (Ancient bones from Mdaga.)
Raoul Hartweg, Françoise Treinen. N'Djamena: INTSH, [n.d.]. 24p.
(Etudes et Documents Tchadiens, Série A, 2).

This study constitutes a report from excavations carried out in February and March 1964 north of N'Djamena, on the Sao site of Mdaga, under scrutiny since 1960. It refers to a number of skeletons found on this site, inhabited until around 1875. The study deals only with the anatomical features of the skeletons and does not refer to the archaeological context or to the conditions of the site, published in a subsequent study of Mdaga. The items were in the process of being carbon-dated at the time of publication.

131 **Transition du néolithique à l'âge du fer dans la plaine péritchadienne: le cas de Mdaga.** (The transition from the Neolithic to the Iron Age in the Peri-Chadian Plain: the case of Mdaga.)
Augustin Holl. In: *Le milieu et les hommes – Recherches comparatives dans le bassin du lac Tchad. Actes du 2ème colloque Méga-Tchad, ORSTOM Bondy, le 3 et 4 octobre 1985 (The environment and the people – comparative research in the Lake Chad Basin. Proceedings of the Mega-Chad colloquium, ORSTOM Bondy, 3 and 4 October 1985),* edited by Daniel Barreteau, Henri Tourneux. Paris: ORSTOM, 1988, p. 81-109. map. bibliog.

This article analyses the archaeology of a very short period of the recent prehistory of the Peri-Chadian Plain, which witnessed the beginning of iron working. It examines the Mdagha hill, situated fourteen kilometres north of N'Djamena, which is the largest excavated site in this part of Chad.

132 **Les arts sao. Cameroun, Tchad, Nigeria.** (Sao arts. Cameroon, Chad, Nigeria.)
Annie Lebeuf, Jean-Paul Lebeuf. Paris: Chêne, 1977. 208p. maps. bibliog.

A large illustrated book dealing with the ancient populations collectively called Sao, ancestors of the Kotoko, who used to live in the area now spanning Cameroon, Chad and Nigeria. The work combines an archaeological, ethnological and historical approach and describes the materials used for the making of the objects found during excavation, as well as the objects themselves and their use.

133 **Archéologie tchadienne. Les Sao du Cameroun et du Tchad.**
(Chadian archaeology: the Sao of Cameroon and Chad.)
Jean-Paul Lebeuf. Paris: Hermann, 1962. 147p. maps. bibliog.
(Actualités scientifiques et industrielles, 1295).

Compiled from data collected during four different missions carried out between 1936 and 1952 in the regions of Sahara-Cameroon, Niger-Lake Iro, Logone-Lake Fitri, Borkou, and northern Cameroon, this study describes the excavated sites as well as the various artefacts unearthed. It also discusses some ethnographical features of the excavations and explains the use and symbolism of the main materials used: terracotta and metal. Finally, the author proposes a possible chronology and the history of the sites.

134 **Carte archéologique des abords du lac Tchad (Cameroun, Nigeria et Tchad).** (Archaeological map of the area around Lake Chad (Cameroon, Nigeria and Chad).)
Jean-Paul Lebeuf. Paris: CNRS, 1969. 171p. maps. bibliog.

The map is divided into eleven sections which provide much information on the archaeology of the surroundings of Lake Chad and include such features as main migratory movements, ancient settlements, various excavation sites within the urban perimeter of Fort-Lamy and places of worship. The scale of the sections ranges between 1:20,000 and 1:600,000 and each is accompanied by an introduction, tables and brief comments, as well as a list of ancient sites.

135 **Pipes anciennes à fumer des fouilles de Mdaga (Tchad).** (Ancient smoking pipes of the Mdaga excavation site (Chad).)
Raymond Mauny. *Journal des Africanistes*, vol. 52, no. 1-2 (1982), p. 165-7. bibliog.

Mauny's short article refers to the excavations carried out on Sao sites by Annie and Jean-Paul Lebeuf and their team between 1960 and 1968. It accounts in detail for the fifteen points excavated, providing for each the location, depth, number and characteristics of the pipes found and the age of various layers.

136 **Recherches préhistoriques dans le sud-ouest tchadien.** (Prehistoric research in southwestern Chad.)
Th. Tillet. *Travaux du LAPERMO* (1977). 8p. map.

Southwestern Chad was the subject of only two short prehistoric research missions in 1962 and 1963, in the Sara and Mayo-Kebbi regions. These were followed by three other missions led by the author in 1974 and 1975 in the Mayo-Kebbi region and this article provides an account of his findings. The artefacts described are of Palaeolithic and Neolithic origin and come from excavations in Gamba-Toubouri, Mombaroua, Fianca and Goumadji.

137 **Sahara et Sahel à l'âge du fer, Bourkou, Tchad.** (Sahara and Sahel in the Iron Age, Borku, Chad.)
Françoise Treinen-Claustre. Paris: Société des Africanistes, Musée de l'Homme, 1982. 214p. maps. bibliog.

This study, richly illustrated and based on many artefacts from this part of northern Chad, demonstrates that the 'Koro-Toro culture', which flourished between 300 and 800 AD, developed in an intensive manner the use of iron and refined ceramics which place it among the greatest African civilizations of the Iron Age.

Rapport sur une mission exécutée . . . 1966 et 1967.
See item no. 83.

History

General

138 **The Kanuri factor in Nigeria–Chad relations.**
Ade Adefuye. *Journal of the Historical Society of Nigeria*, vol. 12, no. 3-4 (1984-85), p. 121-37.
One of the effects of the Berlin Conference on Africa (1884-85) was that the Kanuri people found their territory divided between two colonial authorities: the British in Nigeria and the French in Chad. This colonial division did not reflect the Kanuri state and has been a source of conflict between the independent states of Nigeria and Chad.

139 **Les français en Afrique noire de Richelieu à Mitterrand, 350 ans de présence française au sud du Sahara.** (The French in black Africa from Richelieu to Mitterrand, a 350-year-long French presence south of the Sahara.)
P. Biarnès. Paris: Editions Armand Colin, 1987. 448p. maps.
An illustrated historical and political study of French Africa, which also includes references to Chad. It is divided into three parts: the slavery period, the colonial period and independence.

140 **Le Tchad écartelé.** (Chad torn apart.)
Jean Cabot. *Hérodote*, no. 18 (April-June 1980), p. 133-53. maps.
Cabot makes a thorough attempt to explain the Chadian conflict. He observes that the history of this region, characterized by 2000 years of combat, pillage, and razzias [tribal raids], together with the drawing of arbitrary borders, make it difficult to expect a few decades of 'French peace' to create the conditions for the successful creation of a nation-state. He stresses linguistic diversity as an illustration of the sources of conflict which were amplified by colonial economic and cultural impositions. He claims that economic and social discrepancies between North and South caused by colonial administration are at the origins of the rebellion in the

north, centre and east of the country. The author finally examines the rebellion and the splits between its various actors who were not able to overcome the tribal differences exploited by their neighbours.

141 **Le peuple tchadien, ses racines et sa vie quotidienne.** (The Chadian people, their origins and daily life.)
Jean Chapelle. Paris: L'Harmattan, 1980. 304p.

A very thorough socio-historical study, which covers prehistoric times and includes the pre- and post-independence periods. It discusses the internecine fighting and contemporary political problems of the Tombalbaye period. It also examines the origins of the people of Chad, as well as their religious and social structures as animists, Muslims and Christians. A very clear and easy-to-read work, especially on political matters. It provides a good, albeit schematic, overview of the civil war.

142 **Historical dictionary of Chad.**
Samuel Decalo. London: Scarecrow Press, 1977. 413p. maps. bibliog. (African Historical Dictionaries, no. 13).

A very useful dictionary containing entries on all aspects of Chad's recent history and giving summaries about political figures as well as ethnic groups, political parties and events, and geographical entities. It contains a nineteen-page introduction which provides essential information on Chad, a selected chronology and a very extensive bibliography. A second revised edition, in which extra entries have been added and some information amended, was published in 1987 (London: Scarecrow Press. 532p. maps. bibliog.).

143 **A propos du Tchad: la face nord face à l'histoire.** (Chad: the north faces history.)
René Lemarchand. *The Maghreb Review*, vol. 12, no. 1-2 (1987), p. 18-24.

The author of this article attempts to understand the relationship existing between Chad's pre-colonial past and the present and examines the history of the Chad–Libya border region. He analyses the role played by historical determinants in the Libyan intervention and measures the impact of the Sanusiyya on local communities.

144 **Essai de chronologie tchadienne (1707-1940).** (Chad: a chronology (1707-1940).)
Jean Malval, preface by Marie-José Tubiana. Paris: CNRS, 1974. 167p. map. bibliog.

Doctor Malval lived in Chad from 1926 to 1928 as the physician to the colonial forces there, mainly in Kanem and Wadai. His chronology starts in the eighth century with the coming of the first 'white' nomads to the Chad Basin, and it is extremely schematic until the eighteenth century. Events are described in more detail from the beginning of European exploration, starting with Barth's expedition in the 1850s. It is particularly informative about French military movements in Chad and gives a valuable chronology of French penetration into the country. Each entry is presented without commentary.

145 **Eléments pour un dictionnaire biographique du Tchad et du Niger (Téda et Daza).** (A biographical dictionary of Chad and Niger (Teda and Daza).)
Albert Le Rouvreur, Paule Delville, Joseph Tubiana. Paris: Editions du CNRS, 1978. 48p. (Laboratoires Peiresc, Contribution à la Connaissance des Elites Africaines, I).

This short dictionary was inspired by Richard Hill's equivalent *Biographical Dictionary of the Anglo-Egyptian Sudan* and aims to help ethnologists as well as historians in their research. It contains information on characters known for their political, economic and cultural roles in the history of Chad.

146 **Pilgrims in a strange land: the Hausa communities in Chad, 1890-1970.**
John A. Works. Ann Arbor, Michigan: University Microfilms, 1972. 341p. bibliog.

This doctoral thesis centres on the Hausa communities of Abéché and Fort-Lamy and examines the way in which the Hausa manipulated the colonial administration. It analyses the evolution of local communities and of the community at large in order to better understand the significance of migrations during the colonial period, as well as the life of the Hausa abroad.

Pre-colonial (up to 1912)

147 **Rabah, conquérant des pays tchadiens.** (Rabah, conqueror of the Chadian lands.)
Joseph Amegboh. Paris; Dakar; Abidjan: ABC, 1976. 89p. map. bibliog.

A short study which glorifies Rabah and tries to establish a particular status for this African conqueror. Here he is described not as a brutal and bloodthirsty leader, as is often the case, but as a great warrior, who should be praised for his resistance to France. A useful chronology is included.

148 **Documents d'archives I (Tchad, Cameroun, Nigeria, Niger).**
(Archive documents I (Chad, Cameroon, Nigeria, Niger).)
Anon. Fort-Lamy: INTSH, 1968. 180p. (Etudes et Documents Tchadiens, Série B, 1).

This work, introduced by Jean Chapelle, brings together six documents concerned with Chad, most of which are reports by French administrators such as Emile Gentil and refer to Wadai, Baguirmi, Dar al-Kuti and Kanem. Most are between ten and twenty pages long, except for the first report by Capitaine Dubois, Baguimi Resident in 1902, which contains just under one hundred pages.

149 **Documents d'archives II (Tchad et pays limitrophes).**
(Archive documents II (Chad and bordering countries).)
Anon. N'Djamena: INSH, 1975. 173p. (Etudes et Documents
Tchadiens, Série B, 2).

The second volume of archive documents published by the Institut National pour les
Sciences Humaines contains thirty-two texts, many of which emanate from or were
sent to Colonel Largeau. As is the case for the first volume (q.v.), the documents
come from the 'Political Affairs' section of the archives and they are official
documents, letters, instructions or reports.

150 **Organisation politique au Tibesti. Une convention entre Arna et
Temagara.** (Political organization in Tibesti. An agreement between
the Arna and the Temagara.)
Jean d'Arbaumont. *Bulletin de l'Institut Fondamental d'Afrique
Noire*, Vol. XVIII, no. 1-2 (1956), p. 148-55. (Série B).

The translation of a document in Arabic referring to an agreement between two Teda-
Daza tribes of northern Chad is followed by a commentary. The main feature of the
convention, written either in late nineteenth or early twentieth century, is a
demarcation of tribal territories.

151 **Entre Ouaddai et Dar For: Annales des sultans dadjo (1664-1912).**
(Between Wadai and Darfur: annals of the Dajo Sultans (1664-1912).)
Henri Berre. *Le Mois en Afrique*, no. 201-2 (1982), p. 144-8.

Lieutenant Berre occupied an impressive number of important administrative posts in
France and Chad. During his time as administrator of the Dar Sila region between
1942 and 1947 he became acquainted with the Dajo Sultans of that region. He
recounts their history briefly in this article, from their arrival in Chad in the 1660s,
after their eviction from the Darfur region in neighbouring Sudan. He also examines
their relations with neighbouring rulers until 1912, the date of Colonel Largeau's
entry into the Sila.

152 **Sultans dadjo du Sila (Tchad).** (Dajo sultans of the Sila region
(Chad).)
Lieutenant Henri Berre. Paris: CNRS, 1985. 119p. map.
(Laboratoires Pereisc, Contributions à la Connaissance des Elites
Africaines).

This book was written as a complement to Bret's book on Mohammed Bakhit (item
no. 174). The author relates the origins of the Dajo back to the sixteenth century when
they came from Yemen and were united under the banner of Ahmad al-Daj, their first
sultan. He covers their history up to the death of their fifteenth sultan, Mustapha Ould
Bakhit, in 1946.

153 The Shehus of Kukawa, a history of the Al-Kanemi dynasty of
Bornu.
Louis Brenner. Oxford: Clarendon Press, 1973. 145p. bibliog.
(Oxford Studies in African Affairs).

The first attempt by a Western-trained scholar to reconstruct the nineteenth-century
history of Bornu from European and Arabic written sources as well as from
contemporary data. The author traces the course of the Fulani wars in Bornu, the
emergence of Muhammad al-Amin al-Kanemi, the decline and dispersal of the
Saifawa dynasty, and the subsequent reign of the al-Kanemi family until its defeat by
Rabah in the 1890s. Major emphasis is placed upon an analysis of how social and
political structures affected the course of historical developments. The result is a
political history which focuses on the internal dynamics of the Bornu ruling classes.
The work is enhanced by the inclusion of a glossary, tables and illustrations.

154 Les Chefs au Ouaddai. (The tribal chiefs of Wadai.)
M. A. Casenave. Paris: CHEAM, 1952. 7p. (Mémoire, no. 2079).

This short article gives a brief history of the Wadai region in western Chad. It
considers the origins of its dynasty, and examines the principles which determine
dynastic succession and absolute authority as well as administrative institutions and
practices.

155 The Awlad Sulayman of Libya and Chad: power and adaptation
in the Sahara and Sahel.
Dennis D. Cordell. Canadian Journal of African Studies, vol. 19,
no. 2 (1985), p. 319-43. bibliog.

Outlines the history of the Awlad Sulayman, an Arab people from Libya who
dominated the area north of Lake Chad in the 19th century. The Awlad Sulayman
migrated southward in an attempt to gain control over the trans-Saharan commerce.
By the 1840s, they had become the dominant power in the Chad basin. Their control
was based on the use of firearms, camels, and horses, which gave the Awlad
Sulayman a military advantage over their neighbours. During their ascendancy, the
Awlad Sulayman maintained closed political and economic ties with Libya. At the
end of the 19th century, internal political conflict and the presence of the Sanusiyya
and the French in the region undermined the authority of the Awlad Sulayman.

156 Sudanese and Saharan studies.
Humphrey J. Fisher. Journal of African History, vol. 28, no. 2,
p. 281-93.

Reviews Hermann Forkl's Die Beziehungen der Zentralsudanischen Reiche Bornu,
Mandara und Bagirmi sowie der Kotoko-Staaten zu Ihren Südlichen Nachbarn unter
Besonderer Berücksichtigung des Sao-Problems (1983), Hermann Forkl's Der Einfluss
Bornus, Mandaras, Bagirmis der Kotoko-Staaten und der Jukun-Konfäderation auf
die Kulturentwicklung Ihrer Nachbarn Südlich des Tschadsees (1985), Peter Fuch's
Das Brot der Wüste (1983), A. O. Babacar's Tegdaoust III: Recherches sur
Aoudaghost (1983), and Studies in the History of Pre-Colonial Borno (1983), edited
by Bala Usman and Nur Alkali. The five volumes focus on the Lake Chad region of

West Africa from prehistory to the 19th century. They offer a comprehensive historical perspective of the area and, in particular, of the kingdom of Bornu (in northern Nigeria).

157 **Le couteau de jet sacré. Histoire des sar et de leurs rois dans le sud du Tchad.** (The sacred jet knife. A history of the Sar and their kings in southern Chad.)
Joseph Fortier. Paris: L'Harmattan, 1982. 295p. maps. bibliog.

This is a historical and an ethnological study of the Sar people of southern Chad. It starts in the 1850s, with the Baguirmian invasion of southern Chad and the recognition of the Sar king as 'Sun-King' or *Mbang*, by the Baguirmi sultan Abd-el-Kader. The author then examines Rabah's conquest of Chad and French colonization. The rest of the study deals with the king and his power, associated with the sacred jet knife seen only once a year during the 'Sowing Festival', and which enables the king to bring rain and thus ensure good harvests. Illustrations, diagrams and tables are included.

158 **Histoire des Toundjour de Mondo (Kanem).** (A history of the Tunjur of Moundou (Kanem).)
René Gros.   In: *Quelques populations de la République du Tchad. Les Arabes du Tchad* (*Populations of the Republic of Chad. The Arabs of Chad.* CHEAM, 1971, p. 261-80. map. (Recherches et documents du CHEAM, III).

The Tunjur claim Arab descent, possibly from the Beni Hillal in northern Libya. This study traces their origins, their 'Maghribi' and 'Sudanese' phases, their eviction from the Sudan and their incorporation into the two antagonistic empires of Bornu and Wadai.

159 **The life and times of Rabih Fadl Allah.**
W. K. R. Hallam.   Ilfracombe, England: Arthur H. Stockwell, 1977. 367p.

A study of the Sudanese conqueror of central and southern Chad in the latter part of the nineteenth century. Rabah soon acquired notoriety as a slaver and his career was cut short at the Battle of Kusseiri in 1900, when French forces ensured their control of central Chad. This book is based on European secondary source material.

160 **Entre l'Afrique blanche et l'Afrique noire: le Tchad.**
(Chad: between white and black Africa.)
Pierre Hugot.   Paris: *Le Mois en Afrique*, no. 1 (Jan. 1966), p. 43-53.

This article concentrates on the relations between the Arabs and Chad and deals with the former's arrival and influence in pre-colonial Chad. It briefly examines Rabah, the Sanusiyya, slavery and Islam.

161 **Dar Sila, the sultanate in precolonial times, 1870-1916.**
Lidwien Kapteijns. *Cahiers d'Etudes Africaines*, vol. 23, no. 4
(1983), p. 447-70. bibliog.
Traces the political history of Dar Sila, a state on the border of Sudan and Chad, from
1870 until 1916, analysing the social and economic structure as well as the early
impact of French colonial rule.

162 **Le diwan des sultans du Bornou: Chronologie et histoire d'un
royaume africain (de la fin du Xe siècle jusqu'à 1808).** (The diwan
of the sultans of Bornu: chronology and history of an African kingdom
(from the end of the tenth century to 1808).)
Dierk Lange. Wiesbaden, Germany: Franz Steiner Verlag, 1977.
173p.
An historical study of the Kingdom of Kanem-Bornu, situated on both sides of Lake
Chad. It runs from the beginning of the eleventh to the nineteenth century and is
based on written sources from Arab travellers and historians, from other documents
such as letters and dynastic lists, and most importantly from an African document
written in Arabic – the *Diwan salatin Bornu* – which is only five pages long but
contains the history of the Kanem-Bornu kingdom from the beginning of the
thirteenth century to the mid-eighteenth century.

163 **Royaumes et peuples du Tchad.** (Kingdoms and peoples of Chad.)
Dierk Lange. In: *Histoire Générale de l'Afrique IV, L'Afrique du
XIIe au XVIe siècle (A general history of Africa IV, Africa from the
twelfth to the sixteenth century)*. Directeur de volume: D. T. Niane;
Chapter X. Paris: UNESCO, Nouvelles Editions Africaines, 1985,
p. 265-92. maps.
Lange's study deals specifically with the history and the people of the kingdom of
Kanem, the most powerful political entity and therefore the most frequently reported
in the chronicles of the period between the twelfth and sixteenth centuries. It covers
the Sefuwa dynasty, founded in 1075 by Hummay, and describes its political
organization and commercial relations with its neighbours, together with the role it
played in the development of the state.

164 **La région du Tchad en tant que carrefour.** (The Chad region as a
crossroads.)
Dierk Lange, Bawaro W. Barkindo. In: *Histoire Générale de
l'Afrique III, L'Afrique du VIIe au XIe siècle (A general history of
Africa III, Africa from the seventh to the eleventh century)*. Directeur
de volume: M. el Fasi; Chapter XV. Paris: UNESCO, Nouvelles
Editions Africaines, 1990, p. 465-88.
This illustrated article throws light on the geographical distribution and movements of
ethnic groups in the Chad region and focuses on the Zaghawa kingdom which
preceded the Sefuwa dynasty. It also deals with the progress of Islamization from the
seventh century and concludes on the coming to power of the Sefuwa dynasty.

165 **Wars without ends: the political economy of a pre-colonial African state.**
Stephen P. Reyna.   Hanover, Germany; London: University Press of New England, 1990. 210p. maps. bibliog.

This book reconstructs some of the politics and economics of the east-central Sudan, especially those of Baguirmi, for the period between 1870 and 1897. It then formulates a model to account for the frequent warfare in the region. It analyses long-term events as examples of transformations of different types of social structures.

166 **Zones d'influences françaises et anglaises entre le lac Tchad et le Nil.** (French and English zones of influence between Lake Chad and the Nile.)
E. Rouard de Card.   In: *Les territoires africains et les conventions franco-anglaises* (*African territories and Franco-English conventions*), Chap. VI.   Paris: A. Pédone Libraire et Editeur et J. Gamber Libraire et Editeur, 1901, p. 121-78.

An historical study of French colonial policy in the region in the late-nineteenth century in relation to British and Belgian foreign policy.

167 **Tchad 1900-1902: Une guerre franco-libyenne oubliée? Une confrérie musulmane, la Sanusiyya, face à la France.** (Chad 1900-1902: a forgotten Franco-Libyan war? The Sanusiyya, a Muslim brotherhood, against France.)
J. Triaud.   Paris: L'Harmattan, 1987. 203p. (Racines du présent).

A description of the initial moves in the French campaign to subdue northern Chad when the major Sanusi *zawiya* [religious foundation] at Bir Alali was destroyed in 1902. This book also includes a description of the growth of the Sanusi Order in Chad and is based on a set of thirty-eight letters recently discovered in the French archives and written between 1898 and 1902. Both the transcriptions of the original letters and the translations made by the official French interpreter in 1902, the latter heavily annotated, are included.

168 **Abd el-Karim, propagateur de l'Islam et fondateur du royaume du Ouaddai.** (Abd al-Karim, propagator of Islam and founder of the Kingdom of Wadai.)
Marie-José Tubiana, Issa Hassan Khayar, Paule Delville.   Paris: CNRS, 1978. 37p. (Laboratoires Peiresc, Collection Contribution à la Connaissance des Elites Africaines, II).

This study introduces previously unpublished documents or transcripts of interviews with individuals about Abd el-Karim, which reflect widespread opinions on the traditions around him.

169   **Histoire de l'empire du Bornou.** (A history of the Bornu empire.)
Yves Urvoy.   Paris: Librairie Larose, 1949. 166p. maps. (Mémoire de
l'Institut Français d'Afrique Noire, no. 7).
This study, written in 1939, was published posthumously. It spans thirteen centuries
of Chadian history from 700 to 1900 and covers the introduction of Islam, the various
movements of populations caused by conquests and Rabah's empire.

170   **Histoire des arabes sur les rives du lac Tchad.** (A history of Arab
dwellers on the banks of Lake Chad.)
Jean-Claude Zeltner.   *Annales de l'Université d'Abidjan*, vol. 2,
fasc. 2 (1970), p. 109-237. maps. bibliog.
Zeltner tries to establish the circumstances in which Arabs settled on the banks of
Lake Chad from the Sudan, in the eighteenth century, in order to understand their
mentality and way of life. He examines the Arab populations east of the Chari region
and of Bornu and then considers their history in the nineteenth century. He also
examines their role in the state and their relationship with Rabah. Finally he looks at
language and religious life.

171   **Les arabes dans la région du lac Tchad. Problèmes d'origine et de
chronologie.** (Arabs in the Lake Chad region. Origins and
chronology.)
Jean-Claude Zeltner.   Sarh, Chad: Collège Charles Lwanga, 1977.
113p. maps. bibliog.
This study of the history of Arab presence in Chad was based on data gathered from
original documents which were critically assessed. The documents include accounts
by Arab historians and geographers, royal chronicles, travellers' accounts, oral and
written traditions preserved by the Arabs themselves, particularly in genealogy. The
author examines two main Arab groups; the Ahmad al-Ajdam and the Hasan. The
work is much enhanced by diagrams, tables and illustrations.

172   **Les pays du Tchad dans la tourmente (1880-1903).** (The lands of
Chad in turmoil (1880-1903).)
Jean-Claude Zeltner.   Paris: L'Harmattan, 1988. 285p. (Racines du
présent).
A history of the invasions of northern and central Chad towards the end of the
nineteenth century. The author identifies four waves: the Sudanese Mahdi, the Sanusi
from the Libyan desert, the forces of Rabah Fadlallah from the east and, finally,
French forces from the west. His study is based on British and Sanusi archival
material, in addition to the better-known French sources.

173   **Tripolitaine et pays toubou au XIXe siècle.** (Tripolitania and the
Tubu region in the nineteenth century.)
Jean-Claude Zeltner.   *Islam et Sociétés au Sud du Sahara*, no. 3
(May 1989), p. 90-105. map.
Zeltner briefly examines the Fezzen (Libya) and northern Chad in the nineteenth
century, using travellers' writings about the region. He also discusses the demarcation

39

of the border between the two areas. He goes on to describe the relations between three Tubu groups and the Fezzan and examines the Tubu of Borkou, Bahr al-Ghazal and Kanem, the Reshada Tubu of Tibesti and those of Bilma, also known as the Tubu of Kawar.

The Kanuri factor in Nigeria–Chad relations.
See item no. 138.

Colonial period (1912-60)

174 **Vie du sultan Mohammed Bakhit 1856-1916. La pénétration française au Dar Sila, Tchad.** (The life of Sultan Muhammad Bakhit 1856-1916. French penetration into the Dar Sila, Chad.)
Capitaine René-Joseph Bret, preface by Marie-José and Joseph Tubiana. Paris: CNRS, 1987. 258p. maps. bibliog. (Laboratoire Pereisc, Contribution à la Connaissance des Elites Africaines).
This account of the life of Sultan Mohammed Bakhit, ruler of the small semi-independent state of Dar Sila situated between the great sultanates of Darfour and Wadai, was written by this French colonial military commander in charge of the Goz Beida region in 1932 and 1933. The merit of the work lies partly in the sources used by the author (letters, colonial instructions, agreements, reports, as well as the accounts of contemporaries of the Sultan) which have now largely disappeared, and also in his objectivity which was unusual for the time.

175 **La mission Foureau–Lamy et l'arrivée des français au Tchad 1898-1900: Carnets de route du lieutenant Gabriel Britsch.**
(The Foureau–Lamy mission and the arrival of the French in Chad 1898-1900: travel diaries of Lieutenant Gabriel Britsch.)
Jacques Britsch. Paris: L'Harmattan, 1989. 191p. (Racines du présent).
These travel diaries were published by Lieutenant Britsch's son, himself a soldier in Chad in the early 1930s. The study opens with a brief summary of the geopolitical situation of central Africa at the end of the nineteenth century and a description of the diaries. These relate the travels of Lieutenant Britsch as a 23-year-old soldier taking part in the Foureau–Lamy expedition through the Sahara which was to destroy Rabah's empire and open the way to the colonization of Chad.

176 **Les minorités musulmanes du Nord-Est tchadien. Sultanats des Dar Zaghoua et Dar Tama.** (Muslim minorities in northeastern Chad. The Sultanates of Dar Zaghoua and Dar Tama.)
A. Casenave. Paris: CHEAM, 1952. 40p.
This handwritten study by a colonial administrator provides a geographical description of the region occupied by these two sultanates and examines their history, and that of the two powerful and neighbouring sultanates of Darfur and Wadai. It also

looks at the French conquest and what the author inevitably sees as the positive consequences for both sultanates.

177 **Libyens et français au Tchad (1897-1914): La confrérie sénoussie et le commerce transaharien.** (The Libyans and Frenchmen in Chad (1897-1914): the Sanusi Brotherhood and trans-Saharan commerce.) Glauco Ciammaichella. Paris: Editions du CNRS, 1987. 187p. bibliog. (CNRS, Centre Régional de Marseilles).

This book studies the southward extension of Sanusi control from Libya into northern and central Chad after the 1899 Anglo-French convention and the consequent conflict with French forces moving northwards from West Africa and Central Africa. It describes belated Ottoman attempts to occupy the Tibesti and Borkou regions of northern Chad. It also discusses the history of trans-Saharan trade during this period and includes an appendix of French, Sanusi and Ottoman correspondence on the subject of French penetration into the Borkou-Ennedi-Tibesti region (BET) during the 1912-14 period.

178 **Histoire politique du Tchad de 1900 à 1962.** (A political history of Chad from 1900 to 1962.) J. Le Cornec. Paris: R. Pichon et R. Durand-Auzias [or Librairie Générale de Droit et de Jurisprudence], 1963. 374p.

Written by a member of the colonial administration, a former administrator for French Overseas Territories, this study focuses on the role of the chieftains. This role is examined in the pre-colonial, colonial and post-colonial periods with regard to the Sara and Baguirmi regions. It uses thematic and chronological approaches and is formulated around political organizations, events and decisions.

179 **Chefferie traditionnelle, administration française et partis politiques au Ouaddai.** (Traditional chieftains, French administration and political parties in Wadai.) Henri de Courville. Paris: CHEAM, 1959. 19p. (Mémoire, no. 3095).

This article attempts to resolve the future role of rural chieftains before the departure of the French administration. The author, who makes no secret of his distrust and dislike of the chieftain system, examines whether the old system should survive, albeit in a form adapted to the new Chadian state, or whether it should be eradicated in order to open the way to a younger, more 'democratic' system. He decides that the best way forward is an evolutionary approach which would not affect existing social structures.

180 **L'enseignement colonial français au Tchad (1900-1960).** (French colonial education in Chad (1900-1960).) David Gardinier. *L'Afrique et l'Asie Modernes*, no. 161 (Summer 1989), p. 59-71.

Gardinier examines the philosophy behind French colonial education, as well as its strategy and the results it produced, in order to provide a better understanding of the cultural aspects of regional imbalances which have contributed to the conflict in Chad. The authors shows that the educational system, which sought to train Chadians to participate in the administration of their country, failed and even contributed to regional imbalances and divisions which later produced armed conflict.

181 **The Ma'ahad al'Ilmi of Muhammad Awuda Ouléch at Abéché: a reformist Islamic challenge to French and traditionalist interests in Ouaddai, Chad, 1947-1956.**
David E. Gardinier. *Islam et Sociétés au Sud du Sahara*, no. 3 (1989), p. 159-85.
Muhammad Ouléch's creation of an institute of reformist Muslim learning at Abéché in 1947 presented a new challenge to both French and traditionalist interests in eastern Chad. The soon-flourishing Ma'ahad al'Ilmi spurred the French colonial administration to organize a competing institution, the Collège Franco-Arabe of Abéché. It would achieve only a modest success despite the backing of the Ouadaï sultan and notables who were attached to a traditionalist Islam. Though the administration expelled Ouléch from Abéché for his allegedly hostile activities, and though the sultan pressured some of his faqaha [experts in Islamic law and doctrine] to teach at the Collège, thereby crippling the Ma'ahad, they were never able to win over the bulk of the Muslim population or to eliminate all of their sympathy for the reformist and pan-Arab ideas which Ouléch's teaching promoted. These events show the difficulties the French encountered in perpetuating their control over Muslim populations who desired an emancipation different from that defined at the Brazzaville conference and implemented by the French Fourth Republic. They reveal the further decline of traditional political and religious leaders under the impact both of decolonization in sub-Saharan Africa and of the Arab and Muslim awakening to the East.

182 **Le Tchad: décolonisation et indépendance.** (Chad: decolonization and independence.)
Pierre Gentil. Paris: CHEAM, 1965. 331p. (Mémoire, no. 4004).
As a French official in Chad before, during and after decolonization, Gentil was well aware of the decolonization process which led to the independence of Chad. He examines the administration of decolonization in black Africa, by chronicling events rather than analysing the decolonization process itself; he demonstrates a strongly nationalistic attitude.

183 **La conquête du Tchad (1894-1916). Tome 1: Le Tchad d'Emile Gentil (1894-1902). Tome 2: Le Tchad de Victor Emmanuel Largeau (1902-1916).** (The conquest of Chad (1894-1916). Volume 1: The Chad of Emile Gentil (1894-1902). Volume 2: The Chad of Victor Emmanuel Largeau (1902-16).)
Pierre Gentil. Paris: Ministère d'Etat chargé de la Défence Nationale, 1971. 300p. maps. bibliog. (Thesis, Etat Major de l'Armée de Terre, Service Historique, Vincennes).
This doctoral thesis was written by a French civil servant with a prestigious career in Chad as administrator of overseas France, Prefect of Fort-Archambault and Director of the Information Services of Fort-Lamy. It provides a highly jingoistic depiction of the colonization of Chad, which highlights the 'heroic values of the few' involved in the conquest and the development of Chad under the French.

184 **La plus riche des colonies pauvres: la politique monétaire et fiscale de la France au Tchad.** (The richest of poor colonies: France's monetary and fiscal policy in Chad.)
Raymond Gervais. *Canadian Journal of African Studies*, vol. 16, no. 1 (1982), p. 93-112.

This article analyses the active fiscal policy of the military administration in Chad from 1900 to 1920. Using archival data on colonial budgets, taxation revenues and reserve funds, it documents the creation of considerable fiscal surpluses. Despite tight monetary policy, Chad over-achieved as a self-financing colony. This fiscal policy, accompanied by violence and combined with under-investment, laid the foundations for the chronic underdevelopment of Chad: the richest of France's poor colonies.

185 **Le Tchad.** (Chad.)
P. Hugot. Paris: Nouvelles Editions Latines, 1965. 155p.

A very general work which includes one chapter on politics since 1946 and colonization. It is otherwise mainly concerned with the French colonial period, of which it gives a description and historical anecdotes.

186 **Le vide politique du Tchad musulman.** (The political vacuum in Muslim Chad.)
Pierre Hugot. *Le Mois en Afrique*, no. 163-4 (July-Aug. 1979), p. 27-40.

Hugot (one of Chad's colonial administrators) shows how the existing political structures of the Sultanate of Wadai in eastern Chad were dismantled by the French after the conquest of the region early this century. He also demonstrates the lack of an adequate alternative administration and the fallacy of the policy of assimilation which was a characteristic of French colonial policy generally. After describing the failed administrative reforms of the fifties in the Batha region, he analyses the consequences of independence which left Chad with a government dominated by non-Muslim southerners, which soon led to rebellion.

187 **Renaissance d'un sultanat dans l'Afrique centrale française: le Ouaddai.** (Wadai: rebirth of a sultanate in French Central Africa.)
Y. Kelinguen. *L'Afrique et l'Asie*, no. 13 (1951), p. 36-40.

Like most colonial writings, this article stresses the positive role of France as a colonial power in Chad, and more specifically in relation with the sultanate of Wadai, which, the author claims, France helped re-establish and which was strengthened by introducing modern administrative practices.

188 **Le Tchad fait la guerre.** (Chad at war.)
Pierre-Olivier Lapie. Beirut: [n.p.], 1943. 37p. map. (Printed on the printing press of the newspaper *La Syrie et l'Orient*).

This very short study, by one of Chad's governors, endeavours to show how the country benefited from the Second World War by supporting occupied France and by supplying Chadian soldiers. It is excessively enthusiastic and very characteristic of those French colonial studies which sought to emphasize France's 'mission civilisatrice' – its civilizing mission – in Africa and elsewhere.

189 **Un problème politique au Tchad, les arabes myssyriés.** (A political problem in Chad: the Myssire Arabs.)
J. Latruffe. Paris: CHEAM, 1949. 20p. map. (Mémoire, no. 1388).

The Myssire Arabs belong to the Arab group of eastern Chad, situated in the Batha region. As a colonial administrator, Latruffe was able to study their way of life. He identified a specific political problem affecting this group, because of their nomadism and their seasonal migrations. While acknowledging the importance of migration, he stresses its destructive consequences for the environment and he suggests that the Myssire Arabs should be encouraged to sedenterize.

190 **Les émeutes de Fort-Lamy (1946) et Fort-Archambault (1947).**
(The riots of Fort-Lamy (1946) and of Fort-Archambault (1947).)
René Lemarchand. *Le Mois en Afrique*, no. 231-2 (April-May 1985), p. 3-15.

This article presents a series of colonial administration documents relating to riots in what are now N'Djamena and Sarh, in southern Chad. These occurred as a consequence of clashes between the two main political parties in the colony of Chad: the PPT (Parti Progressiste Tchadien) representing the Christian and animist South, and the UDT (Union Démocratique Tchadienne) representing the Muslim North. The author sees these events as illustrating the awakening of a new ethnic awareness in a specifically urban context. The interest of the documents lies in what they reveal of the colonial authorities' attitude towards each faction.

191 **Le Tchad et le RDA: Histoire d'une décolonisation.** (Chad and RDA: the history of a decolonization.)
Yeyon Lisette, Marc Dumas. Paris; Dakar; Abidjan: Présence Africaine, 1986. 346p. (Les Nouvelles Editions Africaines).

A collection of manifestos, speeches, interviews and articles by or about the RDA (Rassemblement Démocratique Africain – African Democratic Union – the first of Francophone Africa's political movements) and Gabriel Lisette, Chad's deputy to the French National Assembly and founder of the Chadian section of the RDA, the Parti Progressiste Tchadien. The documents cover the period between 1946 and 1960.

192 **De l'organisation politique de la région du Tchad.** (The political organization of the Chad region.)
M. Masson. Paris: CHEAM, 1938. 22p. (Mémoire, no. 241).

A short study covering the geography, populations, political organizations and the strategic and political importance of the colony of Chad. As with most studies of this period, it is condescending and jingoistic.

193 **Sur les pistes de l'Oubangui-Chari au Tchad.** (On the tracks of Ubangui-Chari in Chad.)
P. Mollion. Paris: L'Harmattan, 1992. 272p. (Racines du présent).

In the aftermath of the First World War one of the essential problems for the administrators of French Equatorial Africa was that of communications. This is still the case in Chad, a completely landlocked country: over a period of forty years, administrative demands for services and road construction mobilized over 200,000 men in very difficult conditions. This book describes the story of this challenge and its economic and social consequences on the populations of Ubangui-Chari (southern Chad).

194 **Evolution des échanges entre le bassin Tchadien (Tchad, Nord-Cameroun) et la côte du golfe de Guinée pendant la période coloniale.** (Development of trade between the Chad Basin (Chad, North Cameroon) and the Gulf of Guinea coast during the colonial period.)
Marcel Roupsard. In: *Actes du IVe colloque Méga-Tchad, CNRS/ORSTOM, Paris, 14-16 septembre 1988.* Volume III: *Du politique à l'économique, études historiques dans le bassin du lac Tchad (Proceedings of the fourth Mega-Tchad colloquium, CNRS/ORSTOM, Paris, 14-16 September 1988.* Volume III: *From politics to economics, historical studies in the Lake Chad Basin),* edited by Jean Boutrais. Paris: ORSTOM, 1991, p. 107-17.
The author distinguishes three phases of the colonial period in which exchanges evolved, in spite of their weakness, until 1960. The first period stops in 1928, the year until which exchanges were insignificant and commercial structures very poor. Then from 1928 to 1948, Chadian cotton export marked the beginning of an economic development which was only slowed down by the economic crisis and the war, while commercial structure hardly evolved at all. Finally, from 1948 to 1960, the progress of agro-pastoral production generated an increase of exchanges while new infrastructures were created.

195 **Karnu, profeta africano della non violenza.** (Karnu, African prophet of non-violence.)
Carlo Toso. *Africa* (Italy), vol. 45, no. 4 (1990), p. 555-92.
Karnu, a charismatic member of the Baya people, led the peoples of the Ubangui Shari region toward independence preaching non-violent methods. As a keeper of ancestral tradition, he was able to unite different ethnic groups; strengthened by his amulet, they dared to fight against colonial rule. When the Baya assaulted the cattle of the French-allied Bororo, the colonial army launched repressive actions. After the death of the prophet, the rebellion overflowed into Cameroon, the Middle Congo, and Chad, supported by chiefs who received the talisman from Karnu. It took three years for the French army to suppress the rebellion.

196 **Les forces françaises dans la lutte contre l'Axe en Afrique – les forces françaises libres en Afrique 1940-43.** (French forces in the struggle against the Axis in Africa – Free French Forces in Africa 1940-43.)
J. N. Vincent. Vincennes, France: Ministère de la Défense, 1983. 407p. maps. (Etat Major de l'Armée de Terre, Service Historique, Chateau de Vincennes.)
A comprehensive study which includes five chapters on Chad (3e partie: 'Le front autonome du Tchad', chap. X, XI, XII, XIII, XIV). This is mainly a historical study

of military strategy, with some descriptions of the difficulties encountered in the desert due to the nature of the ground, the lack of water and the weather, and comparisons with non-desert fighting conditions. There are detailed descriptions of tactics and strategies, including diagrams and maps of attacks, as well as some of Marshal Leclerc's letters.

Afrique Equatoriale Française.
See items 32, 34.

Independence

197 **Un tchadien à l'aventure.** (A Chadian adventure.)
Mahamat Hassan Abbakar. Paris: L'Harmattan, 1992. 121p.
Originally a school teacher in N'Djamena, Abbakar left his job in Chad in 1972 to join the FROLINAT rebels. He tells here how and why he did not achieve this aim. A lucid and sensitive observer, he recounts his experience and shows through his story some of the hidden realities of black Africa, the Arab world and France.

198 **Tchad 74.** (Chad 74.)
Anon. *Fronts Africains, Bulletin du Groupe d'Information Révolution Africaine*, no. 10-11 (Sept.-Oct. 1974), 56p. map. bibliog.
This issue of the revolutionary African review was written by FROLINAT members. It is divided into five parts which are very critical of the Chadian president, François Tombalbaye, and of French involvement. It contains an interesting chapter on the 'Claustre affair', called here the 'Bardai affair', after the town in which the hostages were originally taken, which is critical of both the regime and Hissen Habré. The last part of the review contains interviews with pro-FROLINAT villagers, FROLINAT fighters, Mohammed Idriss and Abba Siddick, as well as the text of the Forces Populaires de Libération (the FROLINAT armed forces) military code.

199 **Tchad: la réconciliation difficile.** (Chad: A difficult reconciliation.)
Anon. *Afrique Contemporaine*, no. 107 (Jan.-Feb. 1980), p. 20-3.
A narrative of the events which followed the Lagos Agreement of 21 August 1979, with the formation of the GUNT (Transition Government of National Union), headed by Goukouni Oueddei, being the most important. It contains a list of all GUNT members.

200 **Tchad: la deuxième guerre civile.** (Chad: the second civil war.)
Anon. *Afrique Contemporaine*, no. 109 (May-June 1980), p. 31-3.
This short article chronicles the resumption of fighting on 22 March 1980, after the break-up of relations between the various factions which formed the government and the collapse of the precarious relations between Goukouni Oueddei, the President and Hissen Habré, the Defence Minister, which demonstrated the lack of government cohesion and solidarity.

201 **Tchad: la guerre civile.** (Chad: the civil war.)
Anon. *Afrique Contemporaine*, no. 112 (Nov.-Dec. 1980), p. 50-1.
This follows the previous chronicle of events in Chad, still at war after eight months of heavy fighting. It indicates the first signs of Libyan involvement with the bombing of the FAN [Hissen Habré's Forces Armées du Nord] area of N'Djamena by a Tupolev suspected of belonging to Libya.

202 **Le Tchad: Elements d'une géographie de la fragmentation.**
(Chad: elements for a geography of fragmentation.)
Marie-Christine Aquarone. In: *Les frontières du refus. Six séparatismes africains (The limits of refusal. Six African separatist movements)*. Paris: CNRS, 1987, p. 25-40. maps. bibliog. (Mémoires et Documents de Géographie).
This article constitutes a clear summary of basic geographical, historical and political data on Chad. It is mainly descriptive and does not offer a new or challenging analysis. It deals briefly with southern Chad separatist movements and points to the intrinsic weakness of the Chadian state and the north–south divide as the main factors for instability.

203 **Séparatismes et rébellions: comparaison du Soudan et du Tchad.**
(Separatist movements and rebellions: a comparison of Sudan and Chad.)
Marie-Christine Aquarone. In: *Les frontières du refus. Six séparatismes africains (The limits of refusal. Six African separatist movements)*. Paris: CNRS, 1987, p. 41-4. maps. bibliog. (Mémoires et Documents de Géographie).
Aquarone's very brief article makes an interesting comparison between two countries which have a lot in common in terms of their geographical, historical, religious and ethnic characteristics. It examines the birth of both states, the failure of national integration, the intrinsic weakness of protest movements, the internationalization of the conflicts. Finally, the author highlights the divergences between separatism in southern Sudan and rebellion in northern Chad.

204 **Prisonnier de Tombalbaye.** (Prisoner of Tombalbaye.)
Antoine Bangui-Rombaye. Paris: Hatier, 1980. 160p. (Collection Monde Noir Poche).
In 1972, Antoine Bangui, then Minister of Planning and Tombalbaye's right-hand man, was suddenly arrested amidst a wave of denunciations on the order of Tombalbaye himself. He then spent three years in prison. It is these years which he describes here in a short but detailed and vivid account.

205 **Tchad: Genèse d'un conflit.** (Chad: genesis of a conflict.)
Christian Bouquet. Paris: L'Harmattan, 1982. 250p. maps. bibliog. (Racines du présent).
Christian Bouquet, a geographer by training, gives a very clear analysis of the origins of the Chadian conflict and shows how historical factors and ethnic differences

shaped modern Chad. The situation of potential conflict was rendered inevitable by French colonization which drew artificial frontiers, lumping together vast territories which did not reflect ethnic divides and fostering unequal economic development. This was compounded in the post-colonial era by the tribalism it had helped to foster.

206 **Tchad: une saison des pluies chaudes.** (Chad: a hot rainy season.)
Christian Bouquet. In: *Année Africaine 1983*, edited by the Centre d'Etudes d'Afrique Noire de Bordeaux. Paris: A. Pédone, 1985, p. 212-26.
This article recalls the events of the 1981-83 period when power changed hands between Goukouni Oueddei and Hissen Habré. The author deals briefly with the OAU's failure to re-establish peace through the inter-African force. He also explores Habré's search for domestic and foreign recognition, as well as Colonel Qadhafi's intentions in Chad. Most notably, he considers the role of the United States both as a new factor in this part of Africa and as a direct challenge to France's position in Africa, as well as to the French Socialist government. Finally, he examines France's decision to intervene.

207 **L'imbroglio tchadien.** (The Chadian imbroglio.)
Colette Braeckman. *La Revue Nouvelle*, vol. 78, no. 9 (Sept. 1983), p. 125-31.
This article attempts to explain the Chadian situation as it was in 1983. It briefly explains Libyan influence in the North, and how the FROLINAT focused opposition in that area. It then examines Habré's itinerary, the split with Goukouni Oueddei and their conflict over Chadian sovereignty, as well as the role of Libya and France in Chad.

208 **Notes sur l'évolution du Front de Libération Nationale du Tchad.**
(Notes on the evolution of the National Liberation Front of Chad (FROLINAT).)
Robert Buijtenhuijs. *Le Mois en Afrique*, no. 138-9 (June-July 1977), p. 118-25.
The death of Ibrahima Abatcha, Secretary General of the FROLINAT, in February 1968, started a war of succession which laid bare the innate cleavages within the FROLINAT. The accession to power (in dubious circumstances) of a newcomer to FROLINAT, Dr Abba Sidick, resulted in renewed tensions between Dr Sidick and other leaders who were to become prominent in the rebellion, such as Goukouni Oueddei, Hissen Habré, Mahamat Abba. The rebel party subsequently split into five factions, themselves loosely grouped in two camps: the pro- and anti-Sidick factions.

209 **La dialectique Nord–Sud dans l'histoire tchadienne.**
(The North–South dialectic in Chadian history.)
Robert Buijtenhuijs. *African Perspectives*, no. 2 (1977), p. 43-61.
This article is a summary of Buijtenhuijs' later book: *Le FROLINAT et les révoltes populaires du Tchad: 1965-1976*, published in 1978 (see item no. 210).

210 **Le FROLINAT et les révoltes populaires du Tchad: 1965-1976.**
(The FROLINAT and popular revolts in Chad, 1965-76.)
Robert Buijtenhuijs. The Hague; Paris; New York: Mouton, 1978.
526p. (Change and Continuity in Africa).

Although at times critical, Buijtenhuijs demonstrates in this well-informed and very readable study his solidarity with the revolutionary movement of Chad. He deals with the theme of insurrection in Chad by examining its roots, evolution and significance, and he places particular emphasis on the North–South divide. His approach, which combines both the chronology and analysis, provides a detailed and well-balanced study. The book also includes a short but concise analysis of the Claustre affair (the kidnapping of Françoise Claustre, Marc Combe and Dr Staewen on 24 April 1974) which contains a warning against some aspects of Thierry Desjardins' account (q.v.). Several communiqués, interviews and texts of members of the FROLINAT are published in an annexe.

211 **Le Frolinat et les guerres civiles du Tchad, 1977-1984.** (The FROLINAT and the civil wars of Chad, 1977-84.)
Robert Buijtenhuijs. Paris; Leiden, The Netherlands: Karthala ASC, 1987. 479p. maps. bibliog.

This book represents an attempt to answer the questions which emerged after the FROLINAT came to power. It examines the factors which contributed to victory and the consequences. This book should be read as a sequel to *Le FROLINAT et les révoltes populaires du Tchad* (q.v.), in which the author gave the benefit of the doubt to the rebels. Now he accuses them of not having kept their promises.

212 **Tchad: 1985-1986.** (Chad: 1985-1986.)
Robert Buijtenhuijs. Talence, France: Presses Universitaires de Bordeaux; Paris: A. Pédone, 1988, p. 73-85. (Centre d'Etudes d'Afrique Noire).

Buijtenhuijs here provides an analysis of President Hissen Habré's politics between 1985 and 1986, and offers a hopeful interpretation of the conflict in Chad, while recognizing that the Habré government still had a long way to go before peace would be established in the country.

213 **Chad: the narrow escape of an African state, 1965-1987.**
Robert Buijtenhuijs. In: *Contemporary West African States*, edited by Donal Cruise O'Brien, John Dunn, Richard Rathbone.
Cambridge: Cambridge University Press, 1989, p. 49-58.

In this article, Robert Buijtenhuijs describes the slow but steady disintegration of the Chadian state from 1965 till 1982, as well as the recovery that has taken place since Hissen Habré came to power in June 1982. He also analyses the reasons for this withering away and why it was stopped just before final collapse.

214 **La rébellion au Tchad.** (The Chadian rebellion.)
Christian Casteran. *Le Mois en Afrique*, no. 73 (1972), p. 35-53.

An overview of the rebellion, with its origins in the BET, and in the centre and east of the country, its organization and its politicization. The author also explains why a number of rebel leaders joined the government in 1970 and examines briefly the economy and the role of President Tombalbaye.

215 **Warlords and militarism in Chad.**
Roger Charlton, Roy May. *Review of African Political Economy,*
no. 45-6 (1989), p. 12-25.

After considering the inadequacies of the prevailing concern with violence and the collapse of the post-colonial state in African studies, the authors argue that the uses made of the concepts of 'militarism' and 'militarisation' are equally confused and inadequate, particularly in explaining recent Chadian history. They suggest, as an alternative approach, a modification of the warlord model used in Chinese history between 1916 and 1928. They argue that there are striking parallels between the China of that time and Chad from the late 1970s, in the pattern of the collapse of central control, the rise of regional centres of power based on personalized rule and military force, and the consequent prevalence of the politics of conflict and war.

216 **Chad: France in Africa.**
J. J. G. Cox. *Army Quarterly and Defence Journal,* vol. 118, no. 2 (1988), p. 161-7.

Charts French intervention in Chad since 1968, noting that this military presence is welcome in Chad because of the politico-economic stability and bulwark the French provide against Libya.

217 **Tchad: L'Etat retrouvé.** (Chad: the state recovered.)
Abderahman Dadi, preface by J. Chevalier. Paris: L'Harmattan, 1987. 222p. (Points de vue).

Dadi argues that Chad's only crisis arises from defects in the nature of the state and that the country will not disintegrate, because of the lack of any desire for secession. The Chadian state, however, is bound to revive. In order to demonstrate this, Dadi describes structures and modes for national integration and examines the failures of the institutional system of the Chadian state during the original phase of national construction. He then turns to its disintegration.

218 **Regionalism, political decay and civil strife in Chad.**
Samuel Decalo. *Journal of Modern African Studies,* vol. 18, no. 1 (March 1980), p. 23-56. map.

Decalo's article provides a broad overview of Chad and underlines the artificiality of central authority in N'Djamena, before and after independence. It also highlights the process of political decay in Chad. It examines Chad's social and historical background and reactions to French rule as well as its economy. It describes the prelude to independence, the rebellions of the 1960s and the political instability and military upheaval that ensued. The author also looks at the cultural revolution, foreign policy shifts, the post-1975 regime and Goukouni Oueddei's rise to power in March 1979.

219 Chad: the roots of centre–periphery strife.
Samuel Decalo. *African Affairs*, vol. 79, no. 317 (Oct. 1980),
p. 491-509. map.
The purpose of this article is to highlight the factors that brought Chad to the brink of
disintegration, rather than to predict the future evolution of the country or to suggest
possible solutions to the centrifugal tendencies in Chadian politics. The author
examines Chad's socio-economic background, its political decay since independence,
its rebellions and its political disintegration.

220 **Pour le Tchad.** (For Chad.)
Marie-Laure de Decker, Ornella Tondini. Paris: Le Sycomore, 1978.
130p. map.
This large-format book is predominantly a collection of beautiful black-and-white
photographs of the people of Tibesti, many of them of FROLINAT. The sixty pages
of text which precede the photographs constitute a general introduction to the
rebellion and emphasize the devastating effects of French colonization and military
intervention. Some poems are included, as well as the political programme of the
FROLINAT.

221 **Le Tchad, plus d'un quart de siècle de guerre civile.** (Chad, a
twenty-five-year-old civil war.)
Philippe Decraene. In his: *L'Afrique centrale* (*Central Africa*).
Paris: CHEAM, 1989, p. 27-41. maps.
The chapter on Chad focuses on three intertwined aspects of the country, namely
political, economic and foreign affairs. The author argues that, in political terms, the
Chadian crisis derived from the fact that Chad was a completely artificial colonial
creation, that its decolonization occurred too early and that it underwent a violent
power struggle. He also examines French interventions and the conflict with Libya.
He argues that war, drought, economic dependence on a single resource (cotton) and a
landlocked geographical situation all combined to weaken the country and make it
one of the poorest in the world.

222 **L'essor du Tchad.** (The expansion of Chad.)
Georges Diguimbaye, Robert Langue. Paris: Presses Universitaires
de France, 1969. 400p.
A history of the independence of Chad, focusing on economic, infrastructural and
social developments mainly in health and education in the context of inter-African
cooperation.

223 **La rébellion tchadienne.** (The Chadian rebellion.)
Philippe Frémeaux. Paris: Université de Paris 1, 1973. 132p. map.
bibliog. (Thesis in Political Science).
This doctoral thesis was largely written from the author's personal sources which
include interviews with FROLINAT leaders, ethnologists, Chadian personalities, and
FROLINAT communiqués. It deals with the Chadian rebellion in a clear and simply
structured way, starting with the origins of the rebellion, both direct and indirect, its
development and the French intervention. The latter chapter offers a particularly

interesting interpretation of the French role, seen here as a much more pervasive and intense phenomenon than has been acknowledged by French or Chadian authorities, and which now represents a renewed French hegemony over Chad.

224 **Pour en finir avec la guerre du Tchad.** (Putting an end to the war in Chad.)
Gérard Galtier. *Le Mois en Afrique*, no. 223-4 (1984), p. 4-17. map. bibliog.

The author rejects the solutions commonly suggested to end the Chadian conflict: the status quo, a third man or the simultaneous retreat of foreign forces. However, he proposes a durable solution which involves the recognition of Hissen Habré (because he has acquired the support of most African states, as well as that of Western states), negotiations in favour of Colonel Qadhafi, the return to an authentic Chadian dual culture (which would represent both North and South) and finally the opening of the Arab League to Chad and the end to the dictatorship of Hissen Habré's FAN (Forces Armées du Nord).

225 **Tchad: une population déchirée par la guerre.** (Chad: a people torn by war.)
François Gaulme. *Actuel Développement*, no. 56-7 (Sept.-Dec. 1983), p. 9-12. maps.

In this general article, Gaulme sets out the main aspects of the Chadian conflict. He evokes the ethnic diversity of the country and stresses the upheavals caused by the civil war, in particular among the Myssire Arabs whose way of life has been destroyed by the restrictions imposed on their seasonal migrations. Finally he examines the problem of war profiteers and briefly looks at the status and circumstances of war recruits.

226 **A balance sheet on external assistance: France in Africa.**
Robert D. Grey. *Journal of Modern African Studies*, vol. 28, no. 1 (1990), p. 101-14.

Among former colonial powers, France since 1960 has maintained by far the closest political, economic, and military ties to its ex-colonies in sub-Saharan Africa. While the francophone states have experienced large numbers of *coups d'état* since independence, military-political arrangements with Paris have contributed significantly to their security from external interventions and internal civil wars, with the notable exception of Chad after 1975. French military bases within France's four closest allied states – Senegal, Ivory Coast, Cameroon, and Gabon – may well have discouraged coups in these countries. While the franc zone has helped to stabilize currencies and Paris has provided significant amounts of economic assistance, the francophone states have remained tied to France as a trading partner, experiencing increasing indebtedness and decreased economic growth in the 1980s. Franco-African ties have clearly produced more military than economic benefits for the former colonies.

227 **Les guerres du Tchad.** (The Chadian wars.)
Pierre Hugot. *Etudes* (Oct. 1983), p. 303-16. map.
This article recounts the main stages of the Chadian conflict, already nineteen years old at the time of writing. The author analyses how rural areas experienced this ordeal and indicates some of the origins of the conflict.

228 **Le Tchad de N'Garta Tombalbaye au général Malloum.**
(Chad from N'Garta Tombalbaye to General Malloum.)
Edmond Jouve. *Le Mois en Afrique*, no. 146 (Feb. 1978), p. 21-56.
map.
In this article, Edmond Jouve recalls the *coup d'état* of 13 April 1975 in which President Tombalbaye was assassinated. He describes the events that led to the installation of the new military regime, illustrating them with speeches made by Generals Malloum and Odingar. The setting up of the new regime and the eradication of all symbols of its predecessor are described. The new military regime and its relations with France are also analysed.

229 **La fin du régime du président Tombalbaye.** (The end of the
Tombalbaye regime.)
Gustave Jourdren. Paris: CHEAM, 1988. 124p. maps. bibliog.
Jourdren investigates the sudden fall of President Tombalbaye in the *coup d'état* of 13 April 1975 after fifteen years in power. He describes the events between 1969 (the date of Tombalbaye's re-election) and 1975. His analysis of the possible causes of the president's fall, however, is based on earlier events as well, including the arbitrary nature of Chad's frontiers, the country's constitutional structure which was based on the constitution of the French Fifth Republic which gave extensive powers to the president, the suicidal policies of an irrational leader such as Tombalbaye, and – as far as the external world was concerned – French, Libyan, Israeli, American and African strategies and designs in Chad.

230 **Tchad: la fin des mythes.** (Chad: the end of myths.)
Jean-Marc Kalflèche. *Géopolitique Africaine*, 5 (April 1987),
p. 5-32.
An analysis of Chad's domestic politics from 1967 to 1987 and of its conflicts with Libya. It recalls some of the points underlined by President Hissen Habré during an interview with the journal in February 1987, especially in relation to the future of Chad and its economic, social and political reconstruction.

231 **Rébellion et guerre civile au Tchad (1965-1983).** (Rebellion and
civil war in Chad (1965-83).)
Bernard Lanne. *Cultures et Développement*, Vol. XVI, no. 3-4
(1984), p. 757-81.
This article by Bernard Lanne is typical of his views of Chad: favourable to the Christian/animist South and critical of the Muslim North. He traces the roots of the insurrection to the North–South divide, the faster development of education, the economy and Christianity in the South. Both nationalism (also more developed in the South) and internal political developments also played a role. Lanne then examines

the rebellion from the point of view of the first uprising of 1965-69, the French military intervention of 1969-72, the fall of President Tombalbaye and the subsequent military regime of 1972-78, and the civil war of 1979-83.

232 **Les causes profondes de la crise tchadienne.** (The underlying causes of the Chadian crisis.)
Bernard Lanne. *L'Afrique et l'Asie Modernes*, no. 140 (Spring 1984), p. 3-14.

Bernard Lanne here examines the factors which led to the 1965 rebellion, an event he considers as inevitable although its prolongation during the 1970s was not. The issue at the heart of the Chadian dilemma is identified as the existence of a duality, the division between North and South, from which most other factors originate: progress in the South and stagnation in the North, the essentially southern-dominated pre-independence nationalism, the personality and geographical origins of the first Chadian president, François Tombalbaye, and the mistakes committed by a corrupt independent administration.

233 **Plaidoyer pour Tombalbaye I.** (A plea for Tombalbaye I.)
Bernard Lanne. *Le Mois en Afrique*, no. 249-50 (1987), p. 32-45.

The first part of this two-part article is devoted to the life of François Tombalbaye before his accession to power in 1959. It deals with his childhood and youth, his personality and the beginning of his political career as a member of the Parti Progressiste Tchadien. The article is sympathetic to Tombalbaye, whom the author, as his friend and political collaborator, tries to rehabilitate.

234 **Plaidoyer pour Tombalbaye II.** (A plea for Tombalbaye II.)
Bernard Lanne. *Le Mois en Afrique*, no. 251-2 (1987), p. 143-56.

In the second part of Lanne's article, Tombalbaye's life and political career between 1959 and his death in 1975 are examined. While Lanne admits that the president became more dictatorial as the years passed, he tries to demonstrate that this was a result of political necessity.

235 **Quinze ans d'ouvrages politiques sur le Tchad.** (Political studies on Chad over the last fifteen years.)
Bernard Lanne. *Afrique Contemporaine*, no. 144 (Oct.-Dec. 1987), p. 37-47.

In this article, the author examines forty French political studies on Chad published between 1971 and 1987.

236 **Le Tchad et le Frolinat, la révolution dérapée.** (Chad and the FROLINAT, the failed revolution.)
Bernard Lanne. *Marchés Tropicaux*, no. 2219 (20 May 1988), p. 1299.

A critical study of Buijtenhuijs' *Le Frolinat et les guerres civiles du Tchad* (q.v.).

237 **Chad: the misadventures of the North–South dialectic.**
René Lemarchand. *African Studies Review*, vol. 29, no. 3 (Sept. 1986), p. 27-41.
René Lemarchand claims that the attempt to explain the Chadian crisis through the North–South division is too simplistic, although not wrong in itself. He asserts that other parameters such as Sara *vs* non-Sara, Sara *vs* Sara, Arabs *vs* Tubu, Tubu *vs* Tubu and Arab *vs* Arab issues all combined to create the reality of conflict. In addition to these internal factors, he stresses the role of Libya which created a more ominous dialectic and set in motion a process of escalation containing the threat of more devastating confrontations.

238 **Security and conflict management in Chad.**
Guy Martin. *Bulletin of Peace Proposals*, vol. 21, no. 1 (1990), p. 37-47.
Analyses the causes of the civil war in Chad from 1965 to 1989 and assesses the prospects for a lasting peace throughout the region.

239 **Conflict resolution: the OAU and Chad.**
Bamayangay Joseph Massaquoi. *TransAfrica Forum*, vol. 7, no. 4 (1990-91), p. 83-99.
Outlines the history of the civil war in Chad since 1965 and notes the various initiatives by the Organization of African Unity (OAU) to help resolve the conflict. The framework, principles, and factional disputes among the members of the OAU have prevented it from playing a decisive role in the Chadian dispute.

240 **Chad: France's 'fortuitous success'.**
Roy May, Roger Charlton. *Modern and Contemporary France*, no. 37 (1989), p. 3-13.
Discusses the intervention of France in Chad since decolonization in 1960, noting French efforts to defeat Libyan involvement in the Chadian civil war and to limit American involvement in the region.

241 **Peut-on encore sauver le Tchad?** (Can Chad still be saved?)
Michel Ngangbet. Paris: Karthala, 1984. 139p.
An interpretation of the Chadian civil war by a Southerner. He argues that the survival of the Chadian state depends on cooperation with external powers, particularly Libya and France.

242 **Tchad: Vingt ans de crise.** (Chad: twenty years of crisis.)
Guy Jérémie Ngansop. Paris: L'Harmattan, 1986. 236p. bibliog. (Racines du présent).
Written by a Cameroonian journalist, this study examines the origins and the context of the Chadian crisis. The author goes back to independence and the rule of the first Chadian president, François Tombalbaye, and follows political life throughout the rebellion, the 1975 coup, the Malloum government, and the Habré government. It also reviews French and Libyan involvement. It concludes that, without denying the

importance of the latter, the solution to the Chadian crisis lies with the Chadians themselves and in their ability to find unity.

243 **Tchad: Guerre civile et désagrégation de l'état.** (Chad: civil war and the dissolution of the state.)
Gali Ngothe Gatta. Paris; Dakar: Présence Africaine, 1985. 217p.

A view from within the Chadian transitional government of 1979-82, this book was originally conceived as a doctoral thesis. It analyses the Chadian civil war in terms of the country's social and economic development during the colonial period. It also summarizes the dangers of the war for surrounding states.

244 **Chad: from civil strife to big power rivalry.**
Kola Olufemi. *India Quarterly*, vol. 41, no. 3-4 (1985), p. 376-89.

Examines the 18-year-old civil war in Chad which, from 1980 when Libya sent tanks into Chad, has become the scene of superpower rivalry.

245 **Civil strife and international involvement: the case of Chad (1964-1983).**
S. E. Orobator. *Africa* (Italy), vol. 39, no. 2 (1984), p. 300-16.

The civil war in Chad is the result of regional inequality, competing political factions, ethnic and religious rivalry, depressed economic conditions, and conflict between civil and military authorities. Many of the problems are the legacy of French colonialism, which favoured the appointment of particular ethnic groups to political positions and encouraged the economic development of southern Chad. In 1966 the Front for the National Liberation of Chad (FROLINAT) was formed by northern Chadians who opposed the national government. Despite political changes and peace efforts, FROLINAT and subsequent separatist movements continue to compete for power. The continuing strife is in large part the result of foreign political and military intervention led by Libya, France, and the United States.

246 **Tchad: L'état, le droit et la politique. L'échec de la Charte Fondamentale du 25 Août 1977.** (Chad: state, law and politics. The failure of the Basic Charter of 25 August 1977.)
Joseph Owona. *Le Mois en Afrique*, no. 200 (1982), p. 16-37.

Joseph Owona describes the decision of the August 1978 Chadian–French Mixed Commission to create a Committee of Defence and Security and a consultative organ called the National Council of Unity, and to adopt a Basic Charter. This decision amounted to a remoulding of the Chadian state by General Malloum (who had overthrown Tombalbaye three years earlier) and Hissen Habré the head of the rebel FAN (Forces Armées du Nord) forces.
(**NB** The year of 1977, mentioned in the title as the date of the Basic Charter, appears to be a misprint and should read 1978.)

247 **Conflict in Chad.**
Virginia Thompson, Richard Adloff.   London: C. Hurst & Co., 1981.
180p. bibliog.

This is a modern history of Chad which deals briefly with French colonization and concentrates on post-independence conflicts, starting with President François Tombalbaye. The authors also examine the process of disintegration which took place from 1979 and throughout the 1980s, and analyse Chad's relations with other African states.

248 **Le refus de l'état: l'exemple tchadien.** (Rejection of the state: the Chadian example.)
Jean-Louis Triaud.   *Esprit*, no. 100 (April 1985), p. 20-6.

This brief article is an analysis of the Chadian situation and its background in 1985. The author stresses the predominance of factionalism as a factor in the failure to achieve state building, whilst acknowledging the importance of the North–South divide. Both inter- and intra-regional antagonisms explain why most factions strive to prevent the constitution of a central power. Triaud also takes into account the rapid shifts of allegiance among soldiers and civil servants which ensured that the conflict was in a state of constant fluctuation until 1982 when French policy brought a stability which, however, was not to last.

249 **L'OUA face à la question tchadienne.** (The OAU faces the question of Chad.)
Olela Tshunda.   *Africa* (Italy), vol. 44, no. 2 (1989), p. 263-78.

Although the origins of the civil war in Chad can be linked to longstanding ethnic, geopolitical, and religious rivalries, the struggle, which began in 1975, can be directly traced to conflict among political factions that have involved the foreign interference of France and Libya. The author examines the efforts of the Organization of African Unity (OAU) to negotiate the conflict. Despite its continued diplomatic efforts, the OAU has faced serious problems in resolving the crisis. In large part, the role of external forces – including France, Libya, and the United States – have turned a civil war into an international political conflict. In addition, political factions within the OAU have prevented it from taking a more active role in the area.

250 **The Organization of African Unity and conflicts in Africa: the Chadian crisis.**
Offiong E. Udofia.   *Journal of Asian and African Affairs*, vol. 1, no. 1 (1989), p. 19-33.

Provides a brief history of the Organization of African Unity's (OAU) conflict resolution efforts in African border and intrastate disputes, paying particular attention to the OAU's involvement in Chad. Since the OAU lacks the machinery to handle conflicts, a serious review of its charter is needed.

251 **Guerre coloniale au Tchad.** (Colonial war in Chad.)
Monique Vernhès, Jean Bloch. Lausanne, Switzerland: La Cité
Editeur, 1972. 95p. maps. bibliog.

Given its Marxist bias, this short book is particularly virulent and open in its criticism
not only of the regime of Tombalbaye but also of the French government, which it
sees as a colonial force. The theme of imperialism runs throughout the book which
opens with a quotation from Joseph Stalin. Nonetheless, it is particularly useful
because of its collection of speeches and articles produced by all the parties involved.
It also includes accounts of raids by the French army against Chadian villages and of
violent actions undertaken against Chadian civilians. Most of the documents
reproduced in this book were originally published in the press or in political tracts.

252 **Les grèves de lycéens de Fort-Lamy (N'Djamena) en 1971 et 1972.**
(The student strikes in Fort-Lamy (N'Djamena), 1971 and 1972.)
Nagoum C. Yamassoum. *Le Mois en Afrique*, no. 198-9 (1982),
p. 110-23.

The events of 1971 and 1972 are analysed by a Chadian, a student who participated in
them at the time. After having analysed the events which led to the strikes – identified
here as discriminatory measures against Chadian students – he rejects the assertion
that they were politically motivated. He acknowledges, however, that they had
political consequences.

Languages

253 **Essai de description de la langue bidiya du Guéra (Tchad).**
Phonologie – Grammaire. (Description of the Bidiya dialect of
Guera (Chad). Phonology – Grammar.)
Khalil Alio.   Berlin: Verlag von Dietrich Reimer, 1986. 365p.
bibliog. (Marburger Studien zur Afrika- und Asienkunde. Serie A:
Afrika, Band 45).

This study was carried out in N'Djamena with Bidiye informants as the civil war
made it impossible for the author to travel to the southern area of Chad where this
language is spoken. The Bidiya language is spoken by approximately 12,500 people
in the prefecture of Guera and it has been classified in the Mubi-Karbo group of the
Chado-Hamitic sub-family.

254 **Emprunts et intégration en bidiya.** (Loanwords and integration in
Bidiya.)
Khalil Alio.   In: *Le milieu et les hommes – Recherches comparatives
dans le bassin du lac Tchad. Actes du 2ème colloque Méga-Tchad
ORSTOM Bondy, le 3 et 4 octobre 1985 (The environment and the
people – comparative research in the Lake Chad Basin. Proceedings
of the second Mega-Chad colloquium, ORSTOM Bondy, 3 and 4
October 1985)*, edited by Daniel Barreteau, Henri Tourneux.   Paris:
ORSTOM, 1988, p. 265-73. map. bibliog.

The Bidiya dialect is spoken by approximately 12,500 people in Central Chad. This
study examines the process of integration of Arabic and other loanwords in the Bidiya
dialect and the pidginization of Bidiya among Arabic speakers.

255 **Lexique thématique de l'Afrique centrale, Tchad, Sara-Ngambay. Activités économiques et sociales.** (Thematic glossary of central Africa, Chad, Sara-Ngambay. Economic and social activities.)
Anon.   Paris: Agence de Coopération Culturelle et Technique, 1983. 481p. bibliog.

This glossary is a selection of the technical vocabulary used in various economic sectors such as cattle-breeding, fishing, agriculture and trade, as well as in socio-political activities such as information, political life, social life and social legislation, arts, culture, sports and leisure.

256 **Dictionnaire sara-kaba-na–français.** (Sara-Kaba-Na–French dictionary.)
Anon.   Sahr, Chad: Centre d'Etudes Linguistiques, 1986. 217p.

This is a typescript dictionary of the language spoken in the town of Kyabe. Sara-Kaba is a dialect divided into four main branches, of which Na is the most widely spoken.

257 **Langues et cultures dans le bassin du lac Tchad.** (Languages and cultures in the Lake Chad Basin.)
Daniel Barreteau.   Paris: ORSTOM, 1987. 217p. maps. bibliog. (Colloques et séminaires).

This book contains the proceedings of a two-day meeting held at ORSTOM (Paris) on 4 and 5 September 1984. The subject was the Chadic languages in the Lake Chad Basin. The meeting brought together researchers in archaeology, ethnography, geography, history whose main area of interest was northern Cameroon, northern Nigeria and Chad. The book contains three contributions in English.

258 **Les langues Adamawa.** (Adamawa languages.)
Raymond Boyd.   In: *Le milieu et les hommes – Recherches comparatives dans le bassin du lac Tchad. Actes du 2ème colloque Méga-Tchad ORSTOM Bondy, le 3 et 4 octobre 1985* (*The environment and the people – comparative research in the Lake Chad Basin. Proceedings of the second Mega-Chad colloquium, ORSTOM Bondy, 3 and 4 October 1985*), edited by Daniel Barreteau, Henri Tourneux.   Paris: ORSTOM, 1988, p. 231-5. bibliog.

This short article provides the various classifications of Adamawa languages proposed by specialists in Chadic languages such as Jungraithmayr (q.v.). Mboum, Tupuri, Mundang and Masa are discussed within the context of the Adamawa languages spoken in Chad.

259 **Les langues du groupe boua (Tchad). Etudes phonologiques.**
(Bua dialects (Chad). Phonological studies.)
Pascal Boyeldieu, Pierre Palayer. N'Djamena: INSH, 1975. 219p.
maps. bibliog.
The Bua dialects form a language group in their own right which is distinct from the
Sara or the Chadic groups. This study provides a phonological outline of the Lua or
Niellim dialect, the Tunia language, the Noy language and the languages of Middle-
Chari.

260 **La langue lua ('niellim'). (Groupe Boua – Moyen-Chari, Tchad)**
Phonologie – Morphologie – Dérivation verbale. (The Lua
('Niellim') dialect. (Bua grop – Middle-Chari, Chad) Phonology –
Morphology – Verbal derivation.)
Pascal Boyeldieu. Paris: Editions de la Maison des Sciences de
l'Homme; Cambridge: Cambridge University Press, 1985. 426p.
(Descriptions de langues et monographies ethnolinguistiques, 1).
The Lua dialect (traditionally known as 'Niellim') is spoken by a minority group of
fishermen-farmers located near the Chari river, in southern Chad. This descriptive
linguistics study is a contribution to the general investigation of the many languages
spoken in Chad.

261 **La formation du pluriel nominal en kulaal (Tchad).** (The formation
of nominal plural in Kulaal (Chad).)
Pascal Boyeldieu. *Afrika und Ubersee*, vol. 69, no. 2 (1986),
p. 209-49.
Kulaal belongs to the group of Bua languages, itself a branch of Adamawa. This
study is an attempt to place documents published by C. Pairault (q.v.) in context: the
first such document is an ethnographic work on the Gula or Kulaa population located
in the area in and around the village of Boum-le-Grand on the banks of Lake Iro
(Middle-Chari); the second deals with Kulaal and contains a phonological study, a
collection of texts and grammatical notes.

262 **Présentation sommaire du groupe boua (Tchad) – (Adamawa 13**
de J. H. Greenberg). (A summary presentation of the Bua group
(Chad) – (J. H. Greenberg's Adamawa 13).)
Pascal Boyeldieu. In: *Le milieu et les hommes – Recherches
comparatives dans le bassin du lac Tchad. Actes du 2ème colloque
Méga-Tchad ORSTOM Bondy, le 3 et 4 octobre 1985* (The
environment and the people – comparative research in the Lake Chad
Basin. Proceedings of the second Mega-Chad colloquium, ORSTOM
Bondy, 3 and 4 October 1985), edited by Daniel Barreteau, Henri
Tourneux. Paris: ORSTOM, 1988, p. 275-86. maps. bibliog.
This article begins with a history of the classification of the Bua dialects. The author
then examines some of the dialects' linguistic features, looking in particular at

phonology and morphology, and deals briefly with the classification of this group (which includes thirteen sub-dialects, among which we find Lua and Kulaal).

263 **Comparative tonal systems: Yulu/Kara vs. Sara group (Kenga/Ngambay/Mbay).**
Pascal Boyeldieu. In: *Topics in Nilo-Saharan linguistics*, edited by Lionel Bender. Hamburg, Germany: Helmut Buske Verlag, 1989, p. 249-70. map. (Nilo-Saharan linguistic analyses and documentation, vol. 3).

Boyeldieu describes the tonal system of Yulu and Kara (both spoken in the north of the Central African Republic) and comments on their particularities in order to draw conclusions from a general comparison integrating Kenga, Ngambay and Mbay.

264 **De deux à trois registres tonals: l'exemple des verbes sara-bongo-baguirmiens.** (From two to three tonal registers: the example of Sara-Bongo-Baguirmian verbs.)
Pascal Boyeldieu. In: *Proceedings of the fourth Nilo-Saharan conference, Bayreuth, Aug. 30 – Sept. 2, 1989*, edited by Lionel Bender. Hamburg, Germany: Helmut Buske Verlag, 1991, p. 283-92. map. bibliog. (Nilo-Saharan linguistic analyses and documentation, vol. 7).

The languages of the Sara-Bongo-Baguirmian group, also called Bongo-Baguirmi, are spoken in an area covering parts of Chad, Sudan, the Central African Republic and Zaïre. This study deals with the verbal morphology in this group and presents a genetic outline of the languages.

265 **Les oppositions de tension en Masa.** (Tension oppositions in Masa.)
Claude Caitucoli. *Annales de la Faculté des Lettres et Sciences Humaines*, Université de Dakar, no. 12 (1982), p. 119-36.

This article defines the phonological status of tension oppositions in Masa, a Chadic language spoken in Chad and Northern Cameroon.

266 **Lexique mbay–français.** (A Mbay–French glossary.)
Jean-Pierre Caprile. Lyon, France: Afrique et Language, [n.d.]. 65p. map. bibliog. (Série Document, no. 2).

The Mbay language is used by about 40,000 people in Chad, and particularly in the area of Moissala, southern Chad. It has been classified into the Nilo-Saharan family, Chari-Nile sub-family and central Sudanese grop. This glossary contains over 1000 Mbay words.

267 **La dénomination des couleurs chez les Mbay de Moïssala (une ethnie sara du Sud du Tchad).** (The naming of colours among the Mbay of Moissala (a Sara ethnic group of southern Chad).) Jean-Pierre Caprile. Fort-Lamy: INTSH, 1971. 66p. maps. bibliog. (Etudes et Documents Tchadiens, Série C (Linguistique), 1).

This short study of the different linguistic images of the same reality (colours) proposes a new and precise method of semantic analysis in this field. This takes into consideration evidence which is generally studied separately by linguists or ethnologists. A preliminary comparison is made with other Sara and non-Sara groups.

268 **Lexique Tumak–Français (Tchad).** (Tumak–French glossary (Chad).) Jean-Pierre Caprile. Berlin: Verlag von Dietrich Reimer, 1975. 137p. maps. bibliog. (Marburgen Studien zur Afrika- und Asienkunde, Serie A: Afrika, Band 5).

The main part of this study consists of a comprehensive Tumak–French glossary and a French–Tumak index. It also records a folk tale, 'The hyena and death', together with notes on the grammatical and phonetic structure of the language. A list of place names is also included.

269 **Le groupe des langues 'sara' (République de Tchad).** (The Sara language group (Republic of Chad).) Edited by Jean-Pierre Caprile, Jacques Fédry. Lyon, France: Afrique et Language, 1969. maps. bibliog. (Archives Linguistiques, no. 1).

This constitutes an inventory of linguistic documents on the Sara languages of southern Chad and contains much unpublished material, either in the form of glossaries or recordings made by linguists, missionaries and other scholars. Mention is also made of written documents on the Ngambay language, on Bongo-Baguirmi, on Sara and Mbay, as well as recordings of Sara, Ngambay and Mbay.

270 **Préalable à la reconstruction du proto-tchadique.** (A preamble to the reconstruction of proto-Chadic.) Edited by Jean-Pierre Caprile, Herrmann Jungraithmayr. Paris: SELAF, 1978. 210p. (Groupe de Travail sur les Langues Tchadiques, LACITO).

This study is the result of the September 1977 meeting of the working group on Chadic languages. The meeting presented its participants with the opportunity to compare their methodology and more specifically the 'descriptivist' and 'interlinguist' approaches of the researchers of the University of Chad and of the CNRS on the one hand, and the 'comparativist' approach of researchers at Marburg (Germany) on the other.

271 **Grammaire et textes teda-daza.** (Teda-Daza grammar and texts.)
Charles Le Coeur, Marguerite Le Coeur. Dakar: IFAN, 1956. 394p.
map. (Mémoires de l'Institut Français d'Afrique Noire, no. 46).
The first part of this study contains a Teda grammar and the second part is made up of
Teda texts accompanied by a French translation and notes.

272 **The Zaghawa verb structure and its relation to other Saharan
languages.**
Norbert Cyffer. In: *Proceedings of the fourth Nilo-Saharan
conference, Bayreuth, Aug. 30 – Sept. 2, 1989*, edited by Lionel
Bender. Hamburg, Germany: Helmut Buske Verlag, 1991, p. 79-90.
bibliog.
The languages of the Saharan group have a close genetic relationship which is visible
in their verb structure. This close coherence is confirmed by Zaghawa verb structure,
despite the lexical distance that exists between the latter and other Saharan languages.
In order to demonstrate this, the author examines Saharan verb-classes, verbal
structures and Class I, II and III verbs.

273 **Les verbaux du Dangaléat de l'Est (Guéra, Tchad): Lexique
français–dangaléat et allemand–dangaléat.** (Eastern Dangaleat
verbal structures (Guera, Chad): French–Dangaleat and
German–Dangaleat glossary.)
Carl Ebobisse. Berlin: Verlag von Dietrich Reimer, 1987. 104p.
bibliog.
This French–Dangaleat and German–Dangaleat glossary complements an earlier work
published in 1979 on the morphology of verbal structures in Eastern Dangaleat, a
language spoken in the mountain region of Guera.

274 **First steps towards proto-Tama.**
John Edgar. In: *Proceedings of the fourth Nilo-Saharan conference,
Beyreuth, Aug. 30 – Sept. 2, 1989*, edited by Lionel Bender.
Hamburg, Germany: Helmut Buske Verlag, 1991, p. 111-31. bibliog.
The languages of the Tama group, spoken in eastern Chad and western Sudan, have
been classified by some linguists as part of the Chari-Nile section of the Nilo-Saharan
phylum, while others regard it as an independent language group. The author belongs
to the latter group and shows that Tama languages form a genetic group whose
distinction from their neighbours is demonstrated by the existence of similar
morphological structures, morphemes and lexemes in all the languages. He also
provides a table consisting of 226 items which, in most cases, have cognates in at
least three Tama dialects.

275 **Masculin, féminin et collectif en Dangaléat (Groupe 'Sokoro-Mubi' – Tchad).** (Maculine, feminine and collective in Dangaleat ('Sokoro-Mubi' group – Chad).)
Jacques Fédry. *Journal of African Languages*, Special Chadic Issue, vol. 10, part 1 (1971), p. 34-46.
This article examines gender structures in Dangaleat. The author analyses tripartite, binary and unilateral structures.

276 **Prières traditionnelles du pays sara.** (Traditional prayers from the Sara region.)
Jacques Fédry, Pascal Djiraingue.   Sahr, Chad: Centre d'Etudes Linguistiques, 1977. 64p. map.
This illustrated booklet records the words pronounced during various rites in the Sara region of southern Chad. The word 'prayer' used in the title is used in its largest sense and means, in the minds of local people, authoritative statements made by a qualified person.

277 **Grammaire Mbaye–Moissala (Tchad – Groupe Sara).** (A Mbay–Moissala grammar (Chad – Sara group).)
Joseph Fortier.   Lyon, France: Afrique et Language, 1971. 112p. map. (Document no. 6, April 1971).
This study deals with one of the dialects of the Sara language of southern Chad. It should originally have been published as a preamble to *Le mythe et contes de Sou* (q.v.), published in 1967, but was revised following an article by Jean-Pierre Caprile published in 1968 in the SELAF *Bulletin*, in which the author questioned previous claims about the language.

278 **Current progress in Chadic linguistics.**
Edited by Zygmunt Frajzyngier.   Amsterdam; Philadelphia: John Benjamins Publishing Company, 1989. 311p.
The proceedings of the Internatinal Symposium on Chadic Linguistics held at Boulder, Colorado, on 1-2 May 1987 bring together papers on general linguistics relating to Chadian languages.

279 **Les styles de discours en sar et leur mode d'emploi.** (Types of speech in Sar and their use.)
Mayange Gakinabay, Ursula Wiesemann.   *Journal of West African Languages*, Vol. XVI, no. 2 (1986), p. 39-48. bibliog.
This is a study of the five types of speech which exist in Sar: direct, indirect, semi-direct, non-quote and embedded speech.

280 **Dictionnaire sara–français.** (Sara–French dictionary.)
Jacques Hallaire, Jean Robinne. Lyon, France: Mission Tchad, 1959.
398p. maps.

Sara languages are spoken by 500,000 people in southern Chad. The Sara group of languages contains nine dialects and this dictionary deals with the Sara Majingaye of Bedaya, spoken by only 5,000 people but understood by 30,000.

281 **Classement des dialectes kanuri-kanembu à partir des verbes de la troisième classe.** (Classification of Kanuri-Kanembu dialects through third-class verbs.)
John P. Hutchinson. In: *Relations interethniques et culture matérielle dans le bassin du lac Tchad. Actes du 3ème colloque Méga-Tchad ORSTOM Bondy, 11-12 septembre 1986 (Inter-ethnic relations and material culture in the Lake Chad Basin. Proceedings of the third Mega-Chad colloquium, ORSTOM Bondy, 11-12 September 1986),* edited by Daniel Barreteau, Henri Tourneux. Paris: ORSTOM, 1990, p. 81-93. bibliog.

The Kanuri and Kanembu people live in the Lake Chad Basin in areas of Niger, Chad, Cameroon and Nigeria. Their languages, which belong to the Saharan branch (Western) of the Nilo-Saharan family, contain many dialects (including Kanembu) which are also spoken in Chad. This article examines third-class verb dialectal differences in order to provide a preliminary classification of these dialects. The Kanembu dialects studied are Tumari, Suwurti, Kubuki and Bol.

282 **Une langue sans conjugaison: le bedjond, parler sara de Bediondo/Tchad.** (A language without conjugation: Bejond, a Sara dialect from Bediondo, Chad.)
Djita Djarangar Issa. *Cahiers Ivoiriens de Recherche Linguistique,* no. 23 (April 1988), p. 62-92. bibliog.

An article on a southern Chad dialect covering subject pronouns and phonological tonal schemes of verbal lexemes. The author concludes that tonal perturbations affect only vocalic initial verbs.

283 **Description phonologique et grammaticale du Bedjond, parler sara de Bebiondo, Tchad.** (Phonological and grammatical description of Bejond, a Sara dialect of Bediondo, Chad.)
Djita Djarangar Issa. Grenoble, France: Université de Grenoble III, 1989.

This doctoral thesis on the Bejond dialect, spoken in southern Chad, contains a sixty-page-long folk tale together with a phonetic and a phonological transcription, a morphological distribution, a literal and a literary translation, as well as a verb glossary.

284 **Etude acoustique du système vocalique du sar (Sara/Tchad).**
(Acoustic study of the Sar vocalic system (Sara/Chad).)
Djita Djarangar Issa. In: *Proceedings of the fourth Nilo-Saharan conference, Bayreuth, Aug. 30 – Sept. 2, 1989*, edited by Lionel Bender. Hamburg, Germany: Helmut Buske Verlag, 1991, p. 293-312. bibliog.

Sar, a Sara language spoken in the Middle-Chari prefecture of southern Chad, contains a number of local variants. The one on which this study is based is the Sar of the town of Douyou, situated between Koumra and Bedaya. The author investigates whether there is a schwa vocalic quality [i.e. a neutral central vowel sound] in Sar and whether there exists an opposition in the Sar vocalic system.

285 **Le Kanembou des Ngaldoukou (Langue saharienne parlée sur les rives septentrionales du Lac Tchad).** (The Ngalduku dialect of Kanembu, a Saharan language spoken on the northern shores of Lake Chad.)
Francis Jouannet. Paris: SELAF, 1982. 166p. maps. bibliog. (Bibliothèque 91-92).

This work on the phonology of the Saharan language Kanembu is a contribution to methodology. It forms a two-part analysis, because the relationships between the segmental sequence discussed in the first part and the prosodic sequence described in the second part do not imply a simultaneous breakdown.

286 **The Chad languages in the Hamito-Semitic-Nigritic border area.**
Edited by Herrmann Jungraithmayr. Berlin: Verlag von Dietrich Reimer, 1982. 269p. maps. (Marburger Studien zur Afrika- und Asienkunde. Serie A: Afrika, Band 27).

This study contains articles by some of the most prominent Hamito-Semitic linguists. The articles are written in English, German or French and deal with Hamito-Semitic, Nigritic, Chadic and Hausa.

287 **Différents héritages culturels et non culturels à l'ouest et à l'est du bassin du Tchad selon les données linguistiques.** (Cultural and non-cultural heritage west and east of the Chad Basin according to linguistic data.)
Herrmann Jungraithmayr. In: *Relations interethniques et culture matérielle dans le bassin du lac Tchad. Actes du 3ème colloque Méga-Tchad ORSTOM Bondy, 11-12 septembre 1986 (Inter-ethnic relations and material culture in the Lake Chad Basin. Proceedings of the third Mega-Chad colloquium, ORSTOM Bondy, 11-12 September 1986)*, edited by Daniel Barreteau, Henri Tourneux. Paris: ORSTOM, 1990, p. 43-52. map. bibliog.

The author examines the dispersal of Chadic languages in eastern Nigeria and western and central Chad and comments on the fact that pockets of Chadic languages are surrounded by other non-Chadic languages. He proposes that this linguistic situation is the result of migrations and inter-ethnic relations which have led to cultural and linguistic superpositions and fusions and would explain why some dialects bear more resemblance to neighbouring, non-genetically related languages than to geographically more distant, but genetically related languages. He illustrates his point by comparing vocabulary of the *Swadesh* list which contains 100 words.

288   **Lexique Migama. Migama–français et français–migama (Guéra, Tchad).** (Migama lexicon. Migama–French and French–Migama (Guera, Chad).)
Herrmann Jungraithmayr, Abakar Adams.   Berlin: Dietrich Reimer Verlag, 1992. 167p. maps. bibliog.

Migama is spoken by approximately 40,000 people in the Djonkor Abou Telfane district of the prefecture of Guera in eastern Chad. It is divided into three dialects: Baro Migama, Doga, and Gamiya. This lexicon deals with the first – Baro Migama – spoken specifically in the towns of Baro, Gourbiti, Mabar and Tchororo. It contains a grammatical introduction which includes remarks on nouns, adjectives, pronouns, verbs, numbers, conjunctions, prepositions and negation.

289   **Cinq textes Tchadiques (Cameroun et Tchad).** (Five Chadic texts (Cameroon and Chad).)
Herrmann Jungraithmayr, Jean-Pierre Caprile.   Berlin: Verlag von Dietrich Reimer, 1978. 247p. (Marburger Studien zur Afrika- und Asienkunde. Serie A: Afrika, Band 12).

This book presents five Chadic texts together with their translations and notes on particularities of the language used in each of them.

290   **Chadic lexical roots. (A first evaluation of the Marburg Chadic Word Catalogue).**
Herrmann Jungraithmayr, Kiyoshi Shimizu.   Berlin: Verlag von Dietrich Reimer, 1982. 269p. map. (Marburger Studien zur Afrika- und Asienkunde. Series A: Afrika, Band 26).

An attempt to improve the understanding of the complex linguistic and historical nature of Chadian languages, which form the southwestern family of the Hamito-Semitic language group. It aims to provide lexical material on a great number of individual Chadian languages and to present this material in a systematic fashion suitable for comparative analysis. It also reconstructs common roots, grades them and indicates their geographical distribution.

291   **Etudes tchadiques: Classes et extensions verbales.** (Chadic studies: classes and verbal extension.)
Edited by Herrmann Jungraithmayr, Henri Tourneux.   Paris: Librairie Orientaliste Paul Geuthner, 1987. 121p. (LACITO, CNRS, Publications du Groupe d'Etudes Tchadiques).

This book contains papers presented at the annual meetings of LACITO in 1984 and 1985. Three branches of Chadic are discussed: the Western branch with Hausa; the

Central branch with Uldeme, Mafa and Munjuk; and the Eastern branch with Bidiya, Mokilko and Mubi.

292   **Etudes Tchadiques: Transitivité et Diathèse. Actes de la XIème réunion du Groupe d'Etudes Tchadiques, LACITO – CNRS – Paris.** (Tchadic Studies: transitivity and diathesis. Proceedings of the sixth meeting of the Chadic Study Group, LACITO – CNRS – Paris.) Edited by Herrmann Jungraithmayr, Henri Tourneux.   Paris: Librairie Orientaliste Paul Geuthner, 1988. 117p.

A very specialized study of Chadic languages, which discusses Hausa, Mopun (western Chad); Mofu-Gudur, Munjuk, Ouldeme (central Chad); and Bidiya, Mokilko and Migama (eastern Chad).

293   **The status of schwa and vowel co-occurrence restrictions in Mbay.** John Keegan.   In: *Topics in Nilo-Saharan linguistics*, edited by Lionel Bender.   Hamburg, Germany: Helmut Buske Verlag, 1989, p. 233-48. (Nilo-Saharan linguistic analyses and documentation, vol. 3).

Mbay is a central Sudanic language which belongs to the Sara group and is spoken in south-central Chad, around the town of Moissala, by approximately 80,000 people. The author's purpose is to provide a clear explanation of schwa in Mbay and specifically of the relationship between its occurrence and two supragmental considerations: the canonical shape of morphemes; and the co-occurrence restrictions which apply to vowels within a single morpheme.

294   **Chadic wordlist. Volume I ('Plateau-Sahel').** Edited by Charles H. Kraft.   Berlin: Verlag von Dietrich Reimer, 1981. 261p. (Marburger Studien zur Afrika- und Asienkunde. Serie A: Afrika, Band 23).

This wordlist contains data on sixty Chadic and four non-Chadic languages. The data were collected in northern Nigeria between August 1966 and July 1967.

295   **Chadic wordlist. Volume II ('Biu-Mandara').** Edited by Charles H. Kraft.   Berlin: Verlag von Dietrich Reimer, 1981. 196p. (Marburger Studien zur Afrika- und Asienkunde. Serie A: Afrika, Band 24).

This volume comprises the first twenty Biu-Mandara lists. They fall into categories II.1 to II.3 of Hoffmann's *Provisional check list of Chadic languages* (1971). The format is the same as that used in Volume I (q.v.).

296   **Chadic wordlist. Volume III ('Biu-Mandara' et al.).** Edited by Charles H. Kraft.   Berlin: Verlag von Dietrich Reimer, 1981. 251p. (Marburger Studien zur Afrika- und Asienkunde. Serie A: Afrika, Band 25).

The third volume of this work contains wordlists from the final twenty-one Chadic languages collected, together with four lists from non-Chadic languages. These languages fall into categories II.4 to II.13 of Hoffmann's *Provisional check list of Chadic languages* (1971).

297 **A Chadic language bibliography (excluding Hausa).**
Paul Newman. *Journal of African Languages*, Special Chadic Issue, vol. 10, part 1 (1971), p. 101-9.
This bibliography contains 164 entries relating to Chadic dialects and a language index.

298 **Nominal and verbal plurality in Chadic.**
Paul Newman. Dordrecht, The Netherlands; Providence, Rhode Island: Foris Publications, 1990. 164p. bibliog. (Publications in African Languages and Linguistics).
This consists of a detailed study of plurality in the Chadic language family, with special attention given to the historical analysis of Hausa.

299 **Le day de Bouna (Tchad). II. Lexique day–français. Index français–day.** (The Bouna dialect of Day (Chad). II. Day–French vocabulary. French–Day index.)
Pierre Nougayrol. Paris: SELAF, 1980. 179p. (Bibliothèque de la SELAF, 77-78).
This volume is a supplement to *Eléments de descriptions linguistiques* (Vol. 1, Bibliothèque 71-72), and contains an extract of the original lexicon, presented as a Day–French vocabulary with some 2,000 entries. The Day words are phonologically transcribed. Information such as grammatical category, definition, and an example of usage are provided for most items. There is a French–Day index at the end of the work.

300 **Note sur la langue kibet.** (A note on the Kibet dialect.)
Pierre Nougayrol. *African Marburgensia*, Vol. XIX, no. 2 (1986), p. 38-55. map. bibliog.
The Dar Kibet region covers the northern part of the Am Timan sub-prefecture, in the Salamat prefecture, southeastern Chad. The people of Dar Kibet, who numbered approximately 4,000 in 1962, speak both the Kibet dialect and Arabic. Kibet is related to its geographical neighbour, Aiki, a dialect spoken by the Runga or Aiki people, which belongs to the Maba group. This study examines Kibet lexicon, expression of numbers, personal pronouns, verbs and negation.

301 **Documents du parler d'Iro. Kulaal du Tchad.** (Documents on Iro dialect. Chadian Kulaal.)
Claude Pairault. Paris: Editions Klincksieck, 1969. 285p. map. bibliog.
This illustrated study is complementary to the ethnographic work titled 'Boum-le-Grand' (q.v.). It is a study of the Iro language and an anthology of songs and poems from this area which have been transliterated and translated.

302 **Eléments de grammaire sar (Tchad).** (Some elements of Sar grammar (Chad).)
Pierre Palayer.   Fort-Archambault, Chad: Collège Charles Lwanga; Lyon, France: Afrique et Langage, 1970. 194p. map. (Etudes Linguistiques, no. 2).

Palayer deals specifically with the Sar dialect of Bedaya (southwest of Sarh), but it can also be applied to the Nar and Pen dialects since all three groups are mutually understandable. The book is not an introduction to the language, but rather a systematic description of it.

303 **Des chants pour les dieux. Analyse d'un vocabulaire codé.** (Songs for the gods. Analysis of a coded vocabulary.)
Suzanne Ruelland.   *Journal des Africanistes*, vol. 57, fasc. 1-2 (1987), p. 225-39.

A semantic approach to the terminology concerning speech in Tupuri, an eastern Adamawa language spoken in Chad and Cameroon, which serves as an introduction to the analysis of a coded vocabulary used by certain women in their songs to the rain god. The concept and attributes of this god, as given in two songs, are described and compared with those of other divinities.

304 **Dictionnaire tupuri–français–anglais. Région de Mindaoré, Tchad.** (Tupuri–French–English dictionary. Mindaore region, Chad.)
Suzanne Ruelland.   Paris: Peeters/SELAF, 1988. 343p. map. (Langues et cultures africaines 10, SELAF 213).

Tupuri is the language of some 250,000 people living in southwest Chad and northeast Cameroon. This trilingual dictionary presents about 3600 dialectical terms spoken in and around the village of Mindaore, in the Fianga sub-prefecture, Chad. The transcription is phonological, and grammatical categories are noted for each term. Translations are in French, the official language of Chad and Cameroon, and in English, also an official language of the latter. Data concerning everyday life has been given whenever possible.

305 **La négation en tupuri.** (Negation in Tupuri.)
Suzanne Ruelland.   *Linguistique Africaine*, no. 4 (1990), p. 181-203.

Tupuri is an Adamawa dialect spoken by approximately 250,000 people in southwestern Chad and northeastern Cameroon. This study deals with the three different kinds of negation found in Tupuri.

306 **Re-employment of grammatical morphemes in Chadic: implications for language history.**
Russell G. Schuh.   In: *Linguistic change and reconstruction methodology*, edited by Philip Baldi.   Berlin; New York: Mouton de Gruyter, 1990, p. 599-618. (Trends and linguistics, Studies and monographs, no. 45).

Chadic is divided into three major branches: West Chadic, Central Chadic and East Chadic. The latter comprises languages spoken in western and central Chad. The author of this article shows that languages genetically related, such as those which form the Chadic group, have undergone the same syntactic changes despite being separated from each other in time and space.

307 **The deep structure of the sentence in Sara-Ngambaye dialogues.**
James Edward Thayer. Dallas, Texas: The Summer Institute of Linguistics, The University of Texas at Arlington, 1978. 221p. bibliog. (Publications in Linguistics, no. 57).

This study focuses on one of the main Sara dialects – Sara-Ngambay – and it provides a grammatical description which covers the higher levels of syntax from text material which is more representative of the total range of speech forms.

308 **Fifty lessons in Sara-Ngambay, a language of southern Chad.**
Linda J. Thayer, James E. Thayer, Noe Kyambe, Adoum Eloi Gondje. Bloomington, Indiana: Indiana University, 1971. 416p. maps.

A three-volume manual designed for Europeans who wish to learn the Sara-Ngambay language of southern Chad. The manual is written in French and English.

309 **Le Bura-Mabang du Ouadai. Notes pour servir à l'étude de la langue Maba.** (The Bura-Mabang dialect of Wadai. Notes for the study of Maba.)
Georges Trenga. Paris: Institut d'Ethnologie, Musée de l'Homme, 1947. 296p. bibliog. (Université de Paris, Travaux et Mémoires de l'Institut d'Ethnologie, XLIX).

Bora or Bura-Mabang is the language of the Maba and has acted as the administrative and commercial language of Wadai for the last three centuries. This study contains a section on phonetics, a vocabulary, a grammar, twenty-two tales, ten songs and a glossary.

310 **Bouche, voix, langage: la parole chez les BèRi (Tchad et Soudan).**
(Mouth, voice, language: speech among the BèRi (Chad and Sudan).)
Marie-José Tubiana. *Le Journal des Africanistes*, vol. 57, fasc. 1-2 (1987), p. 241-53. map.

Using the BèRi vocabulary, this study analyses three terms that refer to verbal acts: *à* ('mouth' and its metaphorical extensions), *tey* (words not taken seriously) and *bàri* (sound words). Through BèRi language behaviour, the underlying relationship between language and identity can be identified as well as the value placed on the sobriety of the speech of men who are, above all, strategists in dealing with their environment and social relations. The singing of women, however, is seen as a mighty weapon.

311 **Le Ngambay-Moundou: phonologie, grammaire et textes.**
(Ngambay-Moundou: phonology, grammar and texts.)
Charles Vandame.   Dakar: IFAN, 1963. 213p. map. (Mémoire de
l'IFAN, no. 69).
Ngambay-Moundou is one of the five dialects which form the larger Ngambay group
of languages. It is spoken in and around Moundou by approximately 110,000 people
in the extreme south of Chad. In addition to grammar and phonology, this study
contains six texts in Ngambay with a French translation.

312 **Grammaire Kenga, exercices enregistrés.** (A Kenga grammar,
recorded exercises.)
Charles Vandame, recording by Pierre Kora.   Lyon, France: Afrique
et Langage, 1968. 68p. maps. (Documents linguistiques, no. 2).
Kenga is spoken by 20,000 people living to the north, west and south of Bitkine in the
region of Guera, east of N'Djamena. It belongs to the group of Sara dialects of
southern Chad and is itself divided into several groups. This study deals specifically
with the group called tàr cénè, used in Ab-Touyour, Mataya, Djerbe, Tcheleme,
Boullong, Birete, Sara, Barama, Doyo and Toumka.

313 **Chadic historical syntax: reconstructing word order in Proto-
Chadic.**
Charles Kingston Williams.   Ann Arbor, Michigan: University of
Microfilm International, 1989. 201p. bibliog.
The aim of this doctoral thesis is to represent the application of the comparative
method to the realm of diachronic syntax, an area of historical language study which
has recently been the topic of much research but for which the proper methods of
linguistic investigation are still under debate. It demonstrates that the comparative
method can be used to make realistic generalizations about the syntax of a proto-
language through an analysis of the variations in word-order patterns which occur in a
number of Chadic languages.

314 **Morphology of the verb–initial consonant in Maba.**
Ekkehard Wolff.   In: *Topics in Nilo-Saharan linguistics*, edited by
Lionel Bender.   Hamburg, Germany: Helmut Buske Verlag, 1989,
p. 67-84. (Nilo-Saharan linguistic analyses and documentation, vol. 3).
This paper on Maba, spoken in eastern Chad and adjacent parts of Sudan, presents the
first results of a study of the highly complex morphophonology of the verb–initial
consonant in this language.

315 **Studies in Chadic and Afroasiatic linguistics.**
Edited by Ekkehard Wolff, Hilke Meyer-Bahlburg.   Hamburg,
Germany: Helmut Buske Verlag, 1983. 479p.
These are the proceedings of the International Colloquium on the 'Chadic Language
Family' and the Symposium on 'Chadic within Afroasiatic' held at the University of
Hamburg on 14-18 September 1981. The papers have been grouped in two categories:
the Chadic language family in historical perspective, and Chadic internal relations
and historical development.

Religion

316 **Les lycéens et les étudiants tchadiens s'interrogent sur leurs croyances.** (Chadian pupils and students reflect on their beliefs.) Collected by Ignacio Bello, Pierre Teisserenc. [n.p.], 1972. 68p.

A collection (in typescript) which reflects the beliefs of a very specific group of students who live in N'Djamena, are Catholic, and many of whom seem to come from privileged backgrounds. It describes their opinions on and experiences of conversion, the way in which they live their faith in the village context, the degree to which it is in contradiction with the animistic beliefs and way of life, how they envisage religion in the context of the modern world, and their opinion on religion as an ideology.

317 **Le conseil des anciens. Islamisation et arabisation dans le bassin tchadien.** (The elders' council. Islamization and Arabization in the Chad Basin.)
Christian Décobert. *Annales. Economies, Sociétés Civilisations,* no. 4 (July-Aug. 1982), p. 764-82. map.

Décobert traces the history of the Babalia, located on the east bank of the Chari river, and the Kotoko, on the west bank, and determines the date of their Islamization and Arabization.

318 **Les mosquées de Fort-Lamy (A.E.F.).** (Mosques of Fort-Lamy, French Equatorial Africa.)
Jean-Paul Lebeuf, Maxime Rodinson. *Bulletin de l'Institut Français d'Afrique Noire,* Vol. XIV, no. 3 (July 1952), p. 970-4.

This very short article reproduces an original list drawn up by El-Haj Omar, a Cameroonian Kanuri from Fort-Lamy. It contains the names of Fort-Lamy mosques and their number in each town district.

319 **Histoire des missions protestantes au Tchad depuis 1920 jusqu'à nos jours: le case de la mission protestante au pays Ngambaye.**
(History of Protestant missions in Chad from 1920 to the present: the Protestant mission in the Ngambaye region.)
Dingamtoudji Maikoubou. Montpellier, France: Université de Montpellier III, 1988.

Maikoubou describes the work of the Protestant mission established in southwestern Chad since 1927. He claims that the evangelization of the Ngambay people, in spite of the questionable methods used, freed them from their ancestral and irrational fears. The author also explains that the existence of hundreds of churches in the region vouches for the wholehearted acceptance of Christianity by the Ngambaye people.

The Ma'ahad al-'Ilmi of Muhammad Awuda Ouléch at Abéché (Chad).
See item no. 181.

Prières traditionnelles du pays sara.
See item no. 276.

Demography

320 **Recensement démographique de Fort-Lamy, mars-juillet 1962. Résultats provisoires.** (Fort-Lamy census, March-July 1962. Provisional results.)
Anon.   N'Djamena: République du Tchad, Bureau de la Statistique, République Française, Ministère de la Coopération, [n.d.]. 89p. maps.

This study analyses the results of the 1962 demographic survey which counted 88,000 individuals. It examines birth and death rates, migrations and structural data such as distribution by sex and age, ethnic groups and ethnic influence on professional distribution. Both African and non-African populations are included.

321 **Enquête démographique au Tchad, 1964. Vol. 1: Analyse des résultats. Vol. 2: Tableau statistique détaillé.** (A demographic survey of Chad, 1964. Vol. 1: Analysis of results. Vol. 2: Detailed statistical table.)
Anon.   Paris: République Française, Secrétariat d'Etat aux Affaires Etrangères; Fort-Lamy: République du Tchad, Service de Statistique, 1966. Vol. 1: 307p. maps; Vol. 2: 196p.

This demographic study deals with the southern region of Chad which contains most of the sedentary population. It establishes the approximate number of inhabitants, the structure of the population by age, sex, ethnic group, activity, the main demographic movements (fertility, mortality, migrations) and the perspectives of change for the years after 1964.

322 **Rapport de mission sur l'évaluation des besoins d'aide en matière de population.** (Report on population needs.)
Anon.   New York: United Nations Fund for Population-Related Activities, 1986. 53p. map. (Report no. 85).

This study of the Chadian population includes recommendations to the Chadian government and examines the national environment, demographic tendencies, population policies, data gathering and analysis, health and family planning, education, information and communications, women's participation in development and foreign demographic assistance.

323 **Projections de la population au Tchad – 1964-2009.** (Chadian population projections – 1964-2009.)
Oumar Caman Bedaou, Idris Banguita Nelym.   Bamako, Mali: Institut du Sahel, [n.d.]. 41p. bibliog.

This report is the result of a seminar organized by the Sahel Institute and the Demographic Data for Development Project. It examines demographic trends in the 1960s and 1970s, formulates different hypotheses and presents the results and conclusions which place special emphasis on the socio-economic implications of the results.

Ethnic Groups

General

324 **Notes sur l'âme du mil.** (A note about the soul of millet.)
Bernard Champion. *Journal des Africanistes*, vol. 61, fasc. 2 (1991),
p. 91-103.

Champion claims that by using a few elementary notions from plant genetics, we can
penetrate the objective reasons and symbolic depth of a set of African rites of passage
referring to the 'soul of millet'. Whereas interpretations usually emphasize
metaphorical values, we can, on the basis of native concepts and farming practices,
make another assessment of the parallel established between education and the
process of the domestication of the cereal. It is suggested that more is involved than a
figure of speech if the procedure of symbolic circumcision, called for during the
harvest ceremony, conceptualizes the actual selection of seed grain, a selection
necessitated by the cross-fertilization of millet.

325 **Le sort des femmes dans les contes du Tchad.** (Women's destiny in
Chadian tales.)
Herrmann Jungraithmayr. In: *Actes du IVe Colloque Méga-Tchad,
CNRS/ORSTOM, Paris, 14-16 septembre 1988.* Volume II: *Les
relations hommes–femmes dans le bassin du lac Tchad* (*Proceedings
of the fourth Mega-Tchad colloquium, CNRS/ORSTOM, Paris, 14-16
September 1988.* Volume II: *Relations between men and women in the
Lake Chad Basin*), edited by Nicole Echard. Paris: ORSTOM, 1991,
p. 59-69.

Ten folk-tales are studied in this article in order to determine the role the female
protagonist plays in them. The basic theme is that woman's image is more positive
than man's. A key question raised by these folk-tales is whether or not they reflect the
relationship that actually exists between men and women in everyday life.

326 **La chefferie chez les ngama.** (Ngama chieftainship.)
Sadinaly Kraton. Paris: L'Harmattan, 1993. 125p. (Pour mieux
connaître le Tchad).

This study describes the effective power of the Ngama chief and his role in a society
which believes in the supernatural, respect for tradition and for established social
order. It also identifies the unique nature of Ngama institutions.

327 **Scolarisation, fonction publique et relations interethniques au**
Tchad. (Schooling, public service and inter-ethnic relations in Chad.)
Bernard Lanne.   In: *Relations interethniques et culture matérielle*
dans le bassin du lac Tchad. Actes du 3ème colloque Méga-Tchad
ORSTOM Bondy, 11-12 septembre 1986 (Inter-ethnic relations and
material culture in the Lake Chad Basin. Proceedings of the third
Mega-Chad colloquium, ORSTOM Bondy, 11-12 September 1986),
edited by Daniel Barreteau, Henri Tourneux.   Paris: ORSTOM, 1990,
p. 235-66. bibliog.

Bernard Lanne here examines Chadian schooling and public service through the
ethnic looking-glass. He observes that the North–South divide, which has played a
crucial role in the Chadian conflict, was partly caused by education. He explains that
the low level of schooling in the northern Muslim part of Chad (less than 10 per cent
of children were in primary education) in the post-Second World War period, which
is mostly due to hostility towards colonial education and administration, has led to the
predominance of non-Muslim southerners (with a primary schooling rate between 40
and 50 per cent in the same period) in public service. This has resulted in a serious
imbalance whose effects are illustrated by the twenty-year-long civil war which tore
Chad apart.

328 **Les populations du Tchad (nord du 10e parallèle).** (The populations
of Chad (north of the 10th parallel).)
Annie Lebeuf.   Paris: Presses Universitaires de France, 1959. 130p.
map. bibliog.

Annie Lebeuf examines the populations of Chad from the southern rim of the Tibesti
desert to the Chari Basin. The study covers the Teda and Daza of the north, which
were part of the ancient kingdoms of Kanem, Kotoko, Boulala, Baguirmi and Wadai.
It also describes Arabic populations and other groups such as the Yedina, the Kingas
and the Dajo.

329 **Etudes Kotoko.** (Kotoko studies.)
Jean-Paul Lebeuf.   Paris: Mouton, 1976. 105p. bibliog. (Cahiers de
l'Homme, Ethnologie, Géographie, Linguistique, EHESS).

This volume brings together seven studies dealing with a taxonomic system,
numerology and the technique used to establish a calendar of festivals amongst
Kotoko populations.

330   **Jeux éphémères.** (Ephemeral games.)
      Jean-Paul Lebeuf. *Journal des Africanistes*, vol. 61, fasc. 1 (1991),
      p. 109-44.

The games described in this article were observed between 1936 and 1937 in
Cameroon and in 1939 in Chad, among Peul, Fali, Mafa, Namchi, Kotoko and Goula
boys. Six games consisting of drawings in the sand are explained and illustrated.

331   **Peuple, ethnies et nations: le cas du Tchad.** (People, ethnic groups
      and nations: the case of Chad.)
      Jean-Pierre Magnant. *Droits et Cultures*, no. 8 (1984), p. 29-50.
      map.

The author of this article claims that the tendency to reduce the Chadian civil war to
an ethnic conflict is erroneous, as is the belief that tribal consciousness would prevent
the rise of a Chadian nation. He asserts that pre-colonial history shows that the ethnic
group never constituted a self-conscious community. He argues that, in stateless
societies, many ethnic groups were divided either on the military or religious level,
while people of different ethnic backgrounds or languages often celebrated the same
gods. The advent of European colonization, however, imposed state structures which
were never questioned by anti-colonialist leaders and while some antagonisms may
exist between neighbouring populations, the basic elements of Chadian society never
participated in generalized racial attacks. The Chadian nation, the author maintains, is
a reality.

332   **Boum-le-Grand: Village d'Iro.** (Boum-le-Grand: a village of Iro.)
      Claude Pairault.   Paris: Institute d'Ethnologie, 1966. 470p. maps.
      (Université de Paris, Travaux et Mémoires de l'Institut d'Ethnologie,
      LXXIII).

This study of life in the village of Boum-le-Grand (southeastern Chad, near Lake Iro)
is divided into three parts: ecology, sociology and metaphysics. These three
categories constitute the basic and most important aspects of village life.

333   **Saheliens et Sahariens du Tchad.** (The populations of the Sahel and
      the Sahara in Chad.)
      Albert Le Rouvreur, preface by Joseph Tubiana.   Paris: L'Harmattan,
      1989. 535p. (Bibliothèque Peiresc, no. 6).

This book was originally published in 1962 and has not been revised since. It is a
detailed study of the ethnography and material cultures of the complex populations of
northern and central Chad. It also includes considerable detail on the local economies
of different regions of the country in the late 1950s.

334 **De la communauté ethnique à la communauté nationale: les lycéens d'Abéché et de Sarh (Tchad).** (From ethnic to national community: the lycée students of Abéché and Sarh.) Pierre Teisserenc. Paris: EPHE, Université de Paris V, 1972. Vol. 1: 281p., Vol. 2: 521p. bibliog.

As a teacher at the Charles Lwanga College in Sarh between 1965 and 1967, Pierre Teisserenc was able to identify what he calls a crisis among the students. This doctoral thesis is the result of his observations. It examines the origins as well as the social, political and personal dimensions of this crisis and the processes of reconciliation between the students and their family, their friends and ultimately, the political authority. It concludes with a description of the potential future of the students and their concept of success.

335 **Le protoptère et le déluge.** (The lungfish and the flood.) Henri Tourneux. In: *Le milieu et les hommes – Recherches comparatives dans le bassin du lac Tchad. Actes du 2éme colloque Méga-Tchad ORSTOM Bondy, le 3 et 4 octobre 1985 (The environment and the people – comparative research in the Lake Chad Basin. Proceedings of the second Mega-Chad colloquium, ORSTOM Bondy, 3 and 4 October 1985)*, edited by Daniel Barreteau, Henri Tourneux. Paris: ORSTOM, 1988, p. 127-38. bibliog.

Henri Tourneux examines the mythological role of the lungfish in the local interpretation of the cyclical movement of water along the Logone river. He shows that the measure of time which separates the Logone's successive floods is determined by the lungfish, which buries itself in mud during the dry season.

336 **Notes sur les populations du District de Bongor (Mayo-Kebi).** (Notes on the populations of the Bongor District (Mayo-Kebi).) J. Vossart. In: *Quelques populations de la République du Tchad. Les Arabes du Tchad (Populations of the Republic of Chad. The Arabs of Chad)*. (Recherches et documents du CHEAM, III). Paris: CHEAM, 1971, p. 127-230. maps. bibliog.

This paper concentrates on the populations of southeastern Chad and covers their environment, ethnic divisions, political and social organization, history and village toponymy, as well as some ethnographic considerations on marriage, birth, illness, death and heritage. It also examines food resources, techniques, games and beliefs.

Le peuple tchadien, ses racines et sa vie quotidienne.
See item no. 141.

Arabs

337 **Les arabes du Tchad.** (The Arabs of Chad.)
M. Boujol. Paris: CHEAM, 1939. 12p. (Mémoire, no. 603).
This study by a former colonial administrator offers a very general view of the Arabs
in Chad. He examines five Arab groups settled there in terms of their lifestyles
(sedentary or nomadic), living conditions, dress, attitude towards other Chadians,
women and religion.

338 **Habitation et vie quotidienne chez les arabes de la rive sud du lac
Tchad.** (Dwellings and daily life among the Arabs of Lake Chad's
southern bank.)
Edouard Conte, Frank Hagenbucher-Sacripanti. *Cahiers ORSTOM,
Série Sciences Humaines*, Vol. XIV, no. 3 (1977), p. 289-323. map.
bibliog.
This article, which deals with the Suwa Arabs, is an account of their architectural and
domestic technology. It offers a description of a particular form of Sahelian Arab
habitat which developed at the crossroads of the former states of Bornu and Baguirmi
and attempts to find interrelations between sedenterization and habitat technology. It
relates gestural, verbal and attitudinal habits to habitat and underlines small daily
occurrences which help to define 'Suwa' life.

339 **Les Arabes Mohamid du District de Biltine. (Ouaddai).** (Mohamid
Arabs of the Biltine District (Wadai).)
L. Courtecuisse. In: *Quelques populations de la République du
Tchad. Les Arabes du Tchad* (*Populations of the Republic of Chad.
The Arabs of Chad*). (Recherches et documents du CHEAM, III).
Paris: CHEAM, 1971, p. 75-125. bibliog.
This study is divided into two parts. The first is a general presentation of the Morcha
region in Wadai, where the Mohamid Arabs live; it provides information on the
geography, geology, climate, hydrography, fauna and, most importantly, flora of this
area. The second part constitutes a physical and social portrait of the Mohamid.

340 **Magie et sorcellerie chez les arabes 'suwa' (Rives sud du lac
Tchad).** (Magic and witchcraft among Suwa Arabs (Lake Chad
southern bank).)
Frank Hagenbucher-Sacripanti. N'Djamena: ORSTOM, 1974. 33p.
The author focuses on the methods of bewitchment, magical aggression and
protection used in conflict and conflict resolution between individuals and groups.

341 **Note sur les alliances et les marques de bétail chez les arabes du nord-Kanem (Tchad).** (Alliances and cattle branding among the Arabs of northern Kanem (Chad).)
Frank Hagenbucher-Sacripanti. *Cahiers ORSTOM, Série Sciences Humaines*, Vol. XVI, no. 4 (1979), p. 351-80. map. bibliog.
The modes of alliance and solidarity which are described in this study have been restrained by new political and socio-economic conditions for about a century. In Kanem, the distribution of nomad population was altered by migrations and by the resulting phenomenon of acculturation which came from continuous desertification and was worsened by famine in the 1970s. The advantageous strategy of alliance embodied in cattle branding is therefore seldom revealed by the records. However, old alliances are still in existence while other types of solidarity gain ground, though they are sometimes temporary, when faced with unexpected and variable situations. This mobility characterizes Arab society in Kanem as it is forced to find water and grazing land in southern regions, to adapt to a new physical and human environment, as well as to reflect on ways of preserving its identity.

342 **Les arabes Missirié du district d'Oum Hadjer (Batha).** (Myssire Arabs of the Oum Hadjer District (Batha).)
Jean Latruffe. In: *Quelques populations de la République du Tchad. Les Arabes du Tchad (Populations of the Republic of Chad. The Arabs of Chad)*. (Recherches et documents du CHEAM, III). Paris: CHEAM, 1971, p. 21-74.
These two studies were originally produced separately. The first deals with the problem of the Myssire, and focuses more specifically on what the author regards as a very delicate political and social problem. He attributes the problem to the concentrated location of this ethnic group, their nomadism and their mode of authority. The second part of the paper focuses on Myssire transhumance and provides data on each tribal group. The information includes the name of the chief, the group's way of life, the location of cultivation zones, of dry and rain season sedentary locations, and the transhumance itinerary.

343 **Nomadisation d'hivernage des Arabes de l'Ouadi Rimé (Batha).** (Winter nomadization of Wadi Rime Arabs (Batha).)
G. Serre. In: *Quelques populations de la République du Tchad. Les Arabes du Tchad (Populations of the Republic of Chad. The Arabs of Chad)*. (Recherches et documents du CHEAM, III). Paris: CHEAM, 1971, p. 1-17. map.
This is a study of the nomadic Arab populations situated in central Chad, which focuses on the difficulties attached to the nomadic way of life, their modes of transhumance and the transhumance pattern.

Baguirmi

344 **Le royaume du Baguirmi.** (The kingdom of Baguirmi.)
Annie Lebeuf. In: *Princes et serviteurs du royaume. Cinq textes de monarchies africaines* (*Princes and servants of the kingdom. Five texts on African monarchies*), edited by Claude Tardits. Paris: Société d'Ethnographie, 1987, p. 171-225. map. (Sociétés Africaines, no. 7).

This article considers the question of power in the Baguirmi kingdom of Chad and how it was shared between princes and royal servants. It does this through the study of a manuscript held in Baguirmi archives which contains an inventory of royalties (*redevances*) received by princes and important royal servants during the period that preceded French colonization.

Day

345 **Les day de Bouna. Notes sur la vie sociale et religieuse d'une population du Moyen-Chari.** (The Day of Bouna. Notes on the social and religious life of a population from the Middle-Chari region.)
Alfred Adler. Fort-Lamy (N'Djamena): INTSH, 1966. 78p. (Etudes et Documents Tchadiens, Serie A, 1). maps.

This study is the result of a three-month visit to the Mbay people of southern Chad (part of the larger Sara ethnic group). Adler examines general aspects of the social and religious life of this population, beginning with some general remarks on history and oral traditions, and then briefly analysing family and marriage, domestic cults, religious hierarchy, and initiation rites (male and female).

Hadjerai

346 **Rite, histoire, structure chez les Kenga.** (Rituals, history and structure among the Kenga.)
Jean Pouillon. In his: *Fétiches sans fétichismes* (*Fetishes without fetishism*). Paris: François Maspéro, 1975, p. 273-89.

In this study, the author examines the ritual which marks the end of agricultural work and during which the Margai or evil spirit of the village speaks through a chosen woman. He describes in detail the ceremony which highlights the role of the Margai as a guardian of traditions, and acts, to a certain extent, as the conscience of village chiefs.

347 **La structure du pouvoir chez les Hadjerai (Tchad).** (Power structures among the Hadjerai of Chad.)
Jean Pouillon. In his: *Fétiches sans fétichismes* (*Fetishes without fetishism*). Paris: François Maspéro, 1975, p. 177-241. maps.
By comparing the history and structures of villages of the Dangaleat region, the author provides an analysis of Hadjerai power structures.

348 **Du sacrifice comme compromis. Note sur le culte dangaleat.**
(Sacrifice as a compromise. A note on Dangaleat cult.)
Jean Pouillon. In: *Sous le masque de l'animal. Essais sur le sacrifice en Afrique noire* (*Under the animal's mask. Essays on sacrifice in Black Africa*), edited by Michel Cartry. Paris: Presses Universitaires de France, 1987, p. 234-9.
This article about the Dangaleat – or Hadjerai – group of eastern Chad explains that animal sacrifices to the Margai – or evil spirits – constitutes a compromise in which certain rules and rituals meant to appease the Margai have been established.

349 **Techniques divinatoires des saba (montagnard du centre-Tchad).**
(Saba divinatory techniques (mountain people of central Chad).)
Jeanne-Françoise Vincent. *Journal de la Société des Africanistes*, Vol. XXXVI, fasc. 2 (1966), p. 45-63. map. bibliog.
Vincent deals with one of the nineteen ethnic groups which make up the Hadjerai people, the Saba. They represent one per cent of the total Hadjerai population and live in the prefecture of Guera, in south-central Chad. The author shows that divination plays an important role in the daily life of the Saba because any event that breaks the expected course of life needs explaining. She explains in detail the methods of divination used and the possible results of a consultation.

350 **Le pouvoir et le sacré chez les Hadjeray du Tchad.** (Power and religion among the Hadjerai of Chad.)
Jeanne-Françoise Vincent. Paris: Editions Anthropos, 1975. 226p.
This ethnological study focuses on social structures and status, religious life and division of power among the Hadjerai. It also describes the formation of Hadjerai society from the fusion of different ethnic groups.

Kanuri/Kanembu

351 **Les populations Kanouri de Fort-Lamy, Chari-Baguirmi.**
(The Kanuri people of Fort-Lamy, Chari-Baguirmi.)
Mahamat Baba Abatcha. N'Djamena: Présidence de la République,
Ecole Nationale d'Administration, 1972. 36p. maps.

The Kanuri people, usually referred to as Bornu, originated from the Kingdom of Kanem-Bornu in northeastern Nigeria. After being dispersed around Lake Chad, part of the population settled in Fort-Lamy, now N'Djamena. It is this population which is examined here, through its history and origins, language, economic life, trade, artisanal techniques, food, social structures and organization, traditions, religion and religious rites. This is a short typewritten work.

352 **Politics and marriage in south Kanem (Chad): a statistical presentation of endogamy from 1895 to 1975.**
Edouard Conte. *Cahiers ORSTOM, Série Sciences Humaines*,
Vol. XVI, no. 4 (1979), p. 275-97. maps. bibliog.

This paper presents the preliminary results of a comparative study of endogamy and lineage organization among the two major social strata of the Kanembu people of southeast Kanem: the 'people of the spear' (Kanembu for 'noble' descent) and the 'people of the bow', better known as the Haddad, who form approximately 20 to 25 per cent of the Kanembu population.

353 **Marriage patterns, political change and the perpetuation of social inequality in southern Kanem (Chad).**
Edouard Conte. Paris: ORSTOM, 1983. 545p.

The introduction to this study is a general discussion of the Kanembu people of the northeastern bank of Lake Chad. It deals with their social structures, socio-political organization and economic patterns. The major part of the study, is devoted to a detailed and thorough examination of Kanembu marriage patterns.

354 **Castes, classes et alliances au sud-Kanem.** (Castes, classes and alliances in south Kanem.)
Edouard Conte. *Journal des Africanistes*, vol. 53, no. 1-2 (1983),
p. 147-69. map. bibliog.

Conte analyses marriage exchange patterns among the Kanembu of south Kanem in terms of descent group membership, consanguinity and locality. The analysis relates to societies manifesting segmentary characteristics but in which marriage between and within unilinearly defined descent groups is regulated neither by an endogamic nor an exogamic restriction. The study discusses how the transformation of alliance structures between the start of the twentieth century and the early 1970s may be interpreted in the light of the socio-political evolution of the two social strata – one based on agro-pastoralism, the other on hunting and artisanal activists – which compose this inegalitarian society.

355 **Nécessité fertile ou le pêcheur sans arbres.** (Fertile necessity or the treeless fisherman.)
Philippe Couty. *Cahiers ORSTOM, Série Sciences Humaines*, Vol. XVII, no. 3-4 (1980), p. 223-6. bibliog.
This short illustrated article, which is part of an issue specially devoted to trees, deals, paradoxically, with the absence of trees and how this problem is remedied by the Buduma people who dwell on the banks of Lake Chad. Couty examines the methods and materials used to build the local pirogue and the process of fish preservation, both of which have replaced the use of reeds, which grow extensively on the banks and the islands of Lake Chad, for more traditional trees, which do not exist in this area.

Masa

356 **Le rôle social et rituel du bétail chez les Massa du Tchad.** (The social and ritual role of cattle among the Masa of Chad.)
Françoise Dumas-Champion. *Africa* (London), vol. 50, no. 2 (1980), p. 161-81.
This article is a preview of the book by the same author which was published in 1983 (see item no. 357).

357 **Les Masa du Tchad – Bétail et société.** (The Masa of Chad: cattle and society.)
Françoise Dumas-Champion. Cambridge: Cambridge University Press; Paris: Editions de la Maison des Sciences de l'Homme, 1983. 276p.
An ethnological study which centres on the role of cattle in Masa society and which analyses its function in marriage, conflict and ritual sacrifice. It shows how cattle provide the Masa with a language and an ideology.

358 **Le droit de maudire: malédiction et serment chez les Masa du Tchad.** (The right to curse. Curses and oaths among the Masa (Chad).)
Françoise Dumas-Champion. *Droit et Cultures*, no. 9-10 (1985), p. 81-93.
This article claims that by analysing the mechanisms through which a curse works, its sociological and judicial significance can be understood. It shows that these mechanisms reveal the existence of a right that, in extreme cases, seem to be exercised through curses and that the 'right to curse' follows from a bond created by real or symbolic consanguinity; it is exercised within the elder–junior relationship. Through the dichotomy that the Masa establish between curses and oaths, the specific nature of the latter can be seen as a penal procedure that reaches beyond the family context.

359 **Le sacrifice ou la question du meurtre.** (Sacrifice or murder.)
Françoise Dumas-Champion. *Anthropos*, vol. 82, no. 1-3 (1987),
p. 135-49.

Dumas-Champion shows how, in the Masa sacrificial system, immolation is not an
essential requirement. The exchange of bodies, which is inherent in the sacrificial
ritual, can take place without killing victims that are endowed with human attributes
and/or by replacing victims with objects. By comparing sacrifice to other forms of
killing, such as homicide, this article demonstrates that the killer and his victim are
symbiotically related. Although, in some way, sacrifice and murder are alike, they
form an antinomy: sacrifice bestows a plentiful progeny upon the sacrifier whereas
the murderer's descendants and procreative powers are threatened.

360 **'Les hommes meurent toujours à cause des femmes', les relations
entre les sexes chez les Masa du Tchad.** ('Men always die because of
women', gender relations among the Masa of Chad.)
Françoise Dumas-Champion. In: *Actes du IVe colloque Méga-Tchad,
CNRS/ORSTOM, Paris, 14-16 september 1988*. Volume II: *Les
relations hommes–femmes dans le bassin du lac Tchad* (*Proceedings
of the fourth Mega-Tchad colloquium, CNRS/ORSTOM, Paris, 14-16
September 1988*. Volume II: *Relations between men and women in the
Lake Chad Basin*), edited by Nicole Echard. Paris: ORSTOM, 1991,
p. 225-47. map.

Among the Masa, cattle are used to mediate relations between men and women.
Cattle belong exclusively to the man, and define his masculinity, not only by enabling
him to obtain wives, but also by contributing to his image as a wrestler. The image of
the woman, corresponding to that of the man as an accomplished herder and wrestler,
has to do with her ability to perform somersaults, which represent her fertility. The
author of this article explains how these symbolic images relate to the marriage
contract on the one hand, and to the interaction between husband and wife on the
other. She concludes that the marriage rites, supported by a rigid matrimonial system,
serve to confine the woman to a single marital union.

361 **Les étrangers, la vengeance et les parents chez les Massa et les
Moussey (Tchad et Cameroun).** (Foreigners, vengeance and parents
among the Masa and the Musey (Chad and Cameroon).)
Igor de Garine. In: *La vengeance. Etudes d'ethnologie, d'histoire et
de philosophie.* Vol. 1: *Vengeance et pouvoir dans quelques sociétés
extra-occidentales* (*Vengeance. Ethnological, historical and
philosophical studies.* Vol. 1: *Vengeance and power in non-Western
societies*), edited by Raymond Verdier. Paris: Editions Cujas, 1980,
p. 91-124. bibliog.

In this comparative study, de Garine shows that in spite of the differences that
separate them, the history and present behaviour of the Masa of Chad and the Musey
of Cameroon are both strongly influenced by the role of vengeance. He deals with
such themes as honour and feud and examines the practice of vengeance in the close
family context. He also looks at supernatural powers, their role and mechanisms in

vengeance, as well as sorcery, bewitchment, poisoning and curses. Finally, the author shows that vengeance is still a powerful feature in modern Masa and Musey societies and that it is a feature of everyday life which has developed and adapted to modern circumstances.

362 **Hina, l'écureuil décepteur. Approche ethnologique d'un conte Musey (Tchad).** (Hina, the deceitful squirrel. The ethnological approach of a Musey tale.)
    Jean Louatron. Paris: EHESS, 1976. 158p. maps. bibliog. (EHESS, Mémoire, Section des Sciences Economiques et Sociales).
The deceitful squirrel seems to be an important figure in Musey mythology, and it is the central figure of the tale analysed here. The author who has recourse to an ethno-linguistic approach in order to understand the symbolism of the tale, and places such tales in the cultural context of the Musey, the two being intrinsically linked.

363 **Wakonga, femme prestigieuse de Holom. Une année de la vie d'une 'possédée' Musey (au Tchad) Avril 1969-Avril 1970.** (Wakonga, a prestigious woman from Holom. A year in the life of a Musey 'possessed woman' (Chad) April 1969-April 1970.)
    Jean Louatron. [n.p., n.d. (1982?)]. 645p. maps.
Louatron discusses a manuscript written by Wakonga, a Musey woman regularly consulted by the elders of her village and who participated in the cultural ceremonies of the Holom clan. It contains Wakonga's 'curriculum vitae', as well as a description of the Musey and the Holom clan, and presents the manuscript record of Wakonga's daily religious activities side by side with a French translation.

364 **La première étape de la vie sociale et les pratiques de puériculture chez les Masa du Tchad.** (The first stages of social life and infant care among the Masa of Chad.)
    Blandine Rondot. Paris: EHESS, 1977. 258p. maps. bibliog. (Diploma, Centre de Recherches Coopératives).
This study examines the rituals and beliefs that surround pregnancy, birth and infant care. It also analyses the names given to newborn babies and classifies them into categories such as: names with a message, those relating to family history, or those inspired by a song, a famous person or religion. The study contains four appendices which present a Masa tale with its analysis, the description of three rituals, death in Masa oral literature and witchcraft among the Masa.

Moundang

365 **La vengeance du sang chez les Moundangs du Tchad.** (Blood feud
among the Moundang of Chad.)
Alfred Adler. In: *La vengeance. Etudes d'ethnologie, d'histoire et de
philosophie.* Vol. 1: *Vengeance et pouvoir dans quelques sociétés
extra-occidentales* (*Vengeance. Ethnological, historical and
philosophical studies.* Vol. 1: *Vengeance and power in non-Western
societies*), edited by Raymond Verdier. Paris: Editions Cujas, 1980,
p. 75-89.
Adler examines the relations and links between the members of Moundang society
and emphasizes the role of the clan as guarantor of identity and security. He also
studies the conciliation ritual which ends the process of violence and deals with royal
power and its sanctions in relation to vengeance.

366 **La mort est le masque du roi – La royauté sacrée chez les
Moundang du Tchad.** (Death is the king's mask – sacred royalty
among the Moundang of Chad.)
Alfred Adler. Paris: Payot, 1982. 427p. maps. (Bibliothèque
Scientifique).
Although this book refers to the history of the Moundang, it is not essentially a
historical study. Instead it is designed to be a modern study of an ethnic group which
survived French occupation and has retained a strong cultural identity with the king
as its focus. Adler examines the clan structure as well as the political and ritual
organization of the Moundang.

367 **La guerre et l'état primitif.** (War and the primitive state.)
Alfred Adler. In: *L'esprit des lois sauvages. Pierre Clastre ou une
nouvelle anthropologie politique* (*Savage laws. Pierre Clastre or the
new political anthropology*), edited by Miguel Abensour. Paris:
Seuil, 1987, p. 95-114.
This article deals with the Moundang kingdom of Lere in southern Chad and shows
how the analysis of fundamental mechanisms of its political life can threaten the
legitimacy of the state.

368 **Le royaume Moundang de Léré.** (The Moundang kingdom of Lere.)
Alfred Adler. In: *Princes et serviteurs du royaume. Cinq textes de
monarchies africaines* (*Princes and servants in the kingdom. Five texts
on African monarchies*), edited by Claude Tardits. Paris: Société
d'Ethnographie, 1987, p. 137-70. map. (Sociétés Africaines, 7).
The author examines the political organization of Moundang society, the question of
royal lineage and slave and royal clans. He shows that clans have an important and
clear role within the political structure which ensures the continuity of Moundang
royalty.

369 **Royauté et sacrifice chez les Moundang du Tchad.** (Royalty and sacrifice among the Moundang of Chad.)
Alfred Adler. In: *Sous le masque de l'animal. Essais sur le sacrifice en Afrique noire* (*Under the animal's mask. Essays on sacrifice in Black Africa*), edited by Michel Cartry. Paris: Presses Universitaires de France, 1987, p. 89-130. map.

In this article, the author presents a concept of royalty among the Moundang entirely based on elements of sacrificial concepts which he examines in great detail.

370 **La fillette amoureuse des masques. Le statut de la femme chez les Moundang.** (The little girl in love with masks. The status of women among the Moundang.)
Alfred Adler. *Journal des Africanistes*, vol. 59, no. 1-2 (1989), p. 63-97. bibliog.

Women's status in Moundang society appears to be mainly a matter of marital alliance in contrast with that of men, which has to do with the order of filiation. This study takes into consideration data from the terminology of affinal relationships and from customs and rites concerning the major stages of women's life-cycle. The linguistic analysis of the system of Omaha-type terms used by the Moundang provides important evidence, but the description and interpretation of the symbols of puberty, matrimonial and funeral ceremonies are even more significant in defining this status and in shaping the Moundang woman's destiny.

371 **Le Bâton de l'aveugle. Divination, maladie et pouvoir chez les Moundang du Tchad.** (The blind man's staff. Divination, illness and power among the Moundang of Chad.)
Alfred Adler, Andras Zempléni. Paris: Hermann, 1972. 224p. map. bibliog. (Collection Savoir).

This work is a careful description of divination in Moundang society, in the Mayo-Kebi area in southwestern Chad. It is examined in the context of illness and power and provides a description as well as an analysis of consultations observed by the authors.

372 **Notes sur les Moundans.** (Notes on the Moundang.)
E. Brussaux. *Bulletin et Mémoires de la Société d'Anthropologie de Paris* (1907), p. 273-95. map.

This illustrated study was one of the first of its kind on the Moundang of southern Chad. It covers the geography of the region, the Moundang's origins, their physical type and character, their beliefs and rituals, their habitat, their farming, hunting and fishing methods, their modes of artistic expression and their political organization.

373 **Myth as reality.**
Luc de Heusch. *Journal of Religion in Africa*, Vol. XVIII, fasc. 3 (Oct. 1988), p. 200-15. bibliog.

This scholarly study on myths and kingship uses Alfred Adler's *La mort est le masque du roi* (see item no. 366) as a springboard and compares the myth about the founding of the Mundang kingship of southwestern Chad and the epic of the origin of the Luba state in Zaïre.

Sara

374 **Sara demographic instability as a consequence of French colonial policy in Chad (1890-1940).**
M. J. Azevedo. Ann Arbor, Michigan: Xerox University Microfilms, 1976. 295p. bibliog.
Based on written and oral sources, this doctoral thesis analyses the reasons for depopulation and demographic instability among the Sara. It identifies three factors: epidemics, forced labour and emigration.

375 **Nourrir les gens, nourrir les haines.** (Feeding people, feeding hatred.)
Helen P. Brown. Paris: Société d'Ethnographie, 1983. 263p. (Etudes et Documents Tchadiens).
This ethnographical study is concerned with the Nar people who belong to the larger Sara group of southern Chad. It looks at the history and practice of authority and its relation with food, itself used to build the social relations which form the focus of this study.

376 **Population du Moyen-Logone. Cameroun et Tchad.**
(The population of the Middle-Logone. Cameroon and Chad.)
Jean Cabot, R. Diziain. Paris: ORSTOM, 1955. 76p. map. bibliog.
(L'Homme d'Outre-Mer, Comptes rendus de missions et d'études).
A demographic study carried out by two geographers, the first a specialist on Chad, the second on the Cameroon. The Middle-Logone region spans the territories of Chad and the Cameroon and covers an area of plains which are flooded by the waters of the Logone river for six months every year. The purpose of the study is to provide information for the development of a dike construction programme to protect local populations from flood.

377 **Tradition et modernisme dans les quartiers de Sarh (République du Tchad).** (Tradition and modernism in Sahr (Republic of Chad).)
Jacques Chauvet. *Les Cahiers d'Outre-Mer*, no. 117 (Jan.-March 1977), p. 57-82. map.
The aim of this study is to describe the African residential quarters of Sarh. It does so by direct observation of the environment and interviews with inhabitants. By analysing data referring to the population's activities and resources, the author attempts to explain the type of population groupings in the various quarters.

378 **Croissance urbaine et incidents de 1979 à Sarh (Tchad). Analyse géographique et problèmes du développement.** (Urban growth and the Sarh incidents (Chad) of 1979. Geographical analysis and development problems.)
Jacques Chauvet. *Les Cahiers d'Outre-Mer*, no. 158 (April-June 1987), p. 205-11.

This article refers to the events in Sahr in March-April 1979 during which 600 black Muslims were killed. The author claims that the killings were not so much the result of communal violence as a consequence of the national political crisis between the North and the South and of the tremendous demographic growth in some parts of this southern Chad city.

379 **Evolution de la famille et croissance des villes moyennes: Sarh (Tchad) et Toumodi (Cote d'Ivoire).** (The evolution of the family and the growth of average size towns: Sarh (Chad) and Toumodi (Ivory Coast).)
Jacques Chauvet. *Cahiers d'Outre-Mer*, no. 158 (April-June 1987), p. 173-203.

In this article the author tries to identify the role of the urban family in the solution of fundamental problems of tropical African towns such as lack of employment and finance. He studies its evolution in developed towns after independence and stresses that priority should be given to the family environment in development.

380 **Essai d'étude démographique des Kaba du District de Kyabe (région du Moyen-Chari).** (Demographic study of the Kaba of the Kyabe District (Middle-Chari).)
Jean Croquevieille. In: *Quelques populations de la République du Tchad. Les Arabes du Tchad (Populations of the Republic of Chad. The Arabs of Chad).* Paris: CHEAM, 1971, p. 231-59. map.
(Recherches et documents du CHEAM, III).

The demographic survey of the Kaba (who belong to the larger Sara group) from which this study stems, was carried out between 1953 and 1954. It investigated questions related to the age pyramid, marriage rate, birth rate, reproduction rate and mortality.

381 **Le mariage en pays Toupouri (Tchad et Cameroun).** (Marriage in the Tupuri region (Chad and Cameroon).)
Laurent Feckoua. In: *Le milieu et les hommes – Recherches comparatives dans le bassin du lac Tchad. Actes du 2ème colloque Méga-Tchad ORSTOM Bondy, le 3 et 4 octobre 1985 (The environment and the people – comparative research in the Lake Chad Basin. Proceedings of the second Mega-Chad colloquium, ORSTOM Bondy, 3 and 4 October 1985)*, edited by Daniel Barreteau, Henri Tourneux. Paris: ORSTOM, 1988, p. 157-94. bibliog.

Tupuri marriage is characterized by very specific and complex rules and customs which are presented here in great detail. The author examines aspects defining engagement, such as the initial encounter between the future spouses, the importance of the choice of witnesses and that of an exogamous relation, as well as the practice of living together before the wedding. He then goes on to study marriage itself through its various forms, the relationship between the spouses' families, the dowry and divorce.

382 **Rituels funéraires Sar. Les Sar en présence de Yo (rites funéraires à Bédaya).** (Sara funerary rituals. The Sara and Yo (funerary rituals in Bedaya).)
Maurice Fournier. *Afrique et Parole*, no. 37-8 (July 1972), p. 5-48.

Yo is the name of the Sara language which can be very approximately translated as 'death'. Because of this linguistic complexity, the author clarifies the meaning and contents of several terms related to the concept of death before describing the stages that separate death and the funeral, the funeral itself, and commemorations of death. He also examines specific types of death, such as infant death, death by drowning and death of the king.

383 **Des noms qui parlent. Hommes et femmes dans la société sar d'après les noms d'initiation.** (Names that speak. Men and women in Sara society: the role of initiation names.)
Jacques Hallaire. Sahr, Chad: Centre d'Etudes Linguistiques, Collège Charles Lwanga, 1977. 354p.

This extensive study highlights the importance of personal names throughout Africa and shows that, in southern Chad in particular, a name has great significance and that a large number of social practices determine its use. The author examines the principles on which name-giving in the Sara region is based and provides a collection of 2,000 names, each translated and briefly explained. He also analyses the characteristics of initiation names and looks at fourteen main themes reflected in them.

384 **Les populations du Moyen-Chari. Esquisse anthropologique.** (The
population of the Middle-Chari. An anthropological sketch.)
Jean Hiernaux. N'Djamena: INTSH, [n.d. (1965?)]. 33p. map.
bibliog. (Etudes et Documents Tchadiens, Série A, 2).

This report is the result of a three-month visit to the Middle-Chari region of southern
Chad commissioned by the Chadian government under the auspices of the Chadian
National Institute for Humanities in N'Djamena (then known as Fort-Lamy). It
concentrates on anthropology and is based on field research amongst the Sara.
Individual members of the Mouvement de la Jeunesse Tchadienne of Fort-
Archambault (now known as Sarh) were picked from widespread geographical
locations within the region occupied by the Sara. Their specific ethnic origins were
noted, as well as their respective biological characteristics.

385 **La mort sara. L'ordre de la vie ou la pensée de la mort au Tchad.**
(Death among the Sara. The pattern of life or the concept of death in
Chad.)
Robert Jaulin. Paris: Plon, 1967. 295p. (Terre Humaine. Civilisations
et Sociétés).

This ethnological study of the Madjingaye and Deme Sara in southern Chad was
carried out in the late 1950s. Its value resides in the author's detailed knowledge as a
result of his own initiation along with Sara young men. His main concern is the
concepts of initiation in the context of death rituals. Initiation is considered more as a
rite of passage from childhood to adulthood, just as death is seen as a similar rite
rather than in its biological sense.

386 **Introduction à la vie et à l'histoire précoloniales des populations
sara du Tchad.** (Introduction to the pre-colonial life and history of the
Sara people of Chad.)
Gayo Jean Kogongar. Paris: Université de Paris I, Centre d'Etudes
Africaines de la Sorbonne, 1971. 275p.

This doctoral thesis is a general introduction to the Sara population of southern Chad
based on a study of the people and their history. Initially, the physical environment of
the Sara is described and their division into groups, languages, racial types is
examined. Then their origins, settlement patterns and relationship to the sultanates of
Central Africa are discussed.

387 **Les populations du Sud du Tchad.** (The populations of southern
Chad.)
Bernard Lanne. *Le Mois en Afrique*, no. 163-4 (July-Aug. 1979),
p. 41-81.

As the Chief Administrator of Overseas Affairs and the director of President
Tombalbaye's cabinet in 1960-61, Bernard Lanne was well informed about the Sara
people of southern Chad. This study is a description of the groups which form the
Sara, a demographic estimate and a discussion of the Sara environment, as well as an
outline of Sara culture and history.

388 **Les dignitaires de la cour de Massenya (Royaume du Barma, République du Tchad).** (The dignitaries of the Massenya court (Kingdom of Barma, Republic of Chad).)
Annie Lebeuf. [n.p.], 1977. 93p. (Paideuma, 23).

This short study focuses on the Kingdom of Barma, which corresponds to the modern province of Chari-Baguirmi in southern Chad. It is based on research carried out in 1966 and 1967, as well as on the accounts from travellers such as Barth (q.v.) and Nachtigal (q.v.).

389 **Terres de lignage et état chez les populations dites 'sara' du Sud du Tchad, XIXe-XXe siècle.** (Lands of lineage and state among the Sara of southern Chad, in the nineteenth and twentieth centuries.)
Jean-Pierre Magnant. *Revue Française d'Histoire d'Outre-Mer,* vol. 68, no. 250-2 (1981), p. 394-426. maps. bibliog.

Magnant discusses the traditional relations that existed between lineages and the spiritual forces of the land which passed through the priest or Mbang. He shows how, in the late eighteenth century, one priest, the Mbang Dai of Bedaya, increased his power by annexing fields on the community's land and constraining peasants into forced labour. This land system was altered by the French conquest as the colonial authorities made the cultivation of cotton compulsory, a modification which finally led to a crisis in 1970. The author also takes into account the introduction of Christianity, the modernization of cotton cultivation, the civil war and its demographic consequences in order to complete the picture of the modern Sara land system.

390 **Terre et pouvoir dans les populations dites 'sara' du sud du Tchad. La famille, l'individu et l'état, leur terroir et leur territoire.** (Land and power among the Sara in southern Chad. Family, the individual and the state, their land and territory.)
Jean-Pierre Magnant. Paris: Université de Paris I, 1983. 745p. maps. bibliog.

This very comprehensive doctoral thesis deals with the notion of law in Sara society and considers the human context of the legal relationship between the individual, the community and the land in the pre-colonial, colonial and post-colonial periods. The author also analyses the impact of colonization on Sara social and economic structures and land systems, and considers prospects for the future.

391 **Les initiations masculines à l'est de l'Adamawa: aires d'extension et problèmes de diffusion.** (Male initiation procedures in the eastern Adamawa region: zone of influence and problems of diffusion.)
Yves Monino. In: *Le milieu et les hommes – Recherches comparatives dans le bassin du lac Tchad. Actes du 2ème colloque Méga-Tchad ORSTOM Bondy, le 3 et 4 octobre 1985 (The environment and the people – comparative research in the Lake Chad Basin. Proceedings of the second Mega-Chad colloquium, ORSTOM Bondy, 3 and 4 October 1985)*, edited by Daniel Barreteau, Henri Tourneux. Paris: ORSTOM, 1988, p. 221-30. maps. bibliog.
A study concerning ethnic groups from the western part of the Central African Republic, southeastern Chad and the eastern part of Central Cameroon. Although ethnically, socially and linguistically different, these groups share certain common characteristics, including male initiation, which marks the passage from childhood to manhood. The author examines in particular the Lá'bi language which is common to the male initiation rites of all the groups concerned.

392 **Le roi pêcheur et le roi chasseur.** (The fisher king and the hunter king.)
Viviana Paques. Strasbourg, France: Travaux de l'Institut d'Anthropologie de Strasbourg, 1977. 237p.
This study of the ancient Baguirmi kingdom, situated on the north bank of the river Chari, describes the complex and subtle relation between the African spiritual world and daily life. It describes aspects of Baguirmi society and analyses the way in which they interact with and are influenced by beliefs which originate from myth.

393 **Marriage payments, household structure and domestic labour-supply among the Barma of Chad.**
Stephen Reyna. *Africa*, vol. 47, no. 1 (1977), p. 81-8. bibliog.
This article investigates the way in which marriage payments affect household structure, specifically the age difference between spouses, between married children and their offspring, and the age of male polygamists. The author also explains how these last two structural parameters contribute to maintain domestic labour supply.

394 **Sara: échanges et instruments monétaires.** (Trade and monetary instruments.)
Josette Rivallain. In: *Le milieu et les hommes – Recherches comparatives dans le bassin du lac Tchad. Actes du 2ème colloque Méga-Tchad ORSTOM Bondy, le 3 et 4 octobre 1985 (The environment and the people – comparative research in the Lake Chad Basin. Proceedings of the second Mega-Chad colloquium, ORSTOM Bondy, 3 and 4 October 1985)*, edited by Daniel Barreteau, Henri Tourneux. Paris: ORSTOM, 1988, p. 195-213. bibliog.
Josette Rivallain begins her study with an introduction to the little-known history of Sara settlement in the region they now occupy. She then examines their currency,

shows the socio-religious role of metallic and other currency, and determines who makes it and who uses it. She concludes by discussing the modes of money exchange and the gradual disappearance of local currency with the introduction of the franc by the French administration.

395 **Fer et forgerons dans le sud du lac Tchad à travers les écrits des premiers colonisateurs.** (Iron and blacksmiths south of Lake Chad through the writings of early colonizers.)
Josette Rivallain.   In: *Actes du IVe colloque Méga-Tchad, CNRS/ORSTOM, Paris, 14-16 september 1988.* Volume 1: *Forge et Forgerons* (*Proceedings of the fourth Mega-Chad colloquium, CNRS/ORSTOM, Paris, 14-16 September 1988.* Volume 1: *Forge and blacksmiths*), edited by Yves Monino.   Paris: ORSTOM, 1991, p. 227-40.

The special place occupied by blacksmiths in most African societies is explored in this volume of the Mega-Tchad colloquium, with a specific reference to the Lake Chad Basin. This particular article is concerned with late-nineteenth-century explorers and what they tell us about blacksmiths and their work. The author describes travelling conditions and the explorers' perceptions of the people they encountered and notes that blacksmiths are among the few craftsmen described in their accounts.

396 **A note on the pre-colonial iron currency of the Laka of southwestern Chad.**
Allen-F. Roberts.   *Journal des Africanistes*, vol. 58, fasc. 1 (1988), p. 99-105. bibliog.

Lar ndul was the name of the iron currency used by the Laka before the arrival of Europeans around 1900. This article describes how the iron used for the manufacture of this currency was obtained and fashioned into shapes which had different functions and then how the currency itself was used in financial and commercial exchanges.

397 **Instruments aratoires du Tchad méridional et du nord-Cameroun.** (Agricultural implements in southern Chad and northern Cameroon.)
Christian Seignobos.   *Cahiers ORSTOM, Série Sciences Humaines,* Vol. XX, no. 3-4 (1984), p. 537-73. (Les instruments aratoires en Afrique tropicale).

Seignobos examines the functions of agricultural implements in Chad. He remarks on the fact that in the north, the iler [a type of hoe] is prevailing and is followed by a series of more or less derivative agricultural implements such as the straight tidging [small-scale] hoes and the straight and short weeders which are used in the whole of southern Chad. The author also establishes that agricultural implements could not be the parameter of agrarian civilizations. Sometimes, the affective value attached to the implement alters its true meaning, thus leading to borrowing or abandoning some of them. Nevertheless the role played by blacksmith societies must not be ignored for, although they adapt to the evolution of the implements, they often contribute to transforming them.

398 **Rôle du forgeron dans la société traditionnelle au Mayo-Kebbi.**
(The blacksmith's role in Mayo-Kebbi traditional society.)
Bouimon Tchago. In: *Actes du IVe colloque Méga-Tchad,
CNRS/ORSTOM, Paris, 14-16 septembre 1988.* Volume 1: *Forge et
Forgerons (Proceedings of the Fourth Mega-Chad colloquium,
CNRS/ORSTOM, Paris, 14-16 September 1988.* Volume 1: *Forge and
blacksmiths*), edited by Yves Monino. Paris: ORSTOM, 1991,
p. 263-80. map. bibliog.
The Mayo-Kebbi region, situated in southwestern Chad, contains a mosaic of ethnic
groups, dominated by the Moundang, the Tupuri and the Masa, among whom
blacksmiths have an important place. The author examines their origins through three
legends and defines their social attributes and their relations with the political and the
military forces.

Teda/Tubu

399 **Notes statistiques sur le Tibesti, le Borkou, l'Ennedi. Notes
bibliographiques.** (Statistical notes on Tibesti, Borkou and Ennedi.
Bibliographical notes.)
Jean d'Arbaumont. Paris: CHEAM, 1953. 31p.
The statistics provided in this study concern the populations, cattle and production of
Borkou, Ennedi and Tibesti, the latter being given more attention than the former two.

400 **Santons du Tibesti oriental. Désignations des chefs coutumiers au
Tibesti et au Borkou. Organisation politique au Tibesti. Comment
appeler les populations du Nord du Tchad?** (Saints of eastern
Tibesti. Titles for the customary chiefs of Tibesti and Borkou. Political
organization in Tibesti. How should the populations of northern Chad
be described?)
Jean d'Arbaumont. Paris: CHEAM, 1953. 47p. map.
This is a compilation of several articles. The first one tells the stories of three local
saints which the author collected from an Ouria chief (part of the Teda group of
northern Chad). The second article describes the way in which chiefs are chosen
amongst the Teda of Tibesti, the Gourma – a small group mainly in the Ennedi region
– the Doza and the Gouroa. The third article, also published in the *Bulletin de
l'Institut Français d'Afrique Noire* in 1956, reviews the structures of political life in
Tibesti. The fourth article attempts to establish a correct name pattern for the
populations of northern Chad.

401 **Le Tibesti et le domaine teda-daza.** (Tibesti and the Teda-Daza region.)
Jean d'Arbaumont. [Paris?]: Centre d'Etude sur l'Histoire du Sahara, 1989; *Bulletin de l'Institut Fondamental d'Afrique Noire*, Série B (July-Oct. 1954). 56p.
This ethnographical study examines the social structures and the Islamization of the tribes and clans of Tibesti.

402 **L'organisation socio-économique Toubou: un système d'échange généralisé du bétail.** (Tubu socio-economic organisation: a widespread system of cattle exchange.)
Catherine Baroin. *Travaux du LAPEPMO* (1980). 5p. bibliog.
According to the author of this article, the Tubu form an anarchic society whose cohesion is based on a specific mode of cattle exchange. The exchange networks are linked to a particular aspect of marriage (marriage between close relatives is forbidden) and lead to a generalized system of exchange of cattle which partly explains the absence of political institutions.

403 **Ecologie et organisation sociale: comparaison de trois sociétés sahariennes (toubou, touarègue, maure).** (Ecology and social organization: a comparison of three Saharan societies (Tubu, Touareg, Moorish).)
Catherine Baroin. *Travaux du LAPEPMO* (1980). 19p. bibliog.
This article shows, by comparing three Saharan societies, how different forms of social organization can develop in one single ecological zone. It highlights the minimal influence that the environment has over the determination of social structures in this area. While this study is not unique in its approach, its interest lies in the powerful contrasts it emphasizes with regard to the three Saharan societies under scrutiny.

404 **Analyse de la famille dans une population pastorale: les toubou.** (An analysis of the pastoral Tubu family.)
Catherine Baroin. *Travaux du LAPEPMO* (1982). 26p.
Baroin describes the problems encountered and the data gathered during a study of the Tubu pastoral family. As an ethnographical study, the survey and its results are qualitative rather than quantitative, but they also have demographic interest as they provide information on the possibilities of demographic survey in such an environment.

405 **Organisation territoriale, organisation sociale: la logique du système toubou.** (Territorial and social organization: the logic of the Tubu system.)
Catherine Baroin. *Journal des Africanistes*, vol. 56, fasc. 2 (1986), p. 7-27. map. bibliog.
This article sheds light on the ties which, in Tubu society, bind a weak territorial organization with a series of other features which characterize Tubu social

organization, such as the geographical dispersion of patrilineal clans, marriage rules excluding close kin, strong economic family ties, the importance of honour and shame, and the weak political role of chiefs.

406　**Gens du roc et du sable: Les toubous. Hommage à Charles et Marguerite Le Coeur.** (People of the rock and sand: The Tubu. Homage to Charles and Marguerite Le Coeur.)
Edited by Catherine Baroin.　Paris: CNRS (Centre Régional de Publication de Marseille), 1988. 286p. maps. bibliog.

This collection of articles contains contributions by some of the most distinguished specialists on Chad, each with a different perspective as colonial administrator, historian or ethnologist. All the studies demonstrate the cultural unity of the Tubu (or Teda as they call themselves) in the Tibesti region in northern Chad. The articles deal with the social structures of the Tubu and their historical and contemporary relations with neighbouring ethnic groups such as the Kanuri or the Ulad Sulayman. The book contains a Teda-Daza bibliography and interviews with Charles and Marguerite Le Coeur, both specialists on the Tibesti in the 1930s.

407　**La règle de mariage et ses conséquences chez les Toubou.**
(Marriage law and its consequences among the Tubu.)
Catherine Baroin.　In: *Le milieu et les hommes – Recherches comparatives dans le bassin du lac Tchad. Actes du 2ème colloque Méga-Tchad ORSTOM Bondy, le 3 et 4 octobre 1985 (The environment and the people – comparative research in the Lake Chad Basin. Proceedings of the second Mega-Chad colloquium, ORSTOM Bondy, 3 and 4 October 1985)*, edited by Daniel Barreteau, Henri Tourneux.　Paris: ORSTOM, 1988, p. 139-56. bibliog.

The author analyses the differences between Tubu marriage law, the Tubu matrimonial system and the social characteristics of Tubu society which are derived from their association with other pastoral populations with which they come in contact. She examines the autonomy of the nuclear family, the nature of rights over cattle, the status of each spouse and the relations between parents and between allies in Tubu society.

408　**Pourquoi les daza assimilent-ils leurs voisins?** (Why do the Daza assimilate their neighbours?)
Catherine Baroin.　In: *Relations interethniques et culture matérielle dans le bassin du lac Tchad. Acts du 3ème colloque Méga-Tchad ORSTOM Bondy, 11-12 septembre 1986 (Inter-ethnic relations and material culture in the Lake Chad Basin. Proceedings of the third Mega-Chad colloquium, ORSTOM Bondy, 11-12 September 1986)*, edited by Daniel Barreteau, Henri Tourneux.　Paris: ORSTOM, 1990, p. 95-102. map. bibliog.

The Daza are a Saharan-Sahelian shepherd people known for assimilating neighbouring Arab groups. The first part of this article looks at the history of the settlement in northern and eastern Chad of such Arab groups as the Hassauna, the

Joheina and the Ulad Sulayman. The second part deals with the manner in which these groups were assimilated by the Daza.

409   **La région du Tchad et du Ouadai. Tomes 1 et 2: Etudes ethnographiques. Dialecte Toubou.** (The region of Chad and Wadai. Volumes 1 and 2: Ethnographic studies. The Tubu dialect.) Henri Carbou.   Paris: Ernest Leroux, 1912. 279p.

This study was written by the Administrateur Adjoint des Colonies (Deputy-Administrator for the Colonies) and complements the work of nineteenth-century travellers such as Barth (q.v.) and Nachtigal (q.v.). It provides an overall view of most ethnic groups which includes their history and general considerations on their geographical, social, political and religious characteristics. Some mention is made, where appropriate, of contemporary events such as rebellions or relations with the Ottoman Empire. It also contains a short practical study of the Tubu language.

410   **Le Nomadisme des Toubous du B.E.T.** (Nomadism amongst the Tubu of the B.E.T. – Borkou–Ennedi–Tibesti.) Capitaine L. J. Caron.   Paris: CHEAM, 1964. 13p. (Mémoire, no. 3967).

This short study examines the history of the nomads of the BET region and describes their environment, before reviewing the different groups which form the Teda-Daza population.

411   **Les Toubous.** (The Tubu.) Commandant Jean Chapelle.   Paris: CHEAM, 1947. 25p.

This very general but exhaustive study of the Tubu of northern Chad examines their origins and history, their religion, their geographical distribution and their economy. A substantial part of the study is devoted to anthropological topics such as tribal organization, family life, childhood, marriage, women, divorce, succession issues, hospitality and blood feud.

412   **Nomades noirs du Sahara, les Toubou.** (Black nomads of the Sahara, the Tubu.) Jean Chapelle.   Paris: L'Harmattan, 1982. 457p.

This is the standard work on the Tubu populations of Tibesti and Borkou in the southern central Sahara, in the surrounding regions of Central Chad to the south and in the Bilma region to the west. Its author was a senior administrator in the region for many years at the end of the colonial period. It covers tribal history, demography and ethnography.

413 **Islam-Afrique Noire: Etude sommaire des races du nord du Lac Tchad: Toubbous, Kredas, Goranes.** (Islam-Black Africa: a basic study of the populations to the north of Lake Chad: Tubu, Kreda, and Gorane.)
Capitaine Jean D'Etat.   Paris: CHEAM, 1950. 7p.

A very short study, derived from the author's own observations, of the Tubu, Kreda and Gorane people, who dwell on the territory now separated by the Niger–Chad border.

Wadai

414 **Tchad: Regards sur les élites Ouaddaiennes.** (A study of Wadai élites.)
Issa Hassan Khayar.   Paris: CNRS, 1984. 231p. (Laboratoire Peiresc, Contribution à la Connaissance des Elites Africaines).

Originally a doctoral thesis entitled 'Aperçus sur la sociologie des élites Ouaddaiennes (Tchad) dans le passé et aujourd'hui' ('A look at the sociology of Wadai (Chad) élites in the past and today'), this book deals with Wadai in southeastern Chad. After a brief analysis of pre-colonial and colonial Chadian power structures, the study concentrates on Wadai élites and examines their relationship with Chadian political parties.

415 **Place et status des forgerons dans la société maba du Tchad.**
(Place and status of blacksmiths in Maba society (Chad).)
Adoum Doutoum Mahamat.   *Journal des Africanistes*, vol. 60, no. 2 (1990), p. 149-60. map. bibliog.

The blacksmiths of the Maba group of eastern Chad form a clan, the Kabartu, regarded as an inferior cast by other Maba clans. This article describes their activities (not limited to iron work, but also including wood work), those of their female members, their life in the midst of other Maba clans, how they are viewed by the latter and how their clan has changed in recent times.

Zaghawa

416 **Un rite de vie: le sacrifice d'une bête pleine chez les zaghawa kobé du Ouaddai.** (A rite of life: the sacrifice of a pregnant animal among the Kobe Zaghawa of Wadai.)
Marie-José Tubiana. *Journal de Psychologie Normale et Pathologique*, no. 3 (July-Sept. 1960), p. 291-310.

This detailed description of the sacrificial ritual among the Zaghawa aims to throw some light on the reasons for this unusual form of sacrifice which goes against economic interests (it constitutes a sacrifice of capital) and religious considerations (because the state of pregnancy is seen as impure). Through her descriptions, the author shows that the focus of such rituals seems to be the sacrifice of the foetus, a symbol of fecundity *par excellence*, which will ensure the fertility of the soil and thereby allow life to continue.

417 **Survivance préislamique en pays Zaghawa.** (Pre-Islamic continuity in Zaghawa lands.)
Marie-José Tubiana. Paris: Institut d'Ethnologie, 1964. 229p. bibliog.

This illustrated study endeavours to describe the survival of pre-Islamic beliefs and rituals amongst a population which regards itself as Muslim. Most of the data used here were collected during a visit to the Zaghawa of Chad in 1956 and 1957 and are the consequence of a concern that these traditions were in the process of disappearing under the influence of the Muslim faqihs. Tubiana shows how the most important of the surviving rituals are concerned with fertility, in a region where life is very precarious and everything depends on rain.

418 **La pratique actuelle de la cueillette chez les zaghawas du Tchad.** (Contemporary fruit, berry and cereal picking among the Zaghawa of Chad.)
Marie-José Tubiana. *Journal d'Agriculture Tropicale et de Botanique Appliquée*, Vol. XVI, no. 2-5 (Feb.-May 1969), p. 55-83. bibliog.

This is a detailed and illustrated study of wild cereal and fruit picking in which the author describes the produce in question and its use, and stresses its importance as a valuable food complement. She also emphasizes the need to continue this practice in a region where agricultural resources are very unreliable.

419 **Pouvoir et confiance. La relation oncle maternel–neveu utérin et le**
système politique des Zaghawa (Tchad-Soudan). (Power and trust.
The Zaghawa maternal uncle–uterine nephew relationship and political
system (Chad-Sudan).)
Marie-José Tubiana. *Cahiers d'Etudes Africaines*, vol. 19, no. 1-4
(1979), p. 55-68. bibliog.

This study shows how closely the relationship between the uterine nephew and the
maternal uncle is linked with political life amongst the Zaghawa. The author clarifies
the ambiguous role and position of the nephew in relation to his uncle, particularly
when the latter occupies a high political position. She also highlights the nephew's
religious function in ritual ceremonies.

420 **L'introduction du numéraire dans les circuits matrimoniaux**
Zaghawas. (The introduction of the cash economy into Zaghawa
matrimonial networks.)
Marie-José Tubiana. *Le Mois en Afrique*, no. 211-12 (1983),
p. 166-73.

This article deals with the introduction of money in commercial transactions and in
marriage and the gradual disappearance of bartering. It stresses, however, that
commercialization is more common than marriage transactions since the use of
money in marriage is still subordinate to the exchange of cattle or other goods such as
clothing or perfume.

421 **Des troupeaux et des femmes – Mariage et transferts de biens**
chez les Beri (Zaghawa et Bideyat) du Tchad et du Soudan. (Cattle
and women – marriage and the transfer of goods among the Beri
(Zaghawa and Bideyat) of Chad and Sudan.)
Marie-José Tubiana. Paris: L'Harmattan, 1985. 390p. (Bibliothèque
Peiresc, 4).

This study of marriage is divided into three parts: autobiographical accounts, the law
and marriage, alliances and exchanges after marriage.

422 **A propos du lévirat chez les Zaghawas, un problème**
méthodologique. (The Levirate among the Zaghawa: a
methodological problem.)
Marie-José Tubiana. In: *De la voûte céleste au terroir, du jardin au*
foyer (From heaven to homeland, from garden to home), edited by B.
Koechlin et al. Paris: EHESS, 1987, p. 647-53.

This study is a comparative analysis of the use of the Levirate [custom by which a
man is obliged to marry his brother's widow] in contemporary and pagan religions in
the Semitic world, in which the author refers to the impact of the Quran on the Arab
concept of the Levirate which has led to a Muslim concept of the custom. This
provides the context for an analysis of the concept among the Zaghawa of eastern
Chad, whose identity is based on Islam and pre-Islamic paganism.

423 **Mariages zaghawa: les changements liés à l'économie et à l'idéologie.** (Zaghawa marriages: changes linked to economy and ideology.)
Marie-José Tubiana. In: *Transformations of African marriage*, edited by David Parkin, David Nyamwaya. Manchester, England: Manchester University Press, 1987, p. 93-109. map.

Tubiana identifies and analyses marriage-pattern changes within Chadian and Sudanese Zaghawa society. The first change studied relates to the introduction of cash into a system based hitherto on bartering. This in turn throws light on the mechanisms of traditional marriage-related exchange of animals. The author then assesses growing Islamization as another more ideological form of change affecting marriage.

424 **Tchad 1989: les changements.** (Chad 1989: changing times.)
Marie-José Tubiana. *Journal des Africanistes*, vol. 59, no. 1-2 (1989). bibliog.

Marie-José Tubiana went back to eastern Chad, after an absence of thirty years, with Joseph Tubiana, her husband, and this illustrated article is the result of their observations. It shows that ecosystems are recovering their former balance after years of drought and that economic change has taken place with the spread of farmers' associations. Progress has also been achieved on a social level, particularly in relation to alliance strategies and the status of women and blacksmiths. There has also been a shift in political and administrative power and an improvement in education, Arabization and Islamization.

425 **Royaume et reconnaissance du chef par le serpent.** (Royalty and the snake's recognition of the chief.)
Marie-José Tubiana. *Systèmes de Pensée en Afrique Noire*, no. 10 (1990), p. 189-205. map. bibliog.

The snake is a major figure in African religions and mythologies and is often thought to be a manifestation of divinity. This is the context in which the author examines its role in the Wadai sultanate, in eastern Chad. She shows that in spite of Islamization, this region has kept some of its pre-Islamic beliefs and customs. These have often been superimposed on to more recent Islamic ones and, until recently, the snake played an important role in enthroning rituals.

426 **The Zaghawa from an ecological perspective: foodgathering, the pastoral system, tradition and development of the Zaghawa of the Sudan and Chad.**
Marie-José Tubiana, Joseph Tubiana, translated from the French by Philip O'Prey. Rotterdam: A. A. Balkema, 1977. 119p.

One of the few studies of the obscure Zaghawa (or Bideyat) tribe of the Ennedi region of eastern Chad and of the Darfur region in Sudan. It discusses in detail the ecological environment and the agricultural–pastoral culture of the Zaghawa and also suggests ways in which agricultural development could be achieved.

Social Services, Health and Welfare

427 **Se nourrir au Sahel. L'alimentation au Tchad 1937-1939.** (Feeding oneself in the Sahel region. The Chadian diet between 1937 and 1939.) Paul Créach. Paris: L'Harmattan, 1993. 302p. maps. (Pour mieux connaître le Tchad).

The author gathered the data used in this study while he was in Chad as a military pharmacist. He describes in detail the food consumed by the population of the Sahel in northern Chad, the variety of cereals grown and the livestock situation. He also describes local cuisine and the nutritional balance of the traditional diet.

428 **The politics of health reform in Chad.** Anne-Marie Foltz, William Foltz. In: *Reforming economic systems in developing countries*, edited by D. H. Perkins, M. Roemer. Cambridge, Massachusetts: Harvard Institute for International Development, Harvard University, 1991, p. 137-57.

This article argues that both the choice of reform and the probability of implementation depend largely on policy-makers' concerns for their own and the regime's political survival and only marginally on the survival of their particular sectors of the bureaucracy. Thus, some variant of a pure political model that takes into account a multiplicity of loyalties, obligations and antipathies seems more appropriate than a standard bureaucratic policy model for analysing the outcome of this proposed reform in Chad.

Food aid

429 **Reducing people's vulnerability to famine. An evaluation of Band Aid & Live Aid financed projects in Africa.**
Coordinated and edited by Luther Banga. [London?]: [n.p.], 1991. 138p. maps. bibliog.

This report follows the 1984 movement of solidarity sparked off by Band Aid and Live Aid which, in addition to emergency aid for drought-stricken African countries, provided $70 million for small-scale development projects to be carried out mainly by non-governmental organizations (NGOs). The report concerns Burkina Faso, Chad, Ethiopia, Mali and Sudan and examines the vulnerability to famine and local mechanisms for dealing with famine situations in each country, as well as their survival strategies and overall management of resources. It assesses the impact of projects funded by Band Aid and describes the participating NGOs, their respective projects in each country and their short- and long-term project budgets.

430 **Evaluation des projets financés par Band Aid au Tchad. Chad, country annexe and case studies.** (Assessment of projects financed by Band Aid in Chad.)
Coordinated and edited by Luther Banga. [n.p.], 1991. 138p. maps. bibliog.

This volume is an annexe to the previous entry (q.v.) and deals specifically with Chad. After describing the country's geography, it examines its economy, the causes of famine and the measures taken by people and state against it. It then examines NGOs and Band Aid action in Chad and assesses projects financed by Band Aid through four case-studies.

431 **An evaluation of the African Emergency Food Assistance Programme in Chad, 1984-1985.**
V. Brown, E. Patterson Brown, D. Eckerson, J. Gilmore, H. Swartzendruber. Washington, DC: AID, 1987. maps. bibliog. (Evaluation Special Study, no. 48).

This report presents data on American aid efforts in Chad, designed to help analyse the impact, immediacy and appropriateness of the 1984-85 emergency food aid programmes in that country and recommends practical measures to improve future programming and impact.

Social Conditions

432 **Etendue du rôle des juridictions tchadiennes dans la protection des droits de la personne.** (Extent of the role of Chadian jurisdiction regarding the protection of the individual.) Nathé Amady. *Revue Juridique et Politique, Indépendence et Coopération*, vol. 36, no. 1 (Jan.-March 1982), p. 244-9.

The author of this article explains that there are no specific institutions or bodies for the effective protection of the rights of the individual. He stresses, however, that tribunals do play a role in sanctioning attacks on these rights, despite the difficulties they may encounter in carrying out their obligations.

433 **Rapport de mission: Mission de coopération et d'enquête effectuée au Tchad pour la F.I.D.H. à la demande de la Ligue Tchadienne des Droits de l'Homme du 12 au 23 juillet 1991.** (Mission report: mission of cooperation and investigation in Chad for the F.I.D.H. (International Federation for Human Rights) at the request of the Chadian League of Human Rights from 12 to 23 July 1991.) Jean-Paul Jean. Paris: Fédération Internationale des Droits de l'Homme, 1991. 22p. (La Lettre de la Fédération Internationale des Droits de l'Homme, Hors série).

The aim of Jean-Paul Jean's mission was twofold as the report's title indicates. On the one hand, it sought to establish cooperation with the Chadian League, with the support of the Ministry of Cooperation, which helped to establish the structures of the L.T.D.H. (Ligue Tchadienne des Droits de l'Homme). The mission investigated the record of Colonel Idriss Déby's new regime on human rights. The main body of the report focuses on the investigative aspect of the mission and deals with the human rights abuses of ex-President Hissen Habré's regime, before focusing on the difficulties facing the new regime. It shows that old habits die hard, especially in a country where judiciary structures are inefficient. The study closes with a warning to

Chadian authorities, pointing to a minor but dangerous attack on the media in July 1991.

434 **Le rôle des juridictions tchadiennes en matière de droits de l'homme dans l'entreprise.** (The role of Chadian jurisdictions in human rights within the enterprise.)
Salmon Yantoingar Mairo. *Revue Juridique et Politique, Indépendance et Coopération*, vol. 43, no. 3-4 (July-Oct. 1989), p. 606-21.

The author, general prosecutor at the Appeal Court in N'Djamena, examines the procedure followed in cases of conflict between employer and employee. In the first instance, there is the mediation of the Employee Welfare Officer and, if this fails, there is recourse to the Labour Court. He also deals with collective conflict and its resolution. Finally he looks at the protection of workers' rights and how they are insured by penal jurisdictions in the case of regulations on hygiene and safety and on minimum wages and working hours.

435 **Le Tchad dans toutes les impasses.** (Chad deadlocked.)
François Misser. *La Revue Nouvelle*, vol. 80, no. 12 (Dec. 1984), p. 525-7.

This short article gives a very vivid evocation of daily life in Chad as well as an intimate insight into Chad's predicament. Rather than a scholarly analysis it is an account of the hardship encountered by many Chadians in their daily life. Finally, it denounces the famine that had already killed many and the executions carried out by Habré's FANT (Forces Armées Nationales Tchadiennes) in the south. It also points an accusatory finger at the Cotontchad company for its role in the famine. The author argues that as long as national reconstruction does not take into account the excesses of the victorious army which have aggravated the drought, international aid will be ineffective.

Politics and
Administration

436 **Discours prononcés à l'ouverture de la deuxième session ordinaire
de l'Assemblée Nationale.** (Opening speeches of the second ordinary
session of the National Assembly).
Anon. N'Djamena: République du Tchad, 1961. 19p.
This booklet contains the speeches of the National Assembly leader and of President
Tombalbaye made at the opening budget session of the National Assembly in 1961.

437 **Les treize préfectures de la république du Tchad.** (The thirteen
prefectures of the Republic of Chad.)
Pierre Gentil. Fort Lamy: Ministère de l'Information et du Tourisme.
1962. 117p.
Pierre Gentil was administrator of the region of Middle-Chari, before being Director
of Information in the newly created republic. In this study he provides information on
the thirteen administrative regions of Chad and deals with detailed as well as general
aspects of each region: people, agriculture, cattle. Each chapter also contains extracts
from a short travel diary concerned with the regions under examination.

438 **La République du Tchad.** (The Republic of Chad.)
P.-F. Gonidec. Paris: Editions Berger-Levrault, 1971. 79p. maps.
bibliog. (Encyclopédie Politique et Constitutionnelle publiée par
l'Institut International d'Administration Publique, Série Afrique).
In this short study Gonidec concentrates on the political institutions of Chad and
examines various aspects of its society (demography, education, economy and social
structures), as well as the political and constitutional evolution from the colonial
conquest until 1962, the political forces and the Tombalbaye regime. The book also
includes a number of documents and texts, including the Constitutional Law of 16
April 1962.

439 **Tchad: Création d'un service national d'archives.** (Chad: The creation of the national archive service.)
C. Gut. Paris: UNESCO, 1973. 33p.

Although the Institut National Tchadien pour les Sciences Humaines assumed archival responsibilities in Chad, there were no governmental archives for it to manage. This is a report on the need and conditions for the creation of a national archive in Chad. It provides a number of solutions for the establishment of an archival system and the laws and regulations which should accompany the creation of the new institution.

440 **Citations et pensées.** (Quotes and thoughts.)
Hissen Habré. N'Djamena: Direction de la Presse Présidentielle, 1984. 119p. map.

This collection covers the period between June 1978 and April 1984 and contains short extracts from speeches and interviews. They relate to such themes as Colonel Qadhafi and the conflict with Libya, FROLINAT, Goukouni Oueddei, and Chadian institutions.

441 **Renoncer à Aouzou ce serait Munich.** (To abandon Aouzou would be a second Munich.)
Hissen Habré. In: *Afrique: les chefs parlent* (*Africa: the leaders speak*). Paris: Editions Pierre Marcel Favre, 1984, p. 157-73.
(Collection: Les grands entretiens).

The transcript of an interview given by the Chadian president on the French international radio station 'Radio France Internationale', in the monthly series 'Club de la Presse du Tiers Monde', in which a group of journalists from the northern hemisphere discuss issues with Third World personalities or journalists. The interview covers the French intervention in Chad and the conflict with Libya, as well as Chad's relations with other African states and with France.

442 **Sovereignty and underdevelopment: juridical statehood in the African crisis.**
Robert H. Jackson, Carl G. Rosberg. *Journal of Modern African Studies*, vol. 24, no. 1 (1986), p. 1-31.

Since formal independence around 1960, new states in sub-Saharan Africa have failed to meet the traditional empirical test of statehood: having governments that exercise effective authority and power over their internationally recognized territories and populations. Personal modes of authority developed within many of these new states, as democratic forms inherited from the West European colonial powers were discarded. Patrimonial systems emerged, while even mendicant states dependent on foreign assistance for their survival have appeared. The new juridical basis of statehood in Africa has been positively sanctioned by the UN and the Organization of African Unity, with no legal recourse offered to dissident movements and population groups. States like Chad, which lack civic or socio-economic unity in any degree, have claimed statehood as their juridical right before the international community.

443 **Problématique de l'administration territoriale au Tchad.**
(Territorial administration in Chad.)
Loumakoye Delwa Kassire. Paris: Université de Paris I, 1988.
This doctoral thesis is divided into two parts. The first is an analysis of neo-traditional institutions and decentralized administration and relates the confused history of an administration which is the result of a process originating in the pre-colonial period and which lasted until 1982. The second part highlights the present problems associated with the Chadian administration, claiming it has not fulfilled its role as the creator of a nation-state, and proposes appropriate solutions.

444 **Petit dictionnaire d'idées reçues sur le Tchad.** (A short dictionary on popular attitudes towards Chad.)
Bernard Lanne. *Le Mois en Afrique*, no. 186-7 (1981), p. 132-42.
This is an article consisting of short sections on topics on which the author seeks to correct popular views. The topics include the Sara; 'white Chadians'; Tombalbaye, Libya and Aozou; Tombalbaye and the initiation programme; schooling and the missions; Tombalbaye and the chiefs.

445 **Liste des chefs des unités administratives du Tchad (1900-1983).**
(A list of heads of administrative units in Chad (1900-83).)
Bernard Lanne. Paris: EHESS, 1983. 194p. bibliog. (Dissertation for DEA in History and Civilization. Mémoire).
Apart from a general overview of Chadian territorial administrative organization, this work is essentially made up of tables which name the head of each administrative unit, the date he took up his post, his rank and the source for this information.

446 **Discours.** (Speeches.)
Gabriel Lisette. [n.p.], [1958-59?]. 68p.
This short book contains speeches made by Gabriel Lisette, Président du Conseil of Fort-Lamy and Deputy Mayor of Fort-Lamy between August 1957 and March 1958.

447 **L'état face au conflit civil: reflexions sur l'Angola, l'Ethiopie et le Tchad.** (The state and civil conflict: reflections on Angola, Ethiopia, and Chad.)
Sam C. Nolutshungu. *Revue Française de Science Politique*, vol. 38, no. 4 (1988), p. 533-54.
The civil conflicts involving significant external intervention in Angola, Ethiopia, and Chad exhibit important similarities. Far from representing the fundamental cleavages of society, the course of these conflicts reflects the divisions within a single stratum of society, with a very specific relation to the state. The article explores three aspects of these wars: the 'autonomy of the state' and its specificity as both a field and an object of struggle; the social traits of those who lead the opposed movements; and the tendency of international intervention to increase the independence of the state and its power in relation to society, and to remove it even further from the real concerns of society.

La normalisation constitutionnelle au Tchad.
See item no. 458.

Les nouvelles institutions politiques au Tchad: la Charte Nationale du 1er mars 1991.
See item no. 460.

Law and Constitution

448 **La codification du droit au Tchad.** (Law codification in Chad.)
Mahamat Hassan Abbakar. *Revue Juridique et Politique,*
Indépendence et Coopération, vol. 40, no. 3-4 (July-Oct. 1986),
p. 447-50.

The author, the president of the Court of First Instance in N'Djamena, explains that
several major obstacles prevented the development of a complete legal code. He
examines the few areas which have been codified since 1960 and asserts that despite
the difficulties, Chad is striving to complete legislation.

449 **La condition des étrangers au Tchad.** (The status of foreigners in
Chad.)
Nathé Amady. *Revue Juridique et Politique, Indépendence et*
Coopération, vol. 34, no. 1 (Jan.-March 1980), p. 237-48.

This article by the public prosecutor of the N'Djamena Appeal Court determines the
status of transit and temporary visitors to Chad's borders. The main issues concern
visas, resident permits and the enjoyment of public or private rights by foreign
physical or moral persons.

450 **Les mouvements de population en République du Tchad.**
(Population movements in the Republic of Chad.)
Ahmat Kinder. *Revue Juridique et Politique, Indépendence et*
Coopération, vol. 34, no. 1 (Jan.-April 1980), p. 218-36.

The author, president of the N'Djamena Labour Court, examines migration to and
from Chad with particular emphasis on neighbouring African countries. He claims
that while nationals are free to leave the country and foreigners to enter it under a
liberal legal system, stricter control of departures abroad has become necessary in
order to curtail the brain drain caused by political tensions. He warns that the brain
drain as well as the drain in manpower threaten the internal stability of the country
both economically and politically.

451 **Les nouvelles institutions de la République du Tchad.** (The new institutions of the Republic of Chad.)
Bernard Lanne. *Revue Juridique et Politique, Indépendence et Coopération*, vol. 30, no. 2 (April-June 1976), p. 141-76.

After evoking the constitutional evolution of Chad up to the overthrow of President Tombalbaye, the author examines the birth of the new regime and its bases. He analyses the situation of the new leaders, the organization of the Conseil Supérieur Militaire (High Military Council) and of the provisional government.

452 **Protection des personnes en République du Tchad, la non-représentation d'enfants et le trafic de stupéfiants.** (Protection of the person in the Republic of Chad, non-representation of minors and drug trafficking.)
El-Hadj Mahamat Oumar Madani. *Revue Juridique et Politique, Indépendence et Coopération*, vol. 37, no. 1-2 (Jan.-March 1983), p. 262-74.

The Basic Charter of 1975 replaced the second constitution of 1962, but, as the author notes, it contains very little provision for the protection of the person. This article examines first the 1962 constitution and then the legal code. It also deals with the legal protection of the person. The second chapter briefly deals with the social and penal protection of minors, and the last chapter is a study of drug-related offences and their sentences.

453 **Les infractions et les peines au Tchad.** (Offences and sentences in Chad.)
Kémian Mbaiguedem. *Revue Juridique et Politique, Indépendence et Coopération*, vol. 38, no. 1 (April-June 1984), p. 398-403.

The first part of this report by the head of general legislation at Chad's Ministry of Justice deals with offences and the second with sentences. It shows that Chad's Penal Code is very similar to its French counterpart although some aspects are peculiar to Chad. This is particularly true of new offences regarding public peace, witch doctors, charlatans and beggars.

454 **La charte fondamentale et les nouvelles institutions transitoires de l'état tchadien.** (The Basic Charter and the new transitional institutions of the Chadian state.)
Thierry Michalon. *Revue Juridique et Politique, Indépendence et Coopération*, vol. 33, no. 1 (Jan.-March 1979), p. 75-90.

Michalon examines the institutions created in the late 1970s, after the overthrow of President Tombalbaye in 1975 by General Malloum, who succeeded him as president. In 1978, the new government welcomed back the hitherto rebellious factions of Hissen Habré. The latter became prime minister, and, together with General Malloum, created the basis for new transitional institutions of government. An annexe contains the Basic Charter.

455 **Tchad: échec d'une constitution ambigüe, ou effondrement d'un certain type d'état?** (Chad: failure of an ambiguous constitution or collapse of a particular type of state?)
Thierry Michalon. *Revue Juridique et Politique, Indépendence et Coopération*, vol. 33, no. 2 (April-June 1979), p. 163-8.

The author of this article examines the institutions created by the Basic Charter, which never really functioned. He shows that, instead of the reforms expected in the post-Tombalbaye era, Chad saw a power struggle develop which led to violent clashes between the army and the prime minister's own troops and resulted in the collapse of the state.

456 **Des institutions pour le Tchad: la paix par le droit?** (Institutions for Chad: peace through law?)
Thierry Michalon, Alain Moyrand. *Revue Juridique et Politique, Indépendence et Coopération*, vol. 43, no. 1-2 (Jan.-March 1989), p. 142-63.

As Chad prepared for a new constitution, the authors reflected on the constitutional reforms that would be necessary for the country. They analyse the previous political situation in order to determine the relevance of the institutional choices that were made, in view of the socio-political situation of Chad.

457 **L'organisation judiciaire au Tchad. Commentaires, bilan et statistiques.** (Chad's judicial organization. Comments, assessment and statistics.)
Alain Moyrand, Aché Nabia. *Penant*, no. 796 (Jan.-May 1988), p. 75-95. bibliog.

This article describes the organization and competence of the Appeal Court. It studies criminal justice as well as first-instance jurisdictions which rule on civil matters and it concludes by discussing the problems relating to judicial staff and to applicable law.

458 **La normalisation constitutionnelle au Tchad.** (Constitutional normalization in Chad.)
Alain Moyrand. Bordeaux, France: CEAN, 1990. 74p. (Travaux et Documents, no. 26).

This short but specialized study discusses three main aspects of Chad's political life: the bases of Chad's republican institutions, the organization of the constitution and administrative operations. The study relies heavily on the 1989 constitution.

459 **Destruction et reconstruction d'un appareil judiciaire: le cas du Tchad.** (Destruction and reconstitution of a judiciary apparatus: the case of Chad.)
Alain Moyrand. *Afrique Contemporaine*, vol. 156, no. 4 (1990), p. 45-50.

The chaos created by the Chadian civil war affected the judiciary because all public services were disrupted by the absence of an effective central power structure. This article assesses the impact of the civil war on the administration of justice and shows how customary justice was substituted for modern justice. It also explains how a parallel justice system administered by the military and police officers developed. Finally, the author studies the reorganization of the judiciary by the Habré government, with its subordination to the authority of the head of state, the reform of judicial institutions and the codification of customary law.

460 **Les nouvelles institutions politiques du Tchad: la Charte Nationale du 1er mars 1991.** (Chad's new political institutions: the National Charter of 1 March 1991.)
Alain Moyrand. *Revue Juridique et Politique, Indépendence et Coopération*, vol. 45, no. 1 (Jan.-March 1991), p. 182-91.

As Chad tried to establish political stability with the drafting of a new constitution, the author comments on the National Charter. He relates this development to Chad's political evolution and attempts to determine the chances of success for the new leadership.

La République du Tchad.
See item no. 438.

Foreign Affairs

461 **Threats to security and stability in Nigeria: perceptions and reality.**

Olusola Akinrinade. *Genève-Afrique*, vol. 26, no. 2 (1988), p. 47-82.

Throughout its post-independence history, Nigeria has faced serious challenges to its internal security and national stability. In spite of the relative advantage it enjoys (in terms of economic and military power) in the subregional system, the chief source of Nigeria's external threats are the frictions in its relations with its neighbours. These include boundary problems with Cameroon, the implications of the civil war in Chad, and the dangerous flirtations of Equatorial Guinea with South Africa. Internally, the primary sources of insecurity include sectarian rivalries and mistrust, economic dislocation and corruption, religious fundamentalism, and the implications of the perennial military intervention in the national political process.

462 **War-torn Chad. Cockpit of international rivalry.**

S. Amjad Ali. *Pakistan Horizon*, Vol. XXXVII, no. 3 (1984), p. 20-36.

This is a narration of the events which have punctuated the Chadian conflict since independence. It focuses on the relations between the various players on the domestic Chadian scene and on the role of France and Libya.

463 **La Jamahiriya et la paix au Tchad.** (The Jamahiriya and peace in Chad.)

Anon. Tripoli: La Jamahiriya Arabe Libyenne Populaire Socialiste, 1982. 89p. (L'Information Extérieure, l'Etablissement Public pour l'Edition, la Distribution et la Publicité).

This short book by the Libyan government is clearly divided into very short chapters, most of them illustrated by one or more photographs with captions, which give very brief and general information about Chad. It also justifies the role of Libya in Chad's internal affairs, and more specifically in the civil struggle as a supporter of FROLINAT.

464   **Kadafi/Tchad. Ingérence, agression, occupation. Livre Blanc.**
(Qadhafi/Chad. Interference, aggression, occupation. White Book.)
Anon.   N'Djamena: [n.p.], 1987. 146p. maps.

This work which emanates presumably from the Chadian government, claims to provide proof of Libyan aggression and of the 'terrorist' activities perpetrated in Chad and elsewhere by Colonel Qadhafi. It also shows the damage caused to Chad's economic infrastructure by Libya.

465   **Mémorandum sur le différend frontalier Tchad–Libye.**
(Memorandum on the Chad–Libya border dispute.)
Anon.   N'Djamena: Ministère des Relations Extérieures, January 1990.

This memorandum refers to the conferences and meetings organized over the Chad–Libya border dispute issue between July and December 1989. Two appendixes are included: the text of the Resolution of the Territorial Dispute and the text of the Agreement on the Pacific Resolution of the Territorial Dispute.

466   **Tchad: guerre de libération nationale.** (Chad: a war of independence.)
Anon.   L'Idiot International, Supplément Livre Journal, no. 7 (June 1970), 32p. map.

This special issue of this French newspaper, known for its revolutionary approach, is entirely dedicated to Chad. It presents FROLINAT texts, condemns French military intervention, accuses the French government of supporting the repressive regime of President Tombalbaye and of acting without the full knowledge of French public opinion. It proposes the creation of a specific organization linked to the Chadian rebels in order to support their fight against France and the Chadian government.

467   **Tchad. Une néo-colonie.** (Chad: a colony in all but name.)
Anon.   Paris: Edition Git-Le-Coeur, [n.d.]. maps.

This study, which denounces France's 'imperialist' policy in Chad, seems to have been published around 1974. It provides a general introduction to Chad's history, geography and economy and examines what it calls 'the revolutionary movement' of Chad between 1963 and 1971. It also analyses the role of the FROLINAT in the 'revolutionary struggle'.

468   **Foreign assistance and dependence: post-colonial Chad (1960-1985).**
Mario J. Azevedo, Gwendolyn Prater.   Journal of African Studies, vol. 13, no. 3 (1986), p. 102-10.

The remote, poverty-stricken, and war-torn Republic of Chad is chronically reliant on foreign assistance for its survival. The most neglected colony in French Africa prior to independence in 1960, independent Chad with no railroads and few miles of adequate roads lacked an adequate infrastructure. Although overwhelmingly rural, Chad's population produced only meagre crop exports and insufficient food to feed itself. Chad's unequal trade, and financial and political ties to France left the government in N'Djamena little room to manoeuvre outside the French sphere of influence in Africa. Hopes for future mineral production and the recent increase of American aid out of fear of Libyan expansion southwards provide possible opportunities for Chad to lessen its extreme dependence on Paris.

469 **Chad: imperialisticheskoe vmeshatel'stvo: prichiny, tseli, rezul'taty.**
(Chad: imperialist intervention: the causes, objectives, and results.)
G. Babaian. *Aziia i Afrika Segodnia* (USSR), no. 5 (1987), p. 21-3.

After installing a manipulatable regime in the 1960s and thus provoking persistent civil war with forces supported by Libya, France seemed by 1984 reluctant to continue to bear the costs of intervention in Chad, but continued to do so in the following two years due to the encouragement of the United States, then pursuing a violent anti-Libyan policy. There is an English summary.

470 **La coloniale du Rif au Tchad. 1925-1980.** (The colonial army from the Rif war to the Chadian conflict, 1925-80.)
Erwan Bergot. Paris: Presses de la Cité, France Loisirs, 1982, p. 227-48. maps.

The history of the French colonial army which participated in battles throughout the French empire from Morocco to Indochina. It was also called in to fight in Chad in 1978.

471 **Le retrait du Tchad de l'U.D.E.A.C.: genèse d'une crise.**
(Chad's withdrawal from C.C.C.A.: origins of a crisis.)
Marc Beringaye. Poitiers, France: Université de Poitiers, 1988. [n.p.].

Created in 1964 by the independent states of former French Equatorial Africa (Central African Republic, Congo, Gabon and Chad) and Cameroon, the C.C.C.A. (Customs Community of Central Africa) suffered four years later from a serious crisis that deprived it of one of its members, Chad, which rejoined the union only in 1984. This doctoral thesis examines the reasons for Chad's withdrawal from the C.C.C.A. and analyses this episode in Central African relations, which was typical of the two decades that followed the independence of these states.

472 **Low-intensity conflict in the 1980s: the French experience.**
Michel L. Castillon. *Military Review*, vol. 66, no. 1 (1986), p. 68-77. map.

In this translation from *Armes d'Aujourdhui* (May 1985), Castillon discusses the lessons learned by the French military in its low-intensity conflict experiences in the early 1980s. He describes the basic principles of crisis prevention and retaliation capability employed by the army ('Diodon') and navy ('Olifant') peacekeeping forces in Lebanon, the 'Manta' interdiction force in Chad, and the navy's mine-sweeping operations in the Red Sea. He analyses the roles of command, intelligence, and logistics elements and emphasizes the need for flexibility, innovation, and professionalism.

473 **Frantsiia i konflikty na Afrikanskom kontinente.** (France and the conflicts on the African continent.)
P. Cherkasov. *Mirovaia Ekonomika i Mezhdunarodnye Otnosheniia* (USSR), no. 8 (1987), p. 41-53.

Discusses French policy in Africa in the 1980s, concentrating mainly on Chad, Libya, Southern Africa, and the Western Sahara.

474   **United States relations with North Africa.**
John Damis. *Current History*, vol. 84, no. 502 (1985), p. 193-6, 232-4.
Surveys US diplomatic, strategic, and economic relations with Morocco, Algeria, Tunisia, Libya, and Chad.

475   **Thierry Desjardins, Madame Claustre et le Tchad.** (Thierry Desjardins, Mrs Claustre and Chad.)
Robert Buijtenhuijs. *Politique Aujourd' hui* (March-April 1976), p. 79-83.
A critical assessment of French journalist Thierry Desjardins' book *Avec les otages du Tchad* (q.v.). The author of this article, an expert on the Chadian rebellion and on FROLINAT, provides a balanced and enlightened review of the book and an appraisal of its author. While acknowledging Desjardins' courage, the rapidity with which he published his book and his ability to assimilate quickly a very complicated situation, the author accuses him of not knowing the situation well enough and of distorting reality. He also deplores Desjardins' habit of trusting only his own judgement as well as that of not checking any of the information given to him. Finally, Buijtenhuijs regrets that the Claustre affair shrouded the activities of Hissen Habré as well as the fact that the Tibesti rebellion obscured FROLINAT's activities in central-eastern Chad.

476   **La mort du commandant Galopin: une mise au point.** (Commandant Galopin's death: a statement.)
Robert Buijtenhuijs. *Politique Africaine*, no. 20 (Dec. 1985), p. 91-5.
This short article investigates the death of a French officer sent to negotiate with the Chadian rebels responsible for the kidnapping of Françoise Claustre and Marc Combe in 1974. It argues that the responsibility for the major's death lies with both the rebels and the French. The latter dispatched this French soldier who was known to have tortured and killed or caused the death of relatives and friends of the rebels with whom he was supposed to negotiate.

477   **La politique militaire de la France en Afrique.** (French military policy in Chad.)
Pascal Chaigneau.   Paris: CHEAM, 1984. 146p. maps. bibliog.
In this study Chaigneau covers France's military relations with Africa, such as the military agreements linking France and Africa, France's strategic conception of Africa, the French control of the African arms market, France's local bases there, its overseas intervention capability and the evolution of French African policy from De Gaulle to Mitterrand.

478   **Du Tchad à la Nouvelle-Calédonie: Le défi de l'Outre-Mer dans la politique militaire de la France.** (From Chad to New Caledonia: the overseas challenge in French military policy.)
Pascal Chaigneau. *Cultures et Développement*, Vol. XVII, no. 3 (1985), p. 519-27.
This article examines French overseas intervention in general and takes Chad as a case-study. The author considers the importance of the stakes and the appearance of new players on the international scene which dictate new approaches to interventionist

powers. He examines these in the context of the 1984 'Operation Manta' in Chad, which involved 3000 French troops but failed to fulfil its objectives.

479 **L'affaire Claustre, autopsie d'une prise d'otage.** (The Claustre affair, autopsy of a hostage crisis.)
Pierre Claustre. Paris: Karthala, 1990. 450p.

In April 1974, two French nationals and a German national were taken hostage by Chadian rebels in the northern Chadian region of Tibesti. This study probably constitutes the most reliable account of the Claustre affair since its author, the husband of one of the hostages, became a hostage himself while trying to obtain his wife's release. It also follows the affair from beginning to end and is particularly critical of Ambassador Touze, whose account (in *370 jours d'un ambassadeur au Tchad*; q.v.) is discredited. In short, the book is a very lucid and honest account of an affair which demonstrated the indifference and inefficiency of the French government.

480 **Otage au Tibesti.** (Hostage in Tibesti.)
Marc Combe. Paris: Flammarion, 1976. (L'Aventure vécue).

Marc Combe was taken hostage at the same time as Françoise Claustre, but managed to escape in May 1975. This is his own story. It provides an insight into the daily life of Habré and his fellow rebels in the Tibesti desert. It is particularly interesting to compare with other accounts of the affair by outsiders such as the journalist Desjardins (q.v.), Ambassador Touze (q.v.) or Pierre Claustre (q.v.).

481 **Moammar Kadhafi et les chimères tchadiennes.** (Muammar Qadhafi and Chadian illusions.)
Raoul Crabbé. *Remarques Arabo-africaines*, no. 547-8 (July 1987), p. 2-5. map.

Crabbé summarizes the Libyan political scene and shows the contradictions in Colonel Qadhafi's domestic and foreign policies. These contradictions are illustrated with reference to the examples of Chad and the conflict over the Aozou strip.

482 **Avec les otages du Tchad.** (With the hostages in Chad.)
Thierry Desjardins. Paris: Presses de la Cité, 1975. 288p. maps.

An account of the first phase of the hostage affair (up to Marc Combe's escape) by a French journalist. It stands between the accounts of those directly involved, such as Combe and Claustre, and the descriptions of government officials, such as Touze. Its conclusions tend to favour those who accuse French authorities of mismanagement and negligence.

483 **Stratégie et tactique des forces armées nationales.** (The strategy and tactics of the national armed forces.)
Pierre Devoluy. *Géopolitique Africaine* (April 1987), p. 33-45.

This article contains an analysis of the Chadian army's victory over Libya on 2 January 1987 at Fada. The author examines its objective, means, organization and the way in which it was used by the victors.

484 **Le conflit des frontières entre le Tchad et la Libye.** (The boundary dispute between Chad and Libya.)
S. Djekery. Poitiers, France: Université de Poitiers, 1980. [n.p.].

This doctoral thesis examines the historical origins of the conflict, which are claimed to be the resurgence of Franco-Italian colonial disputes after Libyan independence.

485 **La France et la crise du Tchad d'août 1983: un rendez-vous manqué avec l'Afrique.** (France and the Chadian crisis of August 1983: missed opportunities in Africa.)
Hesse Elce. *Politique Etrangère*, no. 2 (Summer 1985), p. 411-18.

Throughout the 1983 confrontation between France and Libya over Chad, a combination of analytical errors and lack of decisiveness were at the root of France's failure to meet its historic obligations in Africa. Between 1981 and 1983, French foreign policy-makers seemed to have forgotten the basic geographical and historical factors in the Chadian crisis. They wanted to see it as the result of a local clash between progressive and conservative forces in the continuing process of emancipation in a Third World country. In August 1983, the news of Libya's invasion threw the French authorities into a state of confusion, which partially explains their reluctance to intervene. In 1985 it appeared that Paris had resigned itself to Chad's loss of territorial integrity. Such an attitude, the authors argued, would cause a considerable loss of France's international esteem.

486 **Le baroudeur. Les quatre guerres du général Delayen: 1940-1945, Indochine, Algérie, Tchad 1972-1978.** (The adventurer. The four wars of General Delayen: 1940-45, Indochina, Algeria, Chad 1972-78.)
Georges Fleury. Paris: Grasset, 1979. 428p.

This book is a paean of praise for this French general and through him, for French intervention. It contains one chapter on Chad which covers the period of French intervention between 1972 and 1978.

487 **Au-delà du sanctuaire.** (Beyond the sanctuary.)
André Foures. Paris: Economica, 1986. 270p. maps. bibliog.

The study concerns French military policy and intervention in Africa and the Near East (Lebanon). Chad constitutes a sizeable part of the book and is examined in the context of the 1960s revolt, which led to an internal conflict and to French intervention in the 1970s. The 'Claustre Affair' is also dealt with, as well as the second French intervention of 1978-84.

488 **Tensions in the Chad.**
J. F. Froelich. In: *Conflict in Africa*. London: IISS, 1972, p. 42-52. map. (Adelphi Papers, no. 93).

Froelich claims that the origins of the Chadian rebellion lie in the brutality of the Chadian army in BET and the corrupt administration of the black Prefects, but not in the conflict between Islam and Christianity, nor even between Arabs and Blacks.

489   **La force de maintien de la paix au Tchad: éloge ou requiem?** (The
       peace-keeping force in Chad: praise or requiem?)
       Jean-Claude Gautron.   In: *Année Africaine 1981 (The year in Africa,
       1981)*. Paris: CEAN, Bordeaux, 1983, p. 167-89.

This article analyses the origins, context and consequences of the internationalization of
the Chadian conflict and of the presence of peace-keeping forces in Chad. It examines
the role of Libya and of Nigeria, and deals with French intervention and its replacement
by an inter-African force, which is then discussed in detail.

490   **La Libye et le Tchad devant la Cour Internationale de Justice?**
       (Libya and Chad at the International Court of Justice?)
       Jean-Claude Gautron.   In: *Annuaire Français de Droit International*,
       Vol. XXXV (*French Yearbook of International Law*, Vol. XXXV).
       Paris: CNRS, 1989, p. 205-15.

As an introduction to this article, the author recalls Chad's and Libya's previous
experiences with international mechanisms of conflict resolution and peace-keeping. He
also examines Chadian history from colonization to the 1980 split between Habré and
Oueddei, the organization and role of the OAU Interafrican Peace-keeping Force in
Chad and the 1989 Chad–Libya outline agreement on the resolution of the territorial
conflict over the Aozou strip. He then examines in detail the historical parameters of the
conflict and finally, he analyses the institutional aspects as well as the clauses of the
outline agreement of August 1989.

491   **Les conflits tchadiens.** (The Chadian conflicts.)
       Yewawa Gbiamango.   Paris: 1987. [n.p.].

This doctoral thesis looks at three types of conflicts within Chad: internal Chadian
conflicts, the Chadian–Libyan dispute and international intervention.

492   **Le conflit du Tchad.** (The Chadian conflict.)
       Jean Gibour.   *Défense Nationale* (June 1985), p. 127-38. map.

This article, written by a French general, contains considerable detail on armaments
used in the Chadian conflict since its beginning. It is divided into five parts, each one
corresponding to a particular period of recent Chadian political history. Thus 1965-77
corresponds to the beginning of the rebellion, 1977-80 to the conquest of power by the
rebels, 1980-81 to what the author calls Chad under Libyan control, and 1982-84 to a
sharing of influence between the various parties involved in the Chadian conflict.
Finally, the author asks what the future might hold for Chad in 1985, at a time when
combat had ceased.

493   **Det nordlige Afrika – en områdestudie.** (North Africa: a general
       study.)
       A. H. Hansen.   *Militaert Tidsskrift* (Denmark), vol. 117, no. 4 (1988),
       p. 122-37.

Provides a survey of Morocco, Algeria, Tunisia, Libya, Chad, Niger, Mauritania, Mali,
Malta, and the Cape Verde islands in the 1980s, discussing geographical, economic,
sociological, military, and political factors, development, and relations among the
countries.

494 **La bande territoriale d'Aouzou et le conflit tchado-libyen.**
(The Aozou strip and the Chad–Libya conflict.)
M. Ialbai. Paris: Université de Droit, Economiques et Sciences
Sociales, 1981. [n.p.].

Ialbai's dissertation is divided into two parts: the colonial era from 1894 to 1958, and the Aozou strip. It specifically discusses Franco-British treaties, the Turkish question, Italian claims, the eviction of Italians after the war, the border question in the region after 1947 and the dispute between Chad and Libya, the 1975 military coup, Chad's and the OUA's diplomatic efforts, Libya's expansionist drive and the Libyan military offensive.

495 **Habré's hour of glory.**
Franziska James. *Africa Report*, vol. 32, no. 5 (Sept.-Oct. 1987),
p. 20-3.

James reviews the Chadian victory over Libyan troops in early 1987 and reports on President Hissen Habré's visit to Washington and Paris and on his relations with the OAU.

496 **Libya and Chad.**
E. G. H. Joffé. *Review of African Political Economy*, no. 21 (Spring
1981), p. 82-102. map. bibliog.

This article reviews the background to Libya's claim on the Aozou Strip and Libya's relations with FROLINAT. It argues that Libyan interest in the Aozou strip region long predated the arrival of the Qadhafi regime to power and can be traced back to the Sanusiyya Order.

497 **The international consequences of the civil war in Chad.**
E. G. H. Joffé. *Review of African Political Economy*, no. 25
(Sept.-Dec. 1982), p. 91-104. map. bibliog.

Although this was written long before the development of American interest in the Chadian situation, it warned of the dangers of internationalization as the conflict between the Oueddei and Habré factions worsened. It also pointed to the increasing tribalization of the civil war, a feature which was eventually to dominate in Chad's political life.

498 **The current situation in Chad: Habré tries to win the peace.**
E. G. H. Joffé. *Current History* (April 1990). [n.p.].

As the Habré regime tried to impose its control on Chad in 1989, it became evident that tribal resentment was growing. This article reviews the economic and political problems faced by Hissen Habré shortly before his overthrow by Idriss Déby.

499 **Les tentatives de règlement non-juridictionnel du différend territorial tchado-libyen à propos de la 'bande d'Aouzou'.** (Non-jurisdictional attempts to settle the Chad–Libya territorial dispute regarding the 'Aozou strip'.)
Maurice Kamto. *Revue Juridique et Politique, Indépendence et Coopération*, vol. 45, no. 1 (Jan.-March 1991), p. 292-304.
The Chad–Libya dispute over the Aozou strip has existed since Colonel Qadhafi came to power in 1969, although he refused to acknowledge it for many years. Despite both parties' acknowledgement of the dispute, the various non-jurisdictional attempts by the OAU and others to solve the conflict have failed, according to the author, partly because of Libya's attitude. This failure led both parties to refer the matter to the International Court of Justice in 1990. This illustrates a general trend among African countries to resort to jurisdictional modes of conflict resolution, possibly as a consequence of OAU's inefficiency.

500 **A state in disarray – conditions of Chad's survival.**
M. P. Kelley. Boulder, Colorado; London: Westview Press, 1986. 222p.
The focus of this work is on Chad's main dilemma: external support which is so crucial for Chad's viability but is also the very factor that undermines its international standing. The roles of Libya, France, the United States, the United Nations and the Organization of African Unity, and the trans-Saharan regional subsystem are also analysed.

501 **Weak states and captured patrons: French desire to disengage from Chad.**
Michael P. Kelley. *Round Table*, no. 296 (1985), p. 328-38.
Considers the role of France in Chad's civil war, 1976-84, noting the efforts of the François Mitterrand government both to disengage its troops from the region and to limit Libyan intervention in the struggle.

502 **Tchad–Libye – La querelle des frontières.** (Chad–Libya – the border dispute.)
Bernard Lanne. Paris: Karthala, 1982. 251p.
Bernard Lanne traces Qadhafi's claims over Chadian territory back to the early twentieth century and the Ottoman fear of seeing their last bastion threatened by British and French interests and, later on, by Italy. He also analyses the treaties signed in connection with Chadian–Libyan frontiers and concludes that Libyan pretensions, like the earlier claims of Italy and the Ottoman Empire, have no grounds.

503 **Histoire d'une frontière ou la 'bande Aozou'.** (History of a border or the Aozou strip.)
Bernard Lanne. *L'Afrique et l'Asie Modernes*, no. 154 (Autumn 1987), p. 3-15. map.
This article, like most of Lanne's writings on Chad, argues for Chad's legitimate rights over the Aozou strip in northern Chad and against Libyan claims of sovereignty. In order to support the Chadian claim, Lanne traces the question back to the late

nineteenth century and examines the attitudes of the main powers (the Ottoman Empire, the British, the French and the Italians) towards the question and the treaties they signed to try to determine the fate of the region from that period until independence.

504 **Du droit à la neutralité au regard du conflit tchadien.** (On the right of neutrality with regard to the Chadian conflict.)
Ba Udingam Bahuana Lebbeorran. Toulouse, France: Université de Toulouse I, 1988.

The author of this doctoral thesis claims that French and Libyan involvement in the Chadian conflict is the consequence of the awakening of French nationalism and of its wish for territorial compensation and expansion in the aftermath of the 1870 defeat. The internal Chadian conflict cannot be solved unless Chad adopts a totally neutral posture guaranteed by states such as France and Libya or by regional or international organizations.

505 **Tchad 'Opération Manta', la montée en puissance.** (Chad 'Operation Manta', the rise to power.)
Eric Lefevre, photography by Bernard Sidler, Benoit Dufeutrelle.
Paris: Charles Lavauzelle, 1984. 91p. map.

This is essentially a collection of photographs of French troops in Chad during the August-October 1983 Operation Manta, designed to push back Libyan forces and the GUNT of Goukouni Oueddei.

506 **Putting the pieces back together again.**
René Lemarchand. *Africa Report*, vol. 29, no. 6 (Nov.-Dec. 1984), p. 60-7.

Although President Hissen Habré has succeeded in bringing many former opponents into his government, reconciliation with the rebels led by Goukouni Oueddei is yet to be achieved. This article examines Habré's government and achievements, and also contains a sketch of and an interview with the president.

507 **The case of Chad.**
René Lemarchand. In: *The green and the black*, edited by René Lemarchand. Bloomington, Indiana: Indiana University Press, 1988, p. 106-24.

The author traces the geopolitical background of the Libyan intervention in Chad to the colonial period and before that, to the Sanusiyya. He argues that the interventionist thrust of Libya's policies in Chad can best be seen as a series of calculated responses to specific threats and opportunities. He also examines Libya's strategies of penetration resorting alternatively to proxies, direct military action or diplomacy. Finally, he describes Libya's defeat at Fada, in northern Chad, at the hands of Chadian forces between January and March 1987.

508 **Le Congo et la crise tchadienne.** (Congo and the Chadian crisis.) Maganga-Boumba. In: *Le Congo et l'OUA (Congo and the OAU)*. Paris: L'Harmattan, 1989, p. 127-41. bibliog.

The author of this book, originally written as a doctoral thesis, was head of the OAU Section in Congo's Ministry for Foreign Affairs. As such, he was able to observe relations between the Pan-African organization and Chad since 1985. In this chapter (Section II, Part One, Chapter II), he examines the reasons behind the Congolese involvement in the Chadian crisis, the OAU's attitude towards this crisis, and the stakes involved in the Chadian conflict. He also seeks the reasons behind the Chadian anxieties of external attack, and examines briefly the involvement of other powers such as France and Libya.

509 **Chad.**
Gino J. Naldi. In his: *The Organisation of African Unity. An analysis of its role*. London: Mansell, 1989, Chapter 3, p. 73-87.

The difficult recent history of Chad has not been without consequences for the Organization of African Unity which was faced with a two-fold problem in dealing with the country torn by civil war. As Gino Naldi explains, on the one hand, prolonged civil war and political instability posed the problem of Chad's representation at OAU meeting. On the other hand, the conflict with Libya over the Aozou strip put the OAU mediating parties under such pressure that, compounded by the failure of the peace-keeping forces in Chad, it paralysed the organization and drove it to the brink of disintegration.

510 **The Aozou strip dispute – a legal analysis.**
Gino Naldi. *Journal of African Law*, vol. 33 (1989), p. 72-7.

Naldi analyses Libya's territorial claim to the disputed Aozou strip in northern Chad. He covers the background of the dispute and examines Libya's claims, which, the author concludes, have little chance of success, in view of the prevalence of the principle of *uti possidetis*, according to which the frontiers inherited from colonial powers cannot be altered after independence.

511 **Involvement, invasion and withdrawal – Qaddafi's Libya and Chad 1969-1981.**
Benyamin Neuberger. Tel-Aviv: The Shiloah Center for Middle Eastern and African Studies, Tel-Aviv University, 1982. 78p. (Occasional Paper, no. 83).

The short, essentially chronological, study analyses the historical connection between Libya and Chad, the link between domestic Chadian politics and Libyan involvement, and Libya's policies in Chad as part of Qadhafi's 'Grand Strategy' in Africa and the Arab World.

512   L'état face au conflit civil: réflexions sur l'Angola, l'Ethiopie et le
       Tchad. (The state and civil conflict: some reflections on Angola,
       Ethiopia and Chad.)
          Sam C. Nolutshungu. *Revue Française de Science Politique*, vol. 38,
          no. 4 (Aug. 1988), p. 533-54.

Although there are evident differences between individual civil conflicts involving
significant external intervention, as in Angola, Ethiopia and Chad, there are also
important similarities which emerge from a comparative analysis. Far from representing
the fundamental cleavages of the society, these conflicts reflect much more the divisions
within a single social stratum, with its own specific relation to the state. This analysis
explores three aspects of such conflicts: the 'autonomy of the state' and its role as a
field and an object of struggle; the social characteristics of the leaderships; and the
tendency of international intervention to increase state independence in relation to
society.

513   Strands and strains of 'good neighbourliness': the case of Nigeria
       and its francophone neighbours.
          Emeka Nwokedi. *Genève-Afrique*, vol. 23, no. 1 (1985), p. 39-60.

Analyses Nigeria's relations with four francophone neighbours: Benin, Chad,
Cameroon, and Niger. The notion of a formal 'good neighbour' policy may be an
exaggeration, but continuity has led Nigerian governments to take a special interest in
bordering countries. In economic relations, precolonial trading ties (smuggling) are still
greater than legal trade, but formal economic relations are growing with Niger and
Benin, in particular. Where national security is concerned, Nigeria has emphasized its
national interests.

514   Qaddafi and Africa's international relations.
          Oye Ogunbadejo. *Journal of Modern African Studies*, vol. 24, no. 1
          (1986), p. 33-68.

During recent years, Washington has perceived Libya's dictator Muammar Qadhafi as a
global threat, supporting Soviet expansionism and blending Islamic teachings with
Marxism in his Third Universal Theory. Moscow, while arming Libya, has reason to
distrust his erratic behaviour. Within Africa, Qadhafi has generally manifested his own
fanaticism and support of violence. Unable to construct political mergers with Egypt,
the Sudan, and Tunisia, Qadhafi intervened through terrorism and support of
revolutionaries in these neighbouring states. In the case of Chad, Qadhafi expanded by
militarily occupying territory and supporting a puppet political faction. Qadhafi
alienated moderate African regimes and nearly destroyed the Organization of African
Unity in 1982-83. Economic sanctions are unlikely to curb Libya's foreign adventurism,
but internal dissent may in time topple Qadhafi.

515   The dilemma of Nigeria's African policy.
          R. O. Ogunbambi. *Journal of African Studies*, vol. 12, no. 1 (1985),
          p. 10-13.

Beginning with initiatives by the military regimes of Murtala Muhammed and Olusegun
Obasanjo in the 1970s, Nigeria's foreign policy towards other African states became
more assertive or 'action-oriented'. Lagos began to apply overt pressure to force
changes in what were perceived as anti-Nigerian policies or situations relating to

Ghana, Chad, Libya, and other countries. The 'action-oriented' foreign policy to date has had little success in Africa and has even proved to be counterproductive, by antagonizing foreign leaders like Jerry Rawlings in Ghana. A move toward cooperation could improve Nigeria's relations with other African states.

516   **The OAU and conflict management: the case of Chad.**
Olusola Ojo. *International Problems, Society and Politics*, Vol. XXVII, no. 51 (3-4) (1988), p. 33-47.

This article assesses the Organization of African Unity's (OAU) role in the Chadian conflict as an example of conflict management. It starts with a brief description of the conflict in Chad and then examines general OAU passivity in African affairs before looking at the actual role of the organization in the conflict. It concludes that the Chadian conflict has revealed the OAU's limitations – it failed to prevent the conflict – and potentials – it provided a restraining influence on external intervention – as an instrument for conflict management.

517   **Solidarité arabo-islamique ou stratégie de puissance?** (Arab–Islamic solidarity or power strategy?)
René Otayek. *Revue Tiers-Monde*, Vol. XXII, no. 85 (Jan.-March 1981), p. 157-62.

This article reviews Libyan involvement in the Chadian crisis. It considers the FROLINAT as a destabilizing instrument threatening the Tombalbaye regime and then as an instrument of Qadhafi's 'Saharan designs', which the author defines as the Libyan leader's wish to create a vast Islamic–Saharan federation covering Mauritania, Mali, Niger and Chad – thus continuing the Sanusi tradition of southern expansion.

518   **L'intervention du Nigéria dans le conflict Tchadien.** (Nigerian intervention in the Chadian conflict.)
René Otayek. *Le Mois en Afrique*, no. 209-10 (1983), p. 51-66.

Otayek examines the role of Nigeria's intervention in Chad in March 1979. He comments on the fact that, although Nigerian forces were unable to achieve their mission and had to leave Chad four months after arrival, the initiative was supported by all Chadian factions, and it achieved diplomatic success with the Kano and Lagos accords.

519   **La politique africaine de la Libye.** (Libya's African policy.)
René Otayek. Paris: Karthala, 1986, p. 177-203. bibliog.

This study on Libya's African policy contains three chapters on Chad entitled: '1969-1973: le FROLINAT, instrument de destabilisation du régime de François Tombalbaye' ('1969-73: the FROLINAT as an instrument of destabilisation of the Tombalbaye regime'), '1973-198...: le Tchad comme instrument de la politique saharienne de la Libye' ('1973-198...: Chad as an instrument of Libya's Saharan policy') and 'le Tchad dans la stratégie libyenne globale' ('Chad in Libya's global strategy').

520 **La question de la Libye dans le règlement de la paix.** (The question
of Libya in the peace settlement process.)
J. Pichon. Paris: J. Peyronnet & Cie, 1945. [n.p.].
A study which examines the pre-World War II Franco-Italian and Franco-British
agreements and the southern Libyan border.

521 **Civil war and foreign intervention in Chad.**
Alex Rondos. *Current History*, vol. 84, no. 502 (1985), p. 209-12,
232.
Unilateral interventions by foreign powers – particularly Libya, France, and the United
States – undermined African multilateral efforts after 1979 to mediate Chad's
internecine factional and sectional quarrels.

522 **Le différend franco-italien concernant la frontière méridionale de la
Libye.** (The Franco-Libyan dispute regarding the southern border
of Libya.)
E. Rouard de Card. Paris: A. Pédone & J. Gamber, 1929. [n.p.].
This work deals with the origins and the object of the dispute. It first examines the
conventions between France and England with regards to the limits of their zones of
influence between Niger and Chad, and Chad and the Nile region. It also covers Turkish
and Italian reactions to the conventions, Franco-Italian agreements of 1900-2 with
respect to Tripolitania and Morocco, and those of 12 September 1919 on the
rectification of the western border of Libya. It then deals with the early Italian claims
and French reactions to them. The book argues that Italian claims have no basis in
international law.

523 **Libye et Tchad – Evolution du différend armé entre les deux états
au cours de l'été 1987. Rappel des données juridiques concernant la
controverse relative à l'appartenance de la bande d'Aouzou.** (Libya
and Chad – evolution of the armed conflict between the two states
during the summer of 1987. A reminder of the legal data regarding the
controversy of the Aozou strip.)
C. Rousseau, M. Virally. *Revue Générale de Droit International
Public*, vol. 92, no. 1 (1988), p. 151-5. map. (Chronique des Faits
Internationaux).
The authors focus on the legal aspect of the dispute and include a list of treaties
regarding the Aozou strip from 1899 to 1973, as well as the text of the Franco-British
declaration of March 1899 by Paul Cambon and Lord Salisbury.

524 **Le diamant noir. Comment on devient ambassadeur d'Israël.**
(The black diamond. How to become Israel's ambassador.)
Ovadia Soffer. Paris: Robert Laffont, 1987. 284p. map.
Ovadia Soffer was Israel's ambassador in Chad (1965 and 1969-71) and the Central
African Republic (1963-67), and as such he witnessed the early stages of the Chadian

civil war. In this book he provides a portrait of Tombalbaye and gives his impressions of the Chadian situation.

525 **Opération Manta. Tchad 1983-1984.** (Operation Manta. Chad 1983-84.)
    Colonel Spartacus.   Paris: Plon, 1985. 260p. maps.

The author of this study denounces the technical and political errors committed by France in Chad during its intervention against Tubu rebels.

526 **Victoires dans le désert.** (Victories in the desert.)
    Lieutenant-Colonel Texeraud.   Paris: CHEAM, 1988. 44p. maps. bibliog.

This study deals essentially with the events of December 1986-March 1987 in which the forces of President Hissen Habré routed Libyan forces in northern Chad and recovered the BET. This was achieved only with the help of the French Government which provided heavy and sophisticated armament as well as military advisers. Texeraud describes the various processes which led to this victory, and his work is very favourable to the then president, Hissen Habré, whom the author considers to be a sophisticated and efficient leader who achieved the national unification of a deeply divided country.

527 **370 jours d'un ambassadeur au Tchad.** (370 days of an Ambassador in Chad.)
    R. L. Touze.   Paris: Editions France-Empire, 1989. 394p.

Provides an insight into the professional life of R. L. Touze while he was Ambassador in Chad from April 1974 to April 1975. It is a pro-Tombalbaye and biased work dealing mainly with the Claustre–Combe affair, and includes details of the negotiations to obtain the release of the hostages. It is an official version of the affair and an exercise in self-justification.

528 **Les débuts de la mission de délimitation de la frontière entre le Tchad et le Soudan Anglo-Egyptien (1922).** (The early stages of the border demarcation mission between Chad and the Anglo-Egyptian Sudan (1922).)
    Joseph Tubiana.   *Le Mois en Afrique*, no. 186-7 (1981), p. 113-28.

Joseph Tubiana discusses four handwritten letters from Lieutenant-Colonel Grossard, head of the mission, to the French Capitaine in charge of the post of Goz Beida. The letters show Grossard's worries and concerns at the beginning of the mission.

529 **Libya, Chad and the Central Sahara.**
    John Wright.   London: Hurst & Company, 1989. 168p.

Wright's study is concerned with the historical background to the boundary dispute between Chad and Libya and traces the history of the Central Sahara back to antiquity. A whole chapter is devoted to the Sanusi and eventually forms the main theme of this book which seeks to show that the relationship between white and black Africa was essentially one of exploitation.

530　**French policy in Chad and the Libyan challenge.**
David Yost. *Orbis*, vol. 26, no. 4 (Winter 1983), p. 965-97. map.
The author of this article assesses French interests in relation to the Chadian civil war.
He highlights the Libyan intervention in November 1980, the responses of the Giscard
d'Estaing and the Mitterrand governments to it, the Libyan withdrawal in November
1981, the renewed civil war, OAU decisions on Chad, the miscalculations of
Mitterrand's policy and its fortuitous success, and the implications of the conflict for
French policy in Africa.

Chad: from civil strife to big power rivalry.
See item no. 244.

L'OUA face à la question tchadienne.
See item no. 249.

Economy

General

531 **République du Tchad. Economie et Plan de Développement.**
(Republic of Chad. Economy and Development Plan.)
Anon. Paris: République Française, Ministère de la Coopération,
1961. 26p.

A governmental study containing a large number of tables which provide information
on aspects of the Chadian economy such as resources and employment. It also
examines development trends and programmes up to 1961. The data are, however,
incomplete.

532 **Rapport Annuel, Année 1964.** (Annual Report, Year 1964.)
Anon. Fort-Lamy: Ministère de l'Economie et des Transports, 1964.
64p.

This work contains a variety of information and documents, including a speech made
at the Conference on Arachides [groundnuts] of Moundou, 20 May 1965, and many
statistics. The topics covered include wheat, gum, millet and sorghum, sodium
carbonate, cattle, fishing, transport. It concludes with the outlook for 1965.

533 **Enquête socio-économique au Tchad, 1965.** (A socio-economic
survey of Chad, 1965.)
Anon. Paris: République Française, Secrétariat d'Etat aux Affairs
Etrangères; Fort-Lamy: République du Tchad, Ministère du Plan et de
la Coopération, Service de Statistique Générale, 1965. 33p. maps.

Covers the southern provinces of Mayo-Kebbi, Western and Eastern Logone, Middle-
Chari and Tandjile. The study forms the second part of the survey carried out in
relation to the Social and Economic Development Programme of 1964-65 which
sought to determine family income structure, family food consumption per product,

and the importance of local and imported products in family consumption, as well as assessing the daily calorie intake and the average food composition of individual diets.

534 **Tchad: Relance économique en chiffres. Année 1983.** (Chad: statistics on the economic recovery. Year 1983.)
Anon.   N'Djamena: République du Tchad, Ministère du Plan et de la Reconstruction, Direction de la Statistique, des Etudes Economiques et Démographiques, 1983. 125p.

This governmental study contains data on the geography, demography, administration, population, living conditions, general economy, production activities, finance and reserve of Chad. Most of the information concerns the Chari-Baguirmi region or N'Djamena.

535 **Les populations de la moyenne vallée du Chari. Vie économique et sociale.** (The people of the Middle-Chari Basin, their social and economic life.)
Claude Arditi.   N'Djamena: République du Tchad, Ministère de l'Agriculture et de la Production Animale, 1968. 98p. maps. bibliog.

Although available only in typescript, this is a comprehensive study of the economy of the Middle-Chari Basin in which the author describes the strong links between economy and social life. It provides a statistical summary of the region with special emphasis on those ethnic groups for which statistics are missing. The most common Sara or Masa groups are therefore not studied in great detail.

536 **Du mode de production domestique à l'intégration au système capitaliste: le cas des paysans tchadiens.** (From domestic mode of production to integration to the capitalist system: the case of Chadian farmers.)
Jean Cabot.   In: *Sociétés paysannes du Tiers-Monde* (*Third World peasant societies*), edited by Catherine Coquery-Vidrovitch.   Paris: L'Harmattan, 1990, p. 57-65. bibliog.

Jean Cabot analyses the disintegration of Chadian peasant structures caused by the introduction of the capitalist mode of production. He shows that the traditional domestic mode of production has been destroyed and integrated into a system imposed by development in which commercial food crops have been substituted for subsistence food crops.

537 **Les cadres juridiques de l'intervention économique publique au Tchad.** (The juridical framework of state intervention in Chad.)
Tadin Macra.   Toulouse, France: Université de Toulouse I, 1990. [n.p.].

Macra's doctoral thesis examines Chadian state intervention and claims that the public enterprises created after independence do not, in the present state of the law, constitute a homogeneous juridical reality. It also examines Africa's economic situation in the light of the interventionist drive of many African governments.

538 **Le rôle des sociétés dans le financement du développement au
Tchad.** (The role of companies in the financing of development
in Chad.)
Djibangar Madjirebaye. *Revue Juridique et Politique, Indépendence
et Coopération*, vol. 32, no. 1 (Jan.-March 1988), p. 471-83.
This article was written by the Director General of the Justice Ministry. It shows that
the primary sector is the most important economic sector, generating 90 per cent of
foreign currency supply. Cotton holds by far the largest share of that percentage (80
per cent of the total). Industry and commerce are in an embryonic state due to a lack
of financial support. The financing of development is carried out by the state budget.
The author also provides a structural and functional analysis of the banking system
which participates in the financing of development in Chad. He also recalls the role of
the Caisse nationale d'épargne du Tchad (National Savings Bank of Chad) and the
Chadian Investment Office, which has now disappeared.

539 **Business in Chad.**
Mahamat Senoussi Mahamat. N'Djamena: Ministère du Commerce
et de l'Industrie (Department of Trade and Industry), 1988. 70p. maps.
(Guide de l'Opérateur Economique au Tchad).
This report was produced by the staff of the Department of Trade and Industry and
can be regarded as a government publication. It provides brief data on Chad's natural
resources which cover the 1982-88 period and describes the 1985-88 three-year plan,
its objectives and priorities. It also sets out the conditions necessary to carry out
commercial, industrial and artisanal activities in Chad, examines the Code of
Investments and presents three commercial and industrial promotion bodies. Finally,
it gives embassies and other professional addresses in Chad. It must be noted that,
although the title is in English, the text of the report is in French.

540 **Le Tchad se redresse.** (Chad stands up.)
Roger Pons. *Marchés tropicaux*, no. 2219 (20 May 1988), p. 1301-6.
map.
In this article the author describes Chad's military situation and the efforts made
towards national reconciliation. He also deals with the economic situation and foreign
aid.

541 **Tchad: 'Mise en valeur', coton et développement.** (Chad:
'exploitation', cotton and development.)
Ulrich Stürzinger. *Revue Tiers-Monde*, Vol. XXIV, no. 95 (July-
Sept. 1983), p. 643-52.
The cultivation of cotton was introduced in Chad by the French colonial
administration and, although it uses only a small portion of Chad's southern territory,
it has decisively influenced the country's history. The geographical location of cotton
cultivation has skewed social, economic and political development in the country as a
whole. For this reason, political leaders in Chad have always taken a particular
interest in the crop. The author asks whether what has been called 'development
policy' since the 1960s is not in fact exploitation in a new guise or whether colonial
exploitation was not a development policy?

542 **Chad: Development Potential and Constraints.**
World Bank. Washington, DC: Johns Hopkins University Press,
1974. 133p. (A World Bank Country Economic Report).
This report examines all the basic aspects of Chad's economy and analyses the
current situation and the various development projects being carried out in the
country. It proposes ways of improving the situation. The report also contains sixty-
two pages of statistical tables.

Finance

543 **Evolution monétaire du Tchad.** (The financial evolution of Chad.)
Anon. *Bulletin de l'Afrique Noire*, no. 1393 (28 Jan. 1988), p. 12.
This study examines Chad's global resources, external balance and domestic credit.

544 **Fiscalité et code des investissements au Tchad.** (Taxation system
and investment code in Chad.)
Cotnadji Kossi Djohongona. Paris: Université Paris II, 1990. [n.p.].
This doctoral thesis stresses the importance of the taxation system and of an
investment code in the economic development policy of a developing country like
Chad. Its author also provides a critical analysis of Chadian authorities and shows the
deficiencies and incompetence in their use of these tools of economic development.
He argues for reform which would support the fiscal administration and democratize
political and fiscal institutions.

Foreign aid

545 **Programme national pour l'assistance du Programme des Nations
Unies pour le Développement au Tchad (P.N.U.D.) 1972-1976.**
(National Support Programme for the United Nations Development
Programme in Chad (U.N.D.P.) 1972-76.)
Anon. Fort-Lamy: République du Tchad, 1971. 66p.
A study which examines the state of agriculture, infrastructure and industry in Chad
and assesses the needs and objectives of the country and how to achieve them. It also
lists and explains the various projects in each area which have received assistance
from the U.N.D.P.

Evaluation des projets financés par Band Aid au Tchad.
See item no. 430.

Trade

546 **Le commerce du poisson au Tchad.** (The fish trade in Chad.)
Philippe Couty, Pierre Duran. Paris: ORSTOM, 1968. 252p. bibliog.
(Mémoire ORSTOM, no. 23).

Commissioned by the Centre Technique Forestier Tropical (Tropical Forest Technical Centre), this study was part of a project completed in September 1965 and designed to develop fish production from Lake Chad. The aim of the study was to determine whether an increase in fish production could be absorbed by the Chadian market and whether other markets should be considered. It also examines whether the configuration and strength of the commercial networks used by the fish trade could accommodate such an increase in production.

547 **Le poisson salé-séché du Lac Tchad et du Bas-Chari: prix et débouchés.** (Dried salted fish from Lake Chad and Lower-Chari: prices and outlets.)
Philippe Couty. Dakar, Senegal: ORSTOM, 1968. 68p. bibliog.

This study was stimulated by the results of a previous study by Couty and Duran (see above). The author identifies three new factors affecting trade (the development of Lake Chad by the Chad Basin Commission, the disorganization of commercial networks by the war in Biafra, new fish salting and drying methods) which raise questions over the profitability of 'banda' (dried salted fish). In order to decide on the real profitability of this food product, the author determines minimum production costs and maximum retail prices.

Evolution des échanges entre le bassin Tchadien (Tchad, Nord-Cameroun) et la côte du golfe de Guinée pendant la periode coloniale.
See item no. 194.

Transport

548 **Le chemin de fer Bangui–Tchad dans son contexte économique régional. Etude géographique de l'économie des transports au Tchad et dans le Nord de l'Oubangui-Chari.** (The Bangui–Chad railway in its regional economic context. A geographical study of transport economy in Chad and north Ubangui-Chari.)
Gilles Sautter, Mathiot Guggenbuhl. Bangui, Central African Republic: Société Civile d'Etudes du Chemin de Fer de Bangui au Tchad (SCECFBT), 1958. 325p. maps.

This study was carried out at the request of the S.C.E.C.F.B.T. by the Institut de Géographie de l'Université de Strasbourg and deals in a comprehensive manner with the railway link project between Bangui in the Central African Republic and Chad. A third of the work covers general economic data, while two chapters are devoted to means of transport other than rail (road and river) and the last part of the study examines the road transport system and its dynamics. The objective of this study is to determine the potential problems and possible options of the projected Bangui–Chad railway line.

Industry

549 **Les conditions d'installation d'entreprises industrielles dans les états africains et malgaches associés – Vol. 10: République du Tchad.** (Conditions for the creation of industrial enterprises in the Association of African and Malagasy States – Vol. 10: The Republic of Chad.)
[M.] Le Gall, [Dr] Roider, [M.] Pasquier. Commission des Communautés Européennes, Direction Générale de l'Aide au Développement, 1972. 83p.

Part of a wider study which set out to determine the possibilities for establishing export-orientated industries in the countries of the Association of African and Malagasy States. It provides a basic reference datum on the conditions relating to the setting up and the functioning of industrial enterprises in Chad.

550 **Contribution à l'étude de la stratégie d'implantation des entreprises françaises dans les états de l'Afrique centrale (Cameroun, Centrafrique, Congo, Gabon, Tchad).** (A contribution to the study of the location strategy of French firms in central Africa (Cameroon, Central African Republic, Congo, Gabon, Chad).)
Christophe Ouapou.   Bordeaux, France: Université de Bordeaux I, 1988. [n.p.].
Ouapou's doctoral thesis analyses the fact that the majority of French enterprises in central Africa are large firms with a highly centralized subsidiary organization. It claims that they have little local capital or an established production system and that their sole aim is to beat competition.

Agriculture and fishing

551 **Enquête agricole au Tchad, 1960-1961.** (A farming survey in Chad, 1960-61.)
Anon.   N'Djamena: République du Tchad, Ministère du Plan et de la Coopération, Service de la Statistique Générale; Paris: Secrétariat d'Etat aux Affaires Etrangères chargé de la Coopération, 1967. 166p. map.
The study concerns the region of Chad situated south of the Chari river. It presents the results of a survey carried out in 1960, designed to determine the number of farms, farmland surface-area, farming population, cattle and tools. The data are illustrated with a large number of tables and graphs.

552 **Programme 1987-1991 d'aménagement et de mise en valeur des polders du nord-est du lac Tchad.** (1987-91 programme for the development of polders northeast of Lake Chad.)
Anon.   *Bulletin de l'Afrique Noire*, no. 1380 (15 Oct. 1987), p. 11.
This article deals with the food situation in Chad and proposes projects and perspectives for 1991 and after.

553 **Economie et politiques céréalières dans la zone sahélienne – L'exemple du Tchad.** (Cereal economy and policies in the Sahel zone – the example of Chad.)
Claude Arditi.   Paris: Amélioration des Méthodes d'Investigation et de Recherche Appliquées au Développement (AMIRA), 1991. 67p. maps. bibliog. (Brochure no. 60).
This study provides information on the production and consumption of cereals in Chad. It also contains data on cereal prices and volumes in Anglophone and Francophone Africa and on food aid from the European Community. In addition Arditi analyses other studies on the subject of cereals in Chad.

554 **Les moyens d'exhaure en milieu rural.** (Water extraction in rural areas.)
André Benamour. N'Djamena: République du Tchad, Ministère du Développement, Agricole et Pastoral, Direction de l'Elevage et des Industries Animales (Republic of Chad, Ministry of Agricultural and Pastoral Development, Office for Livestock and Animal Industries), 1977. 71p. bibliog. (Comité Interafricain d'Etudes Hydrauliques (C.I.E.H.). Etude financée par la Banque Mondiale. (Inter-African Committee for Hydraulic Studies. Research financed by the World Bank).)

The aim of this survey, which deals with Senegal, Niger, the Ivory Coast, Ghana, Upper Volta (Burkina Faso) as well as Chad, is to examine water extraction techniques, their advantages and disadvantages and possible improvements in existing equipment. It offers the authorities of the countries concerned the opportunity to evaluate the most appropriate equipment for the best technical and economic solutions to hydraulic equipment programmes.

555 **L'agro-pastoralisme au Tchad comme stratégie de survie: Essai sur la relation entre l'anthropologie et la statistique.**
(Agro-pastoralism in Chad as a strategy for survival: a study of the relationship between anthropology and statistics.)
Angelo Maliki Bonfiglioli. Washington, DC: World Bank, 1992. 57p. (Les dimensions sociales de l'ajustement en Afrique subsaharienne, Document de travail no. 11, Enquêtes et statistiques (Social dimensions of adjustment in sub-Saharan Africa, Working paper no. 11, Surveys and statistics).)

A short but very clear and concise study which examines the Chadian agro-pastoral system in the Sahel region (central Chad) as a coherent entity with its own dynamics determined by an unpredictable environment. The author describes the social structures of rural communities and their socio-economic and socio-political context, as well as their pastoral and agricultural system. The last chapter focuses on agricultural and pastoral activities as complementary means of survival.

556 **La culture du blé dans les polders du lac Tchad.** (Wheat cultivation in the Lake Chad polders.)
Christian Bouquet. *Cahier d'Outre-Mer*, no. 86 (1969), p. 203-14. maps.

After wheat cultivation was introduced to Chad by Fezzanis it spread during the nineteenth century to parts of Lake Chad. This success persuaded the administration to create polders to encourage further cultivation. This new agricultural activity is analysed here, in the context of its natural and human environment.

557 **La maîtrise de l'eau dans les wadi et polders du lac Tchad. Etude comparative et prospective.** (The control of water in the wadis and polders of Lake Chad: a comparative and forecasting study.) Christian Bouquet. In: *Les politiques de l'eau en Afrique, développement agricole et participation paysanne. Actes du colloque de la Sorbonne (The politics of water in Africa, agricultural development and peasant participation. Proceedings of the conference held at the Sorbonne)*, edited by Gérard Conac, Claudette Savonnet-Guyot, Françoise Conac. Paris: Economica, 1985, p. 668-75. map.

This paper deals specifically with the region of Kanem in southern Chad. It examines the water resources of the region as well as the needs of rural societies and looks at the traditional means of water control among the Buduma who live on the Lake Chad islands, the Kanembu and the Kuri who dwell on the banks of the lake. The author shows how the question of water control highlights rules of land division and principles of taxation.

558 **Les malentendus de l'Opération Polders au Tchad.** (Misunderstandings of the Polder Operation in Chad.) Christian Bouquet. *Les Cahiers d'Outre-Mer*, no. 159 (July- Sept. 1987), p. 295-301.

Twenty years after the first study on the Polder Operation in Chad, the author analyses the failures generated by this operation which were attributed particularly to the lack of consideration given to geographical advice.

559 **Stratégie et tactique cotonière au Tchad.** (Cotton strategy and tactics in Chad.) Jean Cabot. *Hérodote*, no. 6 (April-June 1977), p. 92-108. map.

Cotton was forcibly introduced in Chad as a crop in 1927 and imposed mainly in the southern Sara region, where it found a favourable climate. A colonial imposition and the only commercial crop, it became a necessary source of income in order to pay tax and thus forced farmers to neglect vital food crops. Jean Cabot examines the colonial monopoly on cotton before analysing the structures established after independence, with the creation of the Cotontchad company and its mode of operation. He looks at the development of the crop, its yield and the consequences for farmers. Finally, he observes that the cotton crop and industry has had disastrous consequences on the soil and, consequently, on the farmers' way of life and he advocates crop diversification, which, he believes, would benefit the country as a whole.

560 **Quelques rites agricoles chez les Banana-Kolon et les Marba de la région du Logone (Tchad).** (Agricultural rituals among the Banana-Kolon and the Marba in the Logone region (Chad).) M. Catherinet. *Notes Africaines*, no. 62 (April 1954), p. 40-2.

The Banana-Kolon and the Marba are often included in the same group called Marba, Banana or Bana. Their members claim to be divided into four sub-groups whose traditions are very close and they all believe in a rain god, Olona. This article shows that the Banana-Kolon and the Marba have similar rituals related to crop location, sacrifice, sowing and domestic produce and wild grain harvests.

561 **La culture attelée: un progrès dangereux.** (Draught cultivation: a dangerous improvement.)
Georges Charrière. *Cahier ORSTOM, Série Science Humaine,* Vol. XX, no. 3-4 (1984), p. 647-56.

In central and southern Chad, a ten-year period of agricultural mechanization (draught or mechanized cultivation) between 1967 and 1977 revealed the fragility of the majority of the soils of the Sahelian and sub-Sahelian zone. Some techniques which were introduced individually, such as ploughing, lead to an increase in erosion and leaching of the soils under cultivation and can result in desertification within a few cropping seasons. The author argues it is necessary to deal with the question from an ecological point of view in order to develop adequate technical models. Agriculture must be associated with stock breeding and reafforestation. He advocates that farmers be trained in order to understand how different factors interact in changes in soil fertility.

562 **Etude générale des conditions d'utilisation des sols de la cuvette tchadienne.** (A general study of the conditions of soil use in the Chadian Basin.)
B. Dabin. Paris: ORSTOM, 1969. 199p. (Travaux et Documents de l'ORSTOM, no. 2. Contribution à la connaissance du bassin tchadien).

This study constitutes a synthesis of previous reports dealing with the pedology (chemical and physical study of the soil), agronomy and the sociology of the Chadian Basin. It brings together the main conclusions of these reports and draws up some essential rules for soil use in the areas concerned. The soil study is designed to inform agronomists in order to allow them to function more efficiently in their own domains, which occupy the remainder of the study. The problems associated with the cultivation of rice, cotton, sorghum, millet and the groundnut are specifically examined.

563 **Problèmes et perspective du développement de l'Est tchadien. Le casier A – Nord de Bongor.** (Problems and perspectives of development of eastern Chad. North of Bongor.)
Dolmaire, Gaudillot. Paris: B.D.P.A., 1960. 86p.

This is the report of the Dolmaire–Gaudillot mission sent by the French government at the request of the Chadian government to survey possibilities for agricultural development in Chad.

564 **La pêche en pays Sar.** (Fishing in the Sar region.)
Gaby Tidanbay Madjingar, in collaboration with Jacques Fédry.
Sahr, Chad: Centre d'Etudes Linguistiques, Collège Charles Lwanga, 1982. 68p. maps. bibliog.

This booklet provides information on fishing in the Sar region, and explains the various techniques used, as well as the rituals that accompany fishing. It emphasizes the multifarious aspect of fishing and stresses its economic importance as a nutritional supplement. It also touches upon ecological aspects by discussing local views on the decline in stocks of certain varieties of fish.

565 **Quelques grands types de systèmes fonciers traditionnels au Tchad.** (Major types of traditional land tenure systems in Chad.)
Jean-Pierre Magnant. *Cahier d'Outre-Mer*, no. 122 (1978), p. 171-201. maps.

In this illustrated study, the author examines Chadian systems of land tenure. These can be understood only in the context of socio-political and familial organization and environmental factors. Thus a distinction must be made between land tenure systems for farmers and cattle pastoralists. It is on the basis of these different land tenure systems that 'feudal' states appeared in the Sahel region, because royal lineages gained control of the land through their religious and fiscal power.

566 **Les réactions paysannes à un projet de développement rizicole au sud de N'Djamena (Tchad).** (Farmers' reactions to a rice development project south of N'Djamena (Chad).)
Jean-Pierre Magnant. In: *Les politiques de l'eau en Afrique, développement agricole et participation paysanne. Actes du colloque de la Sorbonne (The politics of water in Africa, agricultural development and peasant participation. Proceedings of the conference held at the Sorbonne)*, edited by Gérard Conac, Claudette Savonnet-Guyot, Françoise Conac. Paris: Economica, 1985, p. 677-96. maps. bibliog.

This paper analyses a project financed by the PNUD, the FAO and the Commission du Bassin de Lac Tchad (CBLT), which aimed at developing rice and other food crops in the region of Koundoul, southern Chad. It should have been implemented in 1979 or 1980 but the civil war prevented this. Although the project had not been developed in detail, the general principles had been set and these form the basis of this paper.

567 **L'animation agricole. Un moyen d'accroître l'utilité des fonds destinés au développement rural dans le Tiers-Monde.**
(Agricultural training: a means of increasing the efficiency of fund use for rural development in the Third World.)
Roger Pasquier. Fribourg, Switzerland: Editions Universitaires, 1973. 144p. (Cahiers de l'Institut des Sciences Economiques et Sociales de l'Université de Fribourg, no. 28).

This study offers a method of disseminating information on agricultural techniques aimed at development aid organizations in the Third World in order to enable them to use their funds more efficiently. The technique is called agricultural 'animation' and allows a member of a community to be trained extensively into new practical agricultural techniques so that he/she may, in turn, train other members of his/her community. Agricultural 'animation' is different from community development found in African Anglophone countries which is essentially aimed at female training and the elimination of illiteracy, and does not deal with agricultural matters. The study refers to the 1962-70 period and, besides Chad, it deals with Tanzania, Rwanda, the Ivory Coast, Togo and Senegal.

Employment

568 **Rapport du Séminaire National sur l'Education Coopérative et la Promotion Socio-économique en Milieu Rural et Ouvrier.** (Report on the National Seminar on Cooperative Education and Socio-economic Promotion in Farmers' and Workers' Communities.) Anon. N'Djamena: République du Tchad, Ministère de la Fonction Publique et du Travail, 1975. 154p.

The seminar, of which this is the record, took place between 2 and 9 December 1975 in N'Djamena and received financial assistance from the United Nations Fund for Population-Related Activities. This report deals mostly with the organization and development of the seminar. It mentions the participants, the programme and the resolutions as well as reproducing the papers read at the seminar.

Statistics

569 **Bulletin Mensuel de la Statistique.** (Monthly Statistics Bulletin.) Anon. Fort-Lamy: République du Tchad, April 1961, p. 26-43. (Bulletin no. 94).

This bulletin contains figures on climatology, foreign tade, transport and public finance.

570 **Bulletin Mensuel de la Statistique.** (Monthly Statistics Bulletin.) Anon. Fort-Lamy: République du Tchad, July 1962, p. 45-68. (Bulletin no. 100).

This issue of the *Statistics Bulletin* contains figures on climatology, foreign trade, transport and public finance, as well as data on prices, electricity, cotton and meat production.

Education and Training

571 **Enseignement Secondaire Général: Annuaire Statistique
1988-1989.** (General Secondary Education: Statistics 1988-89.)
Anon. N'Djamena: Ministère de l'Education Nationale, Service de la
Planification de l'Education, [n.d.]. 270p.

A compilation of tables, containing no text apart from a brief introduction. The
information is divided into four parts: state and private schools (C.E.G.), state lycées
and the King Faysal Lycée, and covers statistics on the state of school buildings and
furniture as well as on the number of students, their success rate in exams and details
about teachers.

572 **Réunion de suivi de la Table Ronde de Genève III – Sous-secteur
Education–Formation–Emploi – Document de stratégie.**
(Follow-up meeting to the Third Geneva Round Table – Sub-section
Education–Training–Employment – Strategy report.)
Anon. N'Djamena: Ministère du Plan et de la Coopération, 1990.
109p.

A detailed analysis of the state of education, training and employment in Chad, with
an assessment of needs and costs. It is completed by a thorough analysis of a
proposed strategy and objectives designed to remedy the existing shortcomings of the
system.

573 **Réunion de suivi de la Table Ronde de Genève III – Sous-secteur Education–Formation–Emploi – Compte-rendu des travaux.**
(Follow-up meeting to the Third Geneva Round Table – Sub-section Education–Training–Employment – Proceedings.)
Anon. N'Djamena: Ministère du Plan et de la Coopération, 1990. 59p.

This report contains the proceedings of a meeting held on 7 and 8 November 1990 in N'Djamena as a result of the Geneva Round Table of 19 and 20 June 1990. Its contents include action plans related to secondary and higher education as well as to technical and professional training. It includes a list of delegates and a list of the members of the technical support section of the E.F.E. (Education–Formation–Emploi) sub-section.

574 **Les problèmes posés par la formation des cadres administratifs dans certains pays d'Afrique Tropicale. (République Centrafricaine, Congo-Brazzaville, Gabon, Niger, Tchad).**
(Difficulties encountered in the training of civil servants in some countries of tropical Africa. (Central African Republic, Congo-Brazzaville, Gabon, Niger, Chad).)
Antoine Bernard. Paris: UNESCO, [n.d.]. 31p.

This study examines the needs, potentials, means, and objectives of administrative training. It was written after a trip to tropical Africa between November and December 1963 and concerns civil servants with responsibilities in financial, legal, accounting and other sectors of public administration.

575 **Animation féminine dans les communautés villageoises du Moyen-Chari.** (Female education in villages of the Middle-Chari region.)
Ayélé Antoinette Foly, Alain Laffitte. Douala, Cameroon: Panafrican Institute for Development, 1981. 76p. (PAID Reports, Participation and Communication Series IV, no. 2).

This short study in French is accompanied by a summary in English. It explains the work of the Professional Agricultural Training Centres (CFPA) and how their training programmes initiated social and economic change in the communities in which they were set up.

576 **Le refus de l'école. Contribution à l'étude des problèmes de l'éducation chez les Musulmans du Ouaddai (Tchad).** (The rejection of schooling. A contribution to the study of educational problems among the Muslims of Wadai (Chad).)
Issa Hassan Khayar, preface by Joseph Tubiana. Paris: Librairie d'Amérique et d'Orient, 1976. 140p.

Khayar looks for the roots of the rejection of schooling among Muslim families of the north in tradition, Islamization and Arabization as well as in colonial education. He attributes this refusal to a distrust, on the part of a deeply and traditionally religious people, of the secular education offered by colonial, as well as by independent, authorities.

577　**Education traditionnelle et éducation moderne au Tchad. Conflits et adaptation.** (Traditional and modern education in Chad. Conflicts and adaptation.)
Issa Hassan Khayar.　*Le Mois en Afrique*, no. 163-4 (July-Aug. 1979), p. 82-93.
In this study, the author examines primary education in Chad and tries to establish the relationship between the educational system and the population, especially Muslims.

578　**Le français et l'arabe en milieu scholaire 'Zaghawa' au Tchad.** (French and Arabic in Zaghawa schools, Chad.)
Zakaria Fadoul Khidir.　Paris: Université de Paris III, 1987. [n.p.].
This doctoral thesis examines the problems posed by the use of French and Arabic as teaching languages among Beri children whose native language is BèRi. It points to such factors as the quantitative and qualitative insufficiencies of teaching staff and equipment, low national income, bad living conditions, linguistic diversity and cultural incompatibilities as the causes for these shortcomings and for the high rate of school failure and desertion among Beri children.

579　**L'association des paysans: moyens de formation et d'animation dans les villages africains. Le cas des Maisons Familiales Rurales au Sénégal et au Tchad.** (Farmers' association: training in African villages. The case of Rural Family Houses in Senegal and Chad.)
Yvonne Lefebvre, Michel Lefebvre.　Paris: Institut d'Etude du Développement Economique et Social, Université Paris-1, 1974. 376p. bibliog.
This illustrated study analyses the work done by the Union Nationale des Maisons Familiales Rurales d'Education et d'Orientation (U.N.M.F.R.E.O.: National Union of Rural Family Houses for Education and Career Guidance), an organization which helps create agricultural training centres at the request of African states or people. It considers the influence of the rural family house on development and social change.

580　**Ecole et Islam. Problèmes de l'éducation en milieu musulman au Tchad. L'exemple de l'ethnie 'Maba' de la region du Wadai, Tchad.** (School and Islam. The problems of education in Muslim areas of Chad. The case of the Maba of Wadai, Chad.)
Seidou Traoré.　Paris: EHESS, [n.d.]. 78p. map. bibliog.
In his Master's Dissertation Traoré examines the tensions existing between traditional Muslim education and modern education practices inherited from the colonial administration. He shows that the Maba, a Muslim population which is the most important ethnic group in Wadai, have difficulty reconciling traditional Koranic and modern public education.

581 **L'enseignement arabo-islamique privé et ses conséquences au Ouaddai, Tchad.** (Private Islamic education in Arabic and its consequences in Wadai, Chad.)
Seidou Traoré. Lyon, France: Université de Lyon II, 1989. [n.p.].
This doctoral thesis is organized around three themes. The first one is an historical, sociological, cultural and educational study of the Islamized populations of Wadai since the creation of the Islamic kingdom of Wadai. The second theme is the organization of traditional Koranic education institutions and its consequences on the Chadian Muslim community. The last concerns the outlook for a pedagogical approach which would allow for innovations in Wadai Islamic education and contribute to a reform of the Chadian education system.

582 **Problèmes de scolarisation dans le nord-est tchadien et perspectives.** (Schooling problems and perspectives in northeastern Chad.)
Marie-José Tubiana. *Le Mois en Afrique*, no. 178-9 (1980), p. 128-35.
In this article, Marie-José Tubiana compares the experience of several children of northeastern Chad. She then examines the location and density of schools in the region, the qualifications and origins of teachers and the curriculum they teach.

Culture and the Media

Literature

583 **Tchadiennes.** (Tchadian women.)
Daniel Boulanger. Paris: Gallimard, 1969. 101p.
A collection of short poems inspired by Chad.

584 **Il y a cent ans . . . René Maran.** (A hundred years ago . . . René
Maran.)
Keith Cameron. *Présence Africaine*, no. 3 (1987), p. 8-13.
A discussion of the writings of the anticolonialist Antillean author, René Maran
(1887-1960); particular attention to his Pohirro, which deals with the Sara of southern
Chad.

585 **Le discours autobiographique et ses implications: une lecture de
'Prisonnier de Tombalbaye', d'Antoine Bangui.** (Autobiographies
and their implications: reading 'Prisoner of Tombalbaye' by Antoine
Bangui.)
Kester Echenim. *L'Afrique littéraire*, no. 77 (1985), p. 12-23.
This is a literary criticism of the autobiography of Antoine Bangui (q.v.) in which the
narrator recounts how he went from the status of minister in the cabinet of President
Tombalbaye to that of prisoner in his own country.

586 **Loin de moi-même.** (Far away from myself.)
Zakaria Fadoul Khidir. Paris: L'Harmattan, 1989. 223p.
(Bibliothèque Peiresc, no. 7).
This autobiography was written when the author was away from his country and
family while studying abroad. It helped a homesick young man to forget his

loneliness and recapture his past and his identity. The author is now Head of the Department of Linguistics and Oral Literature at the University of N'Djamena.

587 **Tchad–Cameroun: Le destin de Hamai ou le long chemin vers l'indépendance du Tchad.** (Chad–Cameroon: the destiny of Hamai or the long road to Chad's independence.)
Ahmed Kotoko. Paris: L'Harmattan, 1989. 230p.

Ahmed Kotoko was born in Goulfey (Cameroon) but spent a good part of his life in Chad, occupying the posts of minister of education, minister of finance and president of the National Assembly before being expelled from Chad by President Tombalbaye in 1961. He then became a diplomat in Cameroon and died in 1988.

588 **L'humour populaire tchadien en (160) histoires drôles.** (160 jokes from Chad's tradition of popular humour.)
Abakar Mahamat Mabrouk. [N'Djamena]: Published in cooperation with UNESCO, [n.d.]. 135p.

A small book, prefaced by the minister of culture, youth and sports, Djibrine Hissen Greinky, and containing a short introduction about the Chadian sense of humour. He points out that, due to cultural and other differences, Europeans may not find certain stories amusing.

Oral tradition

589 **Gosota-Kemkarje (Proverbes).** (Gosota-Kemkarje (Proverbs).)
Anon. Yaoundé: Alliance Biblique Universelle, 1983. 74p.

This short booklet contains 780 Ngambay (southern Chad) proverbs divided into thirty-one groups. They are all written in Ngambay.

590 **Douze contes masa avec une introduction grammaticale.** (Twelve Masa tales with a grammatical introduction.)
Claude Caitucoli. Berlin: Verlag von Dietrich Reimer, 1986. 414p. maps. bibliog. (Marburger Studien zur Afrika- und Asienkunde, Serie A: Afrika, Band 40).

The first part of this work, devoted to Masa grammar, deals with phonology, morphology and syntax. The second part presents twelve Masa tales recorded in N'Djamena in 1982, with a transcript and a French translation paraphrasing the Masa text. The tales are generally directed to children and therefore have an educational function.

591 **Contes Sar, Tome 1, Tome 2, Tome 3.** (Sar tales, Vol. 1, Vol. 2, Vol. 3.)
    Albert Cayrac, Pascal Djiraingue, Felix Tedebaye.   Sahr, Chad:
    Centre d'Etudes Linguistiques, 1978. Vol. 1: 186p. Vol. 2: 164p. map.
The first two volumes contain sixty-five tales from the Sar region in southern Chad.
These have been grouped into eight categories: the family, ruse and deceit, food and
greed, challenges, revenge, imitations, negative morality, and tales about sources and
origins. Each tale is accompanied by a phonological transcription of the original
language. A third volume is made up of notes divided into two distinct parts: in part
one they provide a general introduction to the main aspects of Sara society, in part
two they comprise a linguistic or cultural critique of the tales.

592 **Le mythe et les contes de Sou en pays Mbai-Moissala.** (Myth and
    tales of Sou from the Mbai-Moissala region.)
    Edited by Joseph Fortier.   Paris: Julliard, 1967. 334p. maps.
    (Classiques Africains).
This is a collection of myths and tales from the Mbai ethnic group, one of the largest
components of the Sara group of southern Chad. They relate to Sou, the Sara hero
who brought down from heaven the sacred objects which confer power on Sara
chiefs. The fifty tales contained in this book are grouped into eight categories and all
are accompanied by a Mbai transliteration.

593 **Contes Ngambaye.** (Ngambay tales.)
    Edited by Joseph Fortier, Jean-Paul Lebeuf.   Fort-Lamy: Mission
    Catholique, 1972. 254p. map.
This is an illustrated collection of forty-five tales from the area around the town of
Benoy in Western Logone. It is designed for entertainment, but the tales are
accompanied by a transcription and notes which help understand their symbolic
meaning.

594 **Dragons et sorcières. Contes et moralités du pays mbai.** (Dragons
    and witches. Tales and morals of the Mbai region.)
    Edited by Joseph Fortier.   Paris: Armand Colin, 1974. 365p. map.
    (Classiques Africains).
Forty tales from southern Chad are grouped under nine topics such as tales of thieves,
of blacksmith's sons or of elephant women. They are characterized by the fact that
they all end on a moral like the eighteenth-century French *Fables* of La Fontaine. All
are accompanied by a Mbai transliteration.

595 **Au confluent des traditions de la savane et de la forêt. Etude
    thématique des contes sar (Moyen-Chari, Tchad).** (At the
    crossroads of savannah and forest traditions. A thematic study of Sar
    tales (Middle-Chari, Chad).)
    Jacques Hallaire.   N'Djamena: CEFOD, 1987. 578p. map.
This book contains seventy tales, most of which centre on the character of Sou, the
clever and sometimes immoral trickster, present in other African oral traditions. Each

tale is accompanied by a phonological transcription and comments designed to illuminate the nature of Sou.

596 **Contes moundang du Tchad.** (Moundang tales from Chad.)
Collected and translated by Madi Tchazabé Louafaya, introduction by Christian Seignobos. Paris: Karthala, 1990. 213p.

A collection of forty-one tales from this ethnic group of southeastern Chad (one third of its population lives in Cameroun). It constitutes the first written record of Moundang oral tradition. The stories are short, but rich in symbols, and provide an insight into the social behaviour of the Moundang and their moral values.

597 **Au Tchad sous les étoiles.** (Under the stars in Chad.)
Joseph Brahim Seid. Paris: Présence Africaine, 1962. 101p.

A short book which contains fourteen stories taken from the oral tradition of Chadian village life.

598 **Les Mbara et leur langue.** (The Mbara and their language.)
Henri Tourneux, Christian Seignobos, Francine Lefarge. Paris: SELAF, 1986. 317p. maps. bibliog.

The Mbara of the Middle-Logone region (southern Chad) are the descendants of the original population of this area, together with the Kargu, the Budugur and the Kawalke. They belong to the civilization which flourished in this region before the coming of the Baguirmi kingdom. Because their culture was principally based on iron and its transformation, its disappearance has left them with their language as the sole focus of their identity.

599 **Voix de femmes.** (Women's voices.)
Marie-José Tubiana. *Cahiers de Littérature Orale*, no. 10 (1981), p. 79-97.

This article describes a song performed by Zaghawa women which was recorded in Chad in 1961-62, just after independence. The song illustrates the aspirations of women and offers advice on how to achieve a better life. Whether the themes relate to food, clothes or work techniques, whether they ask for luxury or progress, they always go back to the same demand: more money. The author explains that the song must be seen in the context of post-independence Chad, when new commodities were available on market-places, but still out of many people's financial reach.

600 **Mythes, histoire et permanence de problèmes politiques. A propos des 'Arabes' Zaghawa.** (Myths, history and permanence of political problems. On Zaghawa 'Arabs'.)
Marie-José Tubiana. In: *Graines de paroles, puissance du verb et traditions orales (Seeds of speech, power of the verb and oral traditions).* Paris: CNRS, 1989, p. 255-66. maps. (Texts offered to Geneviève Calame-Griaule, collected by the CNRS Language and Culture in West Africa team).
Marie-José Tubiana discusses the origins of Zaghawa Arabs of eastern Chad through a local myth and its interpretation by the author. Her purpose is not so much to establish a chronology or history of Zaghawa Arabs, but rather to demonstrate that the various versions of the same myth on the origins of this people show a pattern common to myths on the origins of settlements.

601 **Contes Zaghawa du Tchad – Trente-sept contes et deux légendes. Tome 1 et 2.** (Zaghawa tales from Chad – thirty-seven tales and two legends. Volumes 1 and 2.)
Collected by Marie-José and Joseph Tubiana, preface by Michel Leiris. Paris: L'Harmattan, 1989. Vol. 1: 125p. Vol. 2: 123p. (La Légende des Mondes).
Collected between October 1956 and November 1957 during research carried out by the Mission du Centre National de la Recherche Scientifique aux Confins du Tchad, these tales and legends reveal food to be a dominant theme and reflect the Zaghawa's constant struggle against a harsh environment. The short, symbolic tales, in which animals play a prominent role, are told by children and illustrated by their drawings.

Le sort des femmes dans les contes du Tchad.
See item no. 325.

The arts

602 **Art ancien du Tchad. Bronzes et céramiques.** (Ancient Chadian art. Bronze and ceramics.)
Anon. Paris: Ministère d'Etat des Affaires Culturelles, 1962. 41p. bibliog.
This illustrated catalogue was published to accompany an exhibition on ancient Chadian art, held in Paris between March and May 1962 and organized by Jean-Paul and Annie Lebeuf, both well-known specialists on Chadian art and archaeology. It contains a thirteen-page introduction by Jean-Paul Lebeuf.

603 **Instruments de musique et musiciens instrumentistes chez les Téda du Tibesti.** (Music instruments and instrumentalist musicians among the Teda of Tibesti.) Monique Brandily. Tervuren, Belgium: Musée Royal de l'Afrique Centrale, 1974. 260p. bibliog. (Série IN-8° – Sciences Humaines, no. 82).

In addition to describing the construction and the symbolism of music instruments such as drums and lute, this study also deals with the sociological aspect of music and the function of instruments in society.

604 **Un chant du Tibesti (Tchad).** (A song from Tibesti (Chad).) Monique Brandily. *Journal des Africanistes*, vol. 46, no. 1-2 (1976), p. 127-93.

Brandily analyses a male solo composed by a youth during a fifteen-day trip by camel from Tibesti to Fezzan in Libya. The article contains a semantic analysis and an analysis of the melody, and raises questions about the nature of the complex relations that exist beween the music and the words.

605 **Les lieux de l'improvisation dans la poésie chantée des Teda (Tchad).** (Improvisation in Teda sung poetry (Chad).) Monique Brandily. In: *L'improvisation dans les musiques de tradition orale (Improvisation in oral tradition music)*, edited by Bernard Lortat-Jacob. Paris: SELF, 1987, p. 73-78. (Ethnomusicologie, no. 4).

This study by a specialist of north Chadian music examines the conditions in which improvisation is performed among the Teda. These conditions can be divided into three categories: the place, which determines certain behaviours in Teda musical culture; the time; and the medium – speech or music.

606 **Tambours et pouvoirs au Tibesti.** (Drums and power in Tibesti.) Monique Brandily. *Cahiers du musiques traditionnelles*, no. 3 (1990), p. 151-60. bibliog.

The author examines the relation which exists between three kinds of drums and the exercise of power among the Teda. She shows that one specific drum can be used by only one specific social group. After describing the drums and how they are played, Monique Brandily analyses their social function as indicators of social status in the community and as symbols of power.

607 **Broderie et symbolisme chez les Kanouri et les Kotoko.** (Embroidery and symbolism among the Kanuri and the Kotoko.) Jean-Paul Lebeuf. *Objets et Mondes*, Vol. X, fasc. 4 (Winter 1970), p. 263-82.

Lebeuf explains how the embroidered dresses traditionally worn by a few Kotoko women are of Kanuri origin and, more anciently, Hausa. Far from being merely decorative, their rich patterns show symbolic meanings deriving from a taxonomic and universalist system with various relationships.

608 **Musique traditionnelle d'Afrique Noire. Discographie. Tchad.**
(A discography of traditional music from Black Africa. Chad.)
Chantal Nourrit, William Pruitt. Paris: Radio-France Internationale,
1980. 86p. map. (Musique traditionnelle de l'Afrique Noire, no. 10).

This unique work contains a list of all the recordings of Chadian music, seven indexes
referring to ethnic groups, instruments, interpreters and authors, locations,
personalities, themes and genres. For each entry there is a description of the
instruments used, the context of the music or song, and the name of the interpreter or
the musician.

609 **Danses zaghawa.** (Zaghawa dances.)
Marie-José Tubiana. *Objets et Mondes*, Vol. VI, fasc. 4 (Winter
1966), p. 279-300.

Zaghawa dances are not only an artistic expression, but also reflect Zaghawa society.
In this article, the author investigates various aspects of dances: who dances? where?
in what way? why? and with whom? She also shows that dances can be an expression
of joy or of respect, or a way of obtaining rain.

Mass media

General

610 **Situation de la presse dans les Etats de l'Union Africaine et
Malgache, en Guinée, au Mali, au Togo.** (The press in the states of
the African and Malagasy Union, in Guinea, Mali, Togo.)
Anon. Paris: La documentation française, 1963, p. 161-6. (Travaux
et recherches, no. 17).

A short study dealing with the organization of the press in the countries mentioned –
Chad being a member of the African and Malagasy Union. It lists daily and weekly
newspapers and provides summary information on them.

611 **'Rugir nos féroces jaguars . . .'.** ('Let our ferocious jaguars
roar . . .'.)
Dominique Larroque-Laborde. *Mots*, no. 11 (Oct. 1985), p. 63-78.

This study examines articles dealing with the August 1983 French military
intervention in Chad published in five daily newspapers (*Le Figaro, Libération, Le
Matin de Paris, Le Monde* and *Le Quotidien de Paris*). The tenor of these articles
created a certain image of France. It is based on a systematic inventory of all phrases
where the words 'France', 'Français', 'français(e)', or synonyms of 'gouvernement
francais' (French government) appear. It brings out, through the syntactic functioning
and distribution, the various values of each term. Moreover, the network of

associations and the lexical stereotype traces, in the background, generate evidence for a pattern of a partial national consensus.

Newspapers and magazines

612 **Al-Bouhera.** (The Lake.)
N'Djamena. 1990[?]- .
Independent weekly general-information newspaper published in Arabic.

613 **Le Canard déchaîné. Journal national de combat.** (The Unchained Duck. National struggle newspaper.)
N'Djamena. 1973-75[?].
Official newspaper and mouthpiece of Tombalbaye created by the president. It is a Chadian counterpart to and mockery of the satirical French newspaper *Le canard enchaîné* (*The chained duck*). It should be noted that in French 'canard' also means a malicious rumour and the titles of both publications is designed to reflect this ambiguity in meaning.

614 **Le combat progressiste.** (The progressist struggle.)
Fort-Lamy. 1959-60.
General information organ of the Parti Progressiste Tchadien, the Chadian section of the Rassemblement Démocratique Africain created by Gabriel Lisette.

615 **Le Contact.** (Contact.)
N'Djamena. 1990[?]- .
Independent weekly newspaper.

616 **Le Démocrate.** (The Democrat.)
N'Djamena. 1990[?]- .
Independent weekly newspaper which originally dealt with political matters and was later reoriented towards economic affairs.

617 **Echanges.** (Exchanges.)
Fort-Lamy. 1964-[?].
Bi-monthly bulletin published by the French Embassy in Chad.

618 **Info Tchad.** (Info Chad.)
N'Djamena. 1983-86.
Daily information bulletin published by the Agence Tchadienne de Presse (Chadian Press Agency).

619   **Info-Tchad.** (Info-Chad.)
N'Djamena. 1985- .
Journal on Chadian press published by the Press services of the Chadian Embassy in France.

620   **Journal Officiel de la République du Tchad.** (Official journal of the Republic of Chad.)
Fort-Lamy. 1958[?]- .
Bi-monthly journal which publishes all official decisions.

621   **Le Patriote.** (The Patriot.)
N'Djamena. 1990[?]- .
Official party weekly newspaper.

622   **Le Phare.** (The Beacon.)
N'Djamena. 1990[?]- .
Independent weekly newspaper.

623   **Le Progrès.** (Progress.)
N'Djamena. 1990[?]- .
Independent weekly newspaper.

624   **Tchad-matin.** (Chad-Morning.)
Fort-Lamy. 1960-[?].
Republican information daily.

625   **L'Unité.** (Unity.)
Fort-Lamy. 1962-[?].
Monthly publication of the Parti Progressiste Tchadien, the Chadian section of the Rassemblement Démocratique Africain, directed by Tombalbaye. Last publication date probably around 1975.

626   **Al-Watan.** (The Nation.)
N'Djamena. 1981-90.
Weekly information magazine of the UNIR (Union Nationale pour l'Indépendence et le Rassemblement) published in French and Arabic.

Radio

627 **Tchad: radio et campagne cotonnière.** (Chad: radio and the cotton campaign.)
Maclaou Ndildoum. *Problèmes audiovisuels*, no. 11 (Jan.-Feb. 1983), p. 23-4.

This short article, extracted from a dissertation, examines radio as a means of instruction for the cotton farmers of southern Chad. The author gives examples of poularizing radio micro-programmes, broadcast in the form of brief stories and riddles, which aim to disseminate simple and practical notions. The information provided is completed by data on the times of broadcast and the languages used.

Official Publications

628 **Le Président Hissein Habré en communion avec le peuple.**
(President Hissen Habré talking to the people.)
Anon. N'Djamena: Service de Press Présidentielle, [n.d.]. 47p. map.
An official brochure containing extracts from Hissen Habré's speeches and an anonymous text which celebrates the regime and the president. It is illustrated with photographs showing the president with Chadians, and Chadians engaged in traditional activities.

629 **L'essential sur le Tchad.** (Essential information about Chad.)
Anon. Paris: Editions Diloutremer, Service d'Information de la République du Tchad, 1960. 80p.
This short governmental booklet provides basic information on political and administrative structures as well as social and economic data. It contains extracts from the constitution, lists of deputies, the composition of the first government and of various commissions.

630 **La République du Tchad.** (The Republic of Chad.)
Anon. Monaco: Editions Paul Bory, Service d'Information du Tchad, 1961. 80p.
A government brochure published in 1961 for Independence Day and made up mostly of photographs and captions. The remainder of the text is characterized by a litany of praise and optimism for the government of President François Tombalbaye and his ministers.

631 **The Republic of Chad. Hour of independence.**
Anon. New York: Ambassade de France, Service de Presse et
d'Information, 1961. 32p. maps.

This publication from the Press and Information Division of the French Embassy to
the United Nations is part of a series on the new republics of Africa, each of which
gives a general idea of the country and its people and traces the main steps of its
progress towards independence. It also shows France as a contributor to the political
and economic development of Chad.

632 **Tchad: affirmation d'une nation d'aujourd'hui.** (Chad: assertion of
a nation of today.)
Anon. Paris: Editions Diloutremer, 1967. 16p. map.

This official brochure intends to give a progressive and positive vision of Chad. It
ignores ethnic and political difficulties and provides a brief introduction to the
geography, history, social organization, economy and finance of the country.

633 **Annuaire Officiel du Tchad.** (Chad official yearbook.)
Anon. Fort-Lamy: Ministère de l'Information, Direction Générale de
l'Information, 1970. 204p. maps.

This official publication provides general information on Chad. It is particularly
useful for public administration and government structures and includes a
presentation of government ministers and National Assembly members.

634 **Notice d'information à l'usage des agents de la coopération.**
République du Tchad. (Information for Cooperation Personnel.
Republic of Chad.)
Anon. Paris: Bureau de Liaison des Agents de Coopération
Technique, 1973. 39p.

A small practical guide aimed at French overseas workers in Chad. It provides
essential information on all aspects of Chad, together with practical advice on daily
life and administrative issues with regard to health and accommodation.

635 **Investiture du Président de la République Son Excellence al Hadj**
Hissein Habré, le 22 décembre 1989. (Investiture of the President of
the Republic, His Excellency al Haj Hissen Habré, 22 December
1989.)
Anon. N'Djamena: Direction de la Presse à la Présidence, January
1990. 15p.

This booklet includes official documents and speeches relating to the appointment of
Hissen Habré as president as a result of the referendum of 10 December 1989. Three
colour photographs of the ceremony are included.

Bibliographies

636 **A concise bibliography of northern Chad and Fezzan in southern Libya.**
Mohamed A. Alawar. Wisbech, England: Arab Crescent Press, 1983. 229p. maps.

This bibliography contains 1991 entries, 741 of which deal with Chad. It also contains an extensive list of abbreviations of journals, reviews, proceedings, occasional publications, institutions and professional bodies.

637 **Liste des études et rapports rassemblés au centre de documentation de la sous-direction des études générales.**
République du Tchad. Liste No. 1. (List of studies and reports in the general studies documentation centre. Republic of Chad. List no. 1.)
Anon. Paris: Ministère de la Coopération, Direction des Affaires Economiques et Financières, 1963. 7p.

A list containing thirty-seven titles on a variety of subjects which cover rail transport, economy, infrastructure, administration and geology. The 'Ministère de la Coopération' is now part of the 'Ministère de la Coopération et du Développement' and the 'Centre de Documentation de la Sous-Direction des Etudes Générales' has been incorporated within the Ministry's 'Centre d'Information et de Documentation, Service de l'Information et de la Communication'.

638 **Bibliographie du Tchad (Sciences Humaines).** (A bibliography of Chad (Humanities).)
Anon. Fort-Lamy: INSTH, 1968. 242p. (Série A, 4).

This bibliography deals only with works belonging to the humanities, with a few exceptions in geology and flora. The entries are organized in alphabetical order irrespective of the subject they deal with and the book includes a section on films and records.

639 **Liste chronologique des études éffectuées par l'ORSTOM en République du Tchad et pour partie dans le Bassin du lac Tchad.** (A chronological list of studies carried out by ORSTOM in the Republic of Chad and in part of the Lake Chad Basin.) Anon. N'Djamena: ORSTOM, 1974. *c*.180p. map.

This list concerns essentially (but not exclusively) scientific projects and is divided into seven parts: geology, geophysics, pedology, hydrology/bioclimatology, hydrobiology, humanities. The last part contains subjects such as botany, entomology and economics.

640 **Recherches scientifiques au Tchad. Liste des publications relatives aux recherches menées sur le territoire de la République du Tchad sous l'égide du CNRS.** (Scientific research in Chad. List of publications on research carried out on Chadian territory under the aegis of the CNRS.) Anon. Paris: CNRS, 1974. 60p.

This useful publication contains 467 titles under twenty different headings ranging from anthropology to audio-visual creations. Only the completed works are mentioned and preliminary studies and reports have been excluded when the information they contained was included in subsequent publications. It includes an index of authors.

641 **Bibliography of documents and reports on the Sahelian countries (1977-1985).** Anon. Paris: OECD, 1989. 198p.

This useful bibliography contains references mainly on unpublished works compiled by the Club du Sahel and transferred to the Sahel branch of the Development Centre based at the Organization for Economic and Cooperation and Development (OECD). It contains nineteen socio-economic categories, including one dealing with geography, hydrology and climatology. Most entries are in French, as well as the four indexes (authors, corporate bodies, geographical and subject) which list fifteen entries on Chad.

642 **Complément à la bibliographie du Tchad (Sciences Humaines).** (A complement to Chad's bibliography. (Humanities).) Marie-Magdeleine Bériel. N'Djamena: INSH, 1974. 103p. (Série A, 6).

This study complements the bibliography published in 1968 (q.v.) by the same institute and deals only with works belonging to the humanities, apart from a few exceptions in geology and flora. As in its predecessors, the entries are organized in alphabetical order irrespective of the subject they deal with.

643 **Elements for a bibliography on the Sahelian countries.**
Françoise Beudot, Siaka Coulibaly, Emma Ato.   Paris: OECD,
1976-92.

The Development Centre of the Organization for Economic Cooperation and Development publishes this annual bibliography (called *Elements for a bibliography of Sahel drought* until 1985) which contains entries referring to monographs or articles kept there as well as in other centres such as the Club du Sahel, CIDARC and IAMM. Entries are organized thematically into nineteen socio-economic topics (including one for geographical and climatological works). The large majority of entries are in French, as are the five indexes (authors, corporate bodies, geography, subjects and periodicals). Each volume contains between twelve and seventy-three entries for Chad.

644 **Africa Bibliography.**
Edited by Hector Blackhurst.   Edinburgh: Edinburgh University
Press, 1984-90.

This bibliography, mainly concerned with social sciences, also contains some entries dealing with medical or other scientific subjects. The first general part is quite exhaustive in terms of the topics it covers, while the rest of the study is divided into seven regional sections, including Indian Ocean islands. It also contains one section of collective volumes, as well as an author and a subject index.

645 **Répertoire des thèses africanistes françaises.** (A repertory of French
theses on Africa.)
Wanda Gaignebet.   Paris: CEA/CARDAN – EHESS, 1966- .

This yearly bibliography of the humanities contains a general section and lists all countries of sub-Saharan Africa together with Indian Ocean islands and the Caribbean. It has one index each for authors, subjects and supervisors.

646 **Les priorités de recherches pour le développement à moyen et
à long terme du Sahel.** (Research priorities for medium- and
long-term development in the Sahel region.)
Jean-Pierre Gontard, René V. L. Wadlow.   *Genève-Afrique*,
Vol. XIV, no. 1 and Vol. XV, no. 1 (1975-76), p. 99-103.

This bibliographical essay, published in several parts, deals with research on the Sahel, including Chad, from a global and multisectoral point of view. It also deals with research on the use of water resources, specifically subterranean water and cheap techniques of exploitation.

647 **International African Bibliography.**
Compiled and edited by David Hall, in association with SOAS.
London: Hans Zell Publishers, SOAS. 1971- .

This quarterly publication, previously published by Mansell, lists studies in English, French, Spanish, German and Italian, in two sections (articles and monographs). Each section contains a general and seven regional sub-sections, including one on the African diaspora. Its subject index refers only to the article section.

648 **Bibliographie de l'Afrique sud-saharienne. Sciences humaines et sociales.** (Bibliography of sub-Saharan Africa. Humanities and social sciences.)
Marcel d'Hertefelt, Anne-Marie Bouttiaux-Ndiaye.   Tervuren, Belgium: Musée Royal de l'Afrique Centrale, 1931-90.

This bibliography was first called *Bibliographie ethnographique du Congo Belge*, before changing to *Bibliographie ethnographique de l'Afrique sud-saharienne* and finally adopting its present name. It is a yearly publication, the latest dealing with the years 1986-87. Each entry is ordered alphabetically according to the author's name and contains the title of the study, year, periodical references and several keywords. It contains a subject index.

649 **Bibliographie du Tchad (Sciences Humaines).** (A bibliography of Chad (Humanities).)
Jacqueline Moreau, Danielle Stordeur.   Fort-Lamy: INSTH, 1970. 354p. (Série A, 5).

This second revised edition of the 1968 bibliography (see item no. 638) contains a supplement as well as an extra section on maps.

650 **Bibliographie des travaux en langue française sur l'Afrique au sud du Sahara (Sciences humaines et sociales).** (Bibliography of French works on Africa south of the Sahara (Humanities).)
Zofia Yaranga.   Paris: EHESS – Centre d'Etudes Africaines, CARDAN, 1979-92.

This useful bibliography contains a thematic and a geographical section. The latter is divided into five regional sub-sections (western, central, eastern, southern and Indian Ocean Africa). It also contains an author and a subject index. The first issue, published in 1979, deals with works published in 1977 and the last issue, published in 1992, covers publications in 1988. Unfortunately, this publication ceased in 1992.

Indexes

There follow three separate indexes: authors (personal and corporate); titles; and subjects. Title entries are italicized and refer either to the main titles, or to many of the other works cited in the annotations. The numbers refer to bibliographical entry rather than page numbers. Individual index entries are arranged in alphabetical sequence.

Index of Authors

Index of Titles

Index of Subjects

finance 2, 31, 534, 543-4
fiscal policy 184, 544, 557
fishing 355, 532, 546-7,
    564
floods 376
flora *see* fauna and flora
folk-tales 325, 362,
    589-601
Food and Agriculture
    Organization (FAO)
    566
food aid 429-31, 553
food consumption 533
food production *see*
    agriculture; fishing
food resources 15, 427
foreign affairs 461-530
foreign aid 540, 545
    see also development;
    food aid
Forces Armées du Nord
    (FAN) 201, 224,
    246
Forces Armées Nationales
    Tchadiennes 435
Forces Populaires de
    Libération *see*
    FROLINAT
Fort-Archambault 70,
    87-8, 190
    see also Sarh
Fort-Lamy 134, 146, 190,
    318, 351
    see also N'Djamena
Foureau–Lamy mission
    13, 175
franc zone 226, 394
France in Africa 207, 216,
    221, 223, 226, 229,
    240-2, 245, 249, 462,
    477, 484-7, 521-2
    see also history:
    colonial
Franco-British treaties
    493, 520, 523
Franco-Italian agreements
    520, 522
French Camel Corps 27
French colonial policy
    166, 180-1
French Equatorial Africa
    11, 26, 193, 471
French language 578

French National Assembly
    191
FROLINAT 197-8, 207-
    11, 220, 223, 236,
    245, 440, 464, 466-7,
    475, 496, 517, 519
Fulani 153

G

Gabon 11, 30-1, 33, 226
games 330, 336
genealogies 19, 171
Gentil, Emile 148, 183
Gentil, Pierre 32, 182-3,
    437
geography 2, 5, 9, 12, 25,
    29-112, 339, 534,
    641, 643
geology 19, 31, 34, 84-5,
    87, 103-5, 111-18,
    339, 637-9, 642
Ghana 515, 554
Gide, André 14, 21
Giscard d'Estaing, Valéry
    530
Gouvernement d'Union
    Nationale de
    Transition (GUNT)
    199, 505
Grossard 528
Guera 349

H

Habré, Hissen 3, 12, 198,
    200-1, 206-8, 212-13,
    224, 230, 242, 246,
    433, 435, 440, 454,
    480, 495, 497-8, 506,
    526, 628, 635
Hadjerai 346-50
Haller, Prosper 13
Hasan 171
Hassauna 408
Hausa 146, 607
health 1, 6, 9, 222, 427-8
    see also diseases
history 2, 5, 9, 12, 25, 31,
    76, 78, 138-46
    ancient 33

pre-colonial 34, 147-73
colonial 26-7, 34, 174-
    96
independence 12, 197-
    252
Holsken 17
Hugot, Pierre 186
human rights 432-4
humanities 638-9, 642,
    645, 648-50
humour 588
hydrology 84-5, 87, 101-2,
    111-12, 639, 641
    see also water resources

I

Idriss, Mohammed 198
income 533, 578
Indochina 470
industry 31, 545, 549-50
infrastructure 32, 34, 194,
    545, 637
initiation 383, 391
International Court of
    Justice 499
Iron Age 137
Islam 160, 169, 422, 488,
    580-1
Islamization 15, 317, 401,
    424, 576
Israel 229
Italy 494, 502-3
Ivory Coast 226, 379, 554,
    567

J

judiciary 459

K

Kaba 380
Kanem 16-17, 75, 100,
    144, 148, 162-3, 173,
    328, 341, 557
Kanembu *see* Kanuri
al-Kanemi family 153
Kanuri 95, 138, 351-5,
    406, 607

185

Map of Chad

This map shows the more important towns and other features.

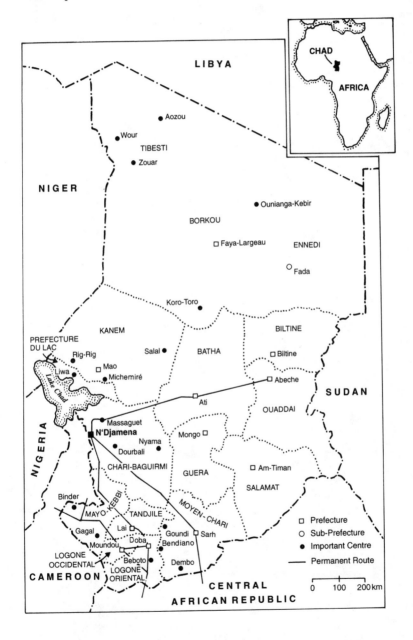

ALSO FROM CLIO PRESS

INTERNATIONAL ORGANIZATIONS SERIES

Each volume in the International Organizations Series is either devoted to one specific organization, or to a number of different organizations operating in a particular region, or engaged in a specific field of activity. The scope of the series is wide-ranging and includes intergovernmental organizations, international non-governmental organizations, and national bodies dealing with international issues. The series is aimed mainly at the English-speaker and each volume provides a selective, annotated, critical bibliography of the organization, or organizations, concerned. The bibliographies cover books, articles, pamphlets, directories, databases and theses and, wherever possible, attention is focused on material about the organizations rather than on the organizations' own publications. Notwithstanding this, the most important official publications, and guides to those publications, will be included. The views expressed in individual volumes, however, are not necessarily those of the publishers.

VOLUMES IN THE SERIES

TITLES IN PREPARATION